A Country Called Prison

A COUNTRY CALLED PRISON

Mass Incarceration and the Making of a New Nation

SECOND EDITION

John D. Carl
Mary D. Looman

OXFORD
UNIVERSITY PRESS

OXFORD
UNIVERSITY PRESS

Oxford University Press is a department of the University of Oxford. It furthers
the University's objective of excellence in research, scholarship, and education
by publishing worldwide. Oxford is a registered trade mark of Oxford University
Press in the UK and certain other countries.

Published in the United States of America by Oxford University Press
198 Madison Avenue, New York, NY 10016, United States of America.

Library of Congress Cataloging-in-Publication Data
Names: Carl, John D., author. | Looman, Mary D., author.
Title: A country called prison : mass incarceration and the making of a
new nation / John D. Carl, Mary D. Looman.
Description: 2nd edition. | New York : Oxford University Press, [2024] |
Includes bibliographical references and index.
Identifiers: LCCN 2024009120 (print) | LCCN 2024009121 (ebook) |
ISBN 9780197768310 (hardback) | ISBN 9780197768334 (epub) |
ISBN 9780197768341
Subjects: LCSH: Imprisonment—United States—History. | Prisons—
United States—History. | Prisoners—United States—History.
Classification: LCC HV9466 .L66 2024 (print) | LCC HV9466 (ebook) |
DDC 365/.973—dc23/eng/20240326
LC record available at https://lccn.loc.gov/2024009120
LC ebook record available at https://lccn.loc.gov/2024009121

DOI: 10.1093/oso/9780197768310.001.0001

Printed by Integrated Books International, United States of America

To my loving wife and children, love you all.
John

To my amazing daughters—Calypso and Adrianna.
Love always, Mary

CONTENTS

PREFACE

> Change is the law of life. And those who look only to the past or the present
> are certain to miss the future.
>
> *John F. Kennedy*

The first thing that you need to know is that this book is about change—big change. We have studied and taught about crime, criminology, and criminal justice for years. We have also worked in the industry. Mary has more than 30 years of experience in the criminal justice system. She has been a prison psychologist for many years and is a college professor. John is a college professor but always a social worker and sociologist. He also has worked inside the walls and teaches classes inside prisons every year. We look at the reality of the criminal justice system through our respective backgrounds.

This book is the result of years of study, thought, and concern for the current state of America as well as its citizens: not just the citizens who have been caught committing a criminal act but also those who have broken the law and not been caught. We believe that the United States has unintentionally built a country within its own borders, a country we call "prison." Prisons are found far and wide. And for the most part they are filled with people who have broken the law. No one denies this fact.

As you read this book, we hope to take you on a journey of understanding that will provide you with up-to-date facts, figures, theories, and research, as well as human stories of life in the Country Called Prison.

Max Weber challenged researchers to practice *Verstehen*, to attempt to understand the actions of an actor from the actor's point of view

(Weber, 1968). This is what we attempt to do in this book. We want to move you, the reader, beyond the mere facts and figures that you can find in a textbook. Through the facts and anecdotes in this book, we want you to see the lives behind the data.

ABOUT THIS BOOK

This book is filled with stories that were created from our memories working in criminal justice organizations and social service agencies. The names and descriptions of people depicted in our stories are representative of those we have met in our professional experience. In every case, names, genders, ages, races, offenses, and towns were changed so that no one specifically could be recognized. The stories are representative of real criminals, prison workers, and politicians we have encountered. We believe these stories strengthen our thesis and help you, the reader, to better understand the human faces behind the data. We stand on the shoulders of Max Weber as we strive to move beyond facts and figures of this social phenomenon.

In Chapter 1, we introduce the reader to the reality of the prison system in the United States. We provide you with comparative data between our country and other nations in how they deal with people they may want or need to punish. This introductory chapter is reworked for this edition with updated data and clear discussion of the current state of incarceration.

In Chapter 2, readers of this new edition will find a new chapter containing a host of information that was not present in the first edition of the book. In "Prison History and Private Prisons," we give the reader the backdrop to the modern, Western prison system, looking specifically at how inmates have for centuries been profit centers for those who desire to make quick, easy money. We provide the history of both public and private prisons to give readers a more complete understanding of how prisons have been used in the past, so that it may enlighten your perspective on the present and the future.

In Chapter 3, "What Makes Prisons a Country?," we review the elements that characterize a country: unified people, geography, history, language, and culture. Then we identify ways that mass incarceration fits those elements. We discuss the ways offenders must assimilate to prison culture to survive. The culture of prison shows inmates ways to behave and interact with others and gives meaning to their lives behind the razor-wire fences. Inmates must adapt to a culture that includes values and beliefs that do not exist anywhere else in the world except prison. Over time, prison inmates learn to live in their new world and, when released, return to a land they no longer understand.

In Chapter 4, "Who Are the People of a Country Called Prison?," we begin by debunking the pervasive myth, popular in the United States, that all people in prison are violent and scary. We then examine the very different way that most people from the Country Called Prison grew up. As children, they frequently experienced a very different psychosocial development process than children in traditional American families. Our examination demonstrates that most prison inmates are not violent and scary but are often poorly educated, poorly socialized, often addicted, and frequently mentally ill. We suggest that the reason for the continued high recidivism rate of former prisoners is that we base solutions and programs on the erroneous assumption that only offenders are at fault.

We believe that the root of the problem lies in an impeded normal childhood development process, as well as social and cultural components that encourage criminality. Therefore, to make the current culture of the Country Called Prison more prosocial, we propose solutions that focus on restoring the psychosocial development process of its citizens.

In Chapter 5, "Living in a Country Called Prison," we deliberate the reasons that prison environments have changed so little since the infamous Stanford prison experiment conducted by Phillip Zimbardo in 1970. In our discussion, we bring to light the four different subcultural groups that coexist within the prison geographic region: inmates, security personnel, administrative staff, and licensed professionals. Each group has its own language, customs and values, perceptions of power, and relationship patterns. Since adults learn new cultural behaviors through observation, instruction, imitation, and reinforcement, we propose strategies that rely on these principles to shift the prison environment toward a milieu that encourages human development and growth rather than human degradation.

In Chapter 6, "Visiting America From a Country Called Prison," we state that most former inmates return to prison within 5 years after their release. Then we ask, "Why?" All over the world, people successfully transition from one country to another, from one culture to another. How does this happen? What can we do differently that will make the homecoming of former inmates permanent and beneficial to society? Through Mary's experiences of helping former inmates during their first year of release, we reveal a constellation of obstacles that former inmates face when they return to the "free world," which for many is a misnomer. However, by understanding these obstacles, we can help explain the steadfast recidivism rate of the last 20 years. With our new insights, we use Abraham Maslow's hierarchy of needs model of human motivation to discuss strategic proposals that aid successful assimilation of citizens from the Country Called Prison into the U.S. culture.

In Chapter 7, "Decarceration: Emigrating From a Country Called Prison," we pose the question, "What can be done for the long haul?" We point out that there is a difference between crime control and punishment. Crime control involves either setting up situations that make crime more difficult to commit or creating citizens who don't want to commit crimes. Prison and punishment are something totally different. This chapter is particularly new in that topics of decarceration and desistance are discussed in detail.

In Chapter 8, "Assimilating a Country Called Prison," we summarize the main reasons that the United States now has a huge problem and the primary justifications for solving it now. The chapter provides the reader with an expanded Marshall Plan to help take down the incarceration mountain. Policy implications are discussed in greater detail than in the previous edition, and new evidence is used to illustrate how decarceration is good for both the incarcerated and the general public.

We conclude that the United States has, through deliberate policy decisions, disenfranchised millions of its own citizens, citizens who could pay taxes, support local schools, and care for their children. Instead, these citizens have become residents of this country we call prison. As you read the book, we hope that you will better understand the reasons we steadfastly believe that within the United States there is a Country Called Prison and that we must transform the criminal justice system now to regain these lost citizens.

WHO CAN BENEFIT FROM THIS BOOK

This book is intended for criminal justice and correctional leadership, policymakers, reformists, interested parties, and the academic community. Since this is such a broad audience, we want readers to first explore and become familiar with universal cultural concepts that are superimposed over the harsh realities of poverty, crime, incarceration, and social alienation. We hope then that policymakers and reformists will close the book with new insights into the vastness of the problem, which goes beyond razor-wire fences. We hope that criminal justice and correctional leaders will realize that they inhabit a brave new world where a century of traditional policies and procedures will no longer be sufficient. We hope academics will be introduced to a perspective of corrections that is humanistic and prosocial rather than regulatory, pejorative, and detrimental. We hope students will become passionate about the possibility of change and bring their fresh insights to an antiquated system.

ACKNOWLEDGMENTS

JOHN D. CARL, MSW, PHD

I cannot overstate my gratitude for the support I receive from my wife, Keven. Your unwavering support for me is the greatest blessing in my life. I also send all my love and appreciation to my father, who continues to show me how to age with dignity. To my daughters, Caroline and Sara, as well as my son-in-law, Gray, and my two lovely grandchildren, Emma and Cooper, I write and work to strive to make the world a better place for all of you. I'm lucky to call you all my family!

I also appreciate the support of many friends, too numerous to list here, as well as colleagues who have served as an "ear" for ideas in this book. I especially thank Mitch Peck, Christopher Hill, and my students who over the years have helped me clarify my thinking on these issues.

Last but certainly *not* least, I thank my coauthor and friend, Mary D. Looman. When Mary came to me and suggested we collaborate on a book, I had no idea where that would end. Her insight, dedication, and effervescent personality have made working on this project a pleasure. Thank you!

MARY D. LOOMAN, MAJ, PHD

To those who made this journey worthwhile I give my affection and thanks: my daughters, Calypso Gilstrap and Adrianna Fernald; Calypso's husband, Rob; and my unique, wonderful grandchildren—Cynthia, Alexandra, Veronica, Ian, Aspen, and Ricarda. I am grateful for all the people, past and present, who have listened to me wonder about all sorts of things, some of which evolved into the concepts found in this book, especially my dear friend, Sue Fischell.

Who would have guessed that when my coauthor agreed to combine our experiences and wisdom in writing this book, I would discover that I now have a buddy who completely understands the value of playing in a sandbox.

JOHN D. CARL AND MARY D. LOOMAN

Of course, no book of any kind is solely constructed by its authors. The process of writing involves many talented people who use their talents to support and improve the book you see before you. Throughout the process of writing this book, the staff and editors at Oxford University Press have been exceptional. They are quite simply the best we have had the privilege to work with. Thanks to the whole team! We especially thank our editor, Dana Bliss, and our title manager, Sarah Ebel, for their enthusiasm, professionalism, and trust.

ABOUT THE AUTHORS

John D. Carl holds a master's degree in social work and a PhD in sociology, both from the University of Oklahoma. He is an associate professor of criminology and sociology at the University of Oklahoma, in Norman, Oklahoma. John teaches criminology and criminal justice–related course work and coordinates the university's "Inside-Out Program" teaching inside a prison each year. He has spent most of his life in Oklahoma, living for brief periods of time in Texas, Indiana, and Mexico. His social work practice experiences include mental health, prisons, disabilities, and hospital- and hospice-related work. Dr. Carl continues to enjoy his life as it unfolds, striving always to be curious. In particular, he finds support from family and friends who enrich his life. In his free time, he gardens, throws pottery, plays his guitar, and occasionally finds a golf course on which he loses a few balls.

Mary D. Looman holds a master's degree in the administration of justice from Wichita State University and a doctorate in clinical psychology from the Fielding Graduate Institute. She spent her early childhood in Virginia and most of her life in Kansas. She returned to Virginia in 2016 to live near her daughter's family and enjoys going to all her grandchildren's activities. Until Dr. Looman retired in 2016, she worked as a forensic psychologist for the Oklahoma Department of Corrections for 8 years. She had a private practice for nearly 20 years providing clinical services to offenders in the community and evaluations for children in foster care who had been severely traumatized. Dr. Looman was an adjunct professor for about 10 years, teaching psychology and criminology courses. As a member of the development teams, Dr. Looman assisted the University of Oklahoma and the University of Southern California start their online programs for a master's degree in criminal justice and taught courses for those programs for about 10 years in total. Dr. Looman always maintains a list of new things to learn and experience alongside the joy of being with her family.

CHAPTER 1

Introduction to a Country Called Prison

> Being unwanted, unloved, uncared for, forgotten by everybody, I think that is a much greater hunger, a much greater poverty, than the person who has nothing to eat.
>
> *Mother Teresa*

What to do with "wrongdoers" is a problem as old as humanity itself. No matter the size, shape, or demographic makeup of an area, there have always been people who break the rules. In pre-literate societies the problem might have been rather simple to solve. First, most population groups were small; therefore, social control was relatively easy. Anyone who has more than one child understands that more people in any social system increases its complexity. Preliterate societies generally handled disputes by assent to an authority figure who made decisions.

As societies became larger and more complex, however, so did questions of laws and fairness. The first legal code with any precision is known as the Code of Hammurabi (1770 BCE). Named after the sixth Babylonian king, the code dates from around 1770 BCE and provides more than 280 laws and punishments. Many of these laws concern legal matters of contract, issues of inheritance, divorce, and family issues. The code also deals with criminality, including appropriate punishments for certain acts. It paints a picture of a society struggling with the meaning of justice. The code attempts to define the tenet of *lex talionis*, better known as the "eye for an eye, tooth for a

A Country Called Prison, Second Edition. John D. Carl and Mary D. Looman, Oxford University Press.
© Oxford University Press 2024. DOI: 10.1093/oso/9780197768310.003.0001

tooth" standard, by providing precise limits on punishments for certain crimes. Some acts that are determined to be "acts of God" can exonerate the individual from responsibility. For example, if a person owes a debt and a storm ruins the grain that he planned to use to pay the debt, then he can avoid paying his debt that year because it is an act of God. If, on the other hand, you merely try to avoid your debt, then punishment can occur.

Early Greek and Roman societies laid the foundation for much of the Western world and our ideas about justice and punishment. These two societies frequently used slavery, banishment, and death as punishments for illegal activities. During that time banishment could be a fate worse than death as the offender lost the protection of the city and had to fend for him- or herself from a host of possible problems including rival bands of people and dangerous packs of wolves. The Romans also crucified thousands hoping to control enemies of the state. Overall, punishment in these societies was quite harsh and the use of death as a punishment was widely accepted.

Later, in Europe, this view of punishment persisted. Throughout Europe's history, harsh punishment abounded. But these punishments did not seem to curb criminality. In fact, severe punishments, such as those listed in Table 1.1, had little effect on the actions of those they were intended to rehabilitate. The table provides a list of punishments used in the Western world throughout the Middle Ages and even into the Reformation. These punishments are only a few of the ways that those in power throughout history have tried to control the behavior of others.

Whenever we take an action to control an entity, whether a person or a dog, some thought process is behind it. If, for example, you housebreak your pet, you do so because you believe that animals should go to the bathroom outside. But you would never expect a human houseguest to use the lawn as their toilet. You have an idea about how each situation should be handled. Decisions about the way to deal with rule breakers are not that much different. Frequently, we decide that punishment is necessary and take for granted the way we do it. Although some of the punishments listed in Table 1.1 seem archaic and inhumane, the people who enforced those punishments thought that they were doing a public service. We are not that much

Table 1.1. PUNISHMENTS

Form of Punishment	Description
Banishment	Forcing the offender to leave his or her home permanently or for a set period.
Beheading	Often carried out with a sword or axe and eventually with the guillotine.
Cane and flogging	Hitting the offender with sticks or a whip. Used on slaves and soldiers to maintain control. Also used in reform schools of the early 17th, 18th, and 19th centuries.
Dunking stool	Involves tying the offender to a seat on a long wooden arm and dunking the seat into the river. Usually used against women.
Flogging	Involves whipping the person. Common throughout history; frequently used in the United States against slaves.
Hard labor	Hard physical work, including rowing in the galleys of military ships.
Mutilation	Blinding or cutting off parts of the body, including hands, feet, tongue, among others. Used throughout history.
Pillory and stocks	Placing a person's hands and head through a wooden frame attached to a pole. Usually used for public shaming.
Slavery	Enslavement of losers in battle and conquered people. In ancient Rome certain crimes could result in the person becoming a slave.
Transportation	Transporting criminals to colonies by European governments.

Sources: Farrington (2000); Lyons (2004).

different today in the way we decide who goes to prison and who does not.

Throughout history, people have been punished for several reasons that seemed valid at the time. Today we try to justify the reasons for punishment as well. Why? In reality, no one likes punishment. We don't like it when we are punished, and we feel uncomfortable punishing others. So, let's look at some theories regarding punishment and see how they fit into the background of the Country Called Prison.

The theory of *retribution* or *retaliation* is as old as life on Earth. Retribution allows the wronged party to impose a suitable punishment on the person who hurt them. When you were a toddler and someone hit you on the playground, you most likely hit the child back. This is retaliation. The "eye for an eye" standard is often quoted as the benchmark for retribution theorists.

Contrary to what many people believe, the "eye for an eye" standard aimed to prevent people from taking *excessive* private vengeance for wrongs committed against them. As we have already discussed, the Code of Hammurabi was an effort to create a system of equitable justice. Our modern notion that the punishment should fit the crime follows this logic. There needs to be a reasonable consequence for the wrong action. Therefore, at least in the United States, we do not put burglars to death because such a punishment does not seem to fit that crime.

Expiation suggests that the criminal has committed a moral wrong. This theory holds to the idea that the guilty party must atone for his or her crime. Historically, crime and sin were linked in the minds of Europeans, and so it was logical that the wrongdoer should "make up" for the offense. If you have read Nathaniel Hawthorne's novel *The Scarlet Letter*, you might recall that it is a tale of expiation. In the story, an adulterous woman must atone for her sins by wearing a scarlet "A" on her clothing so that the community knows she has committed a transgression and that she suffers the shame and indignity of her "wrongdoing."

Today we do not force people in the general population to wear letters on their clothing indicating that they are criminals. In prison, however, "inmate" or "corrections" is printed on the back of shirts that prisoners wear every day—even those in minimum security who are allowed to work outside the prison must wear them. We do believe that people who have wronged society should show remorse for their actions. When society assigns community service to a person who has driven under the influence of alcohol, we are in some respects forcing them to atone for their crime by, for instance, picking up trash in a park. Their community service sentence is imposed to expiate or compensate for their crime.

Deterrence is the best-known theory of punishment. Many parents instinctively use deterrence methods to train their child regarding their society's social/culture rules. If your 4-year-old son takes a cookie when he is not supposed to, if you put him in "time-out," you are practicing deterrence. You believe that temporarily placing your son in a "time-out chair" will somehow teach him a lesson and deter him from acting unsocially again. Deterrence, like all theories of punishment, does nothing to prevent the initial action; it is designed to prevent future crime.

There are two types of deterrence: general and specific. *General deterrence* aims to prevent crime by teaching people that breaking the law brings punishment. When your 3-year-old daughter sees your 4-year-old son in time-out and decides not to try to steal a cookie without permission, she has been generally deterred. Prison works as a general deterrent for most people. When John asks students whether they would be willing to risk incarceration, he always gets a resounding "NO." He then follows up with another question, "What personal experiences have you had that would cause you to feel so strongly about not wanting to go there?" Few in the room can adequately answer the second question. Yet they know they do not want to end up in prison. They are generally deterred by the mere thought of losing their freedom.

Specific deterrence is believed to have its effect on the offender. In theory, it is supposed to limit the likelihood that the lawbreaker will commit future crimes. When your 4-year-old son cries because he has been placed in time-out, he is supposedly "learning his lesson." When former inmates reoffend, society doesn't understand why they did not "learn their lesson." We believe that specific deterrence will correct behavior. When it does not work, society is troubled and often thinks that harsher punishment is needed. In this book, we will identify some reasons that prison does not deter crime, no matter how long the sentence or how harsh the conditions.

It is possible that through punishment your 4-year-old will learn how to be a better thief rather than learn to obey you. Consider your own actions. Were you ever punished for doing something wrong but then did it again later? Have you ever received a speeding ticket and then exceeded the speed limit again? If the answer is yes, then you see that deterrence efforts are not always effective.

The British philosopher Jeremy Bentham (1748–1832) suggested that deterrence will usually work when three clear criteria are met. First, the action taken against the actor must be swift. When the mother sees the little boy reaching for the cookie jar, she must act immediately. Warning him to "wait till your father gets home" will do little to deter his behavior (Figure 1.1).

Second, there must be certainty. In other words, the boy must know for certain that if he goes for the illicit cookie, his mother will catch him and punish him. A lack of certainty is why people continue to exceed the speed limit, even after they have received a ticket. If you

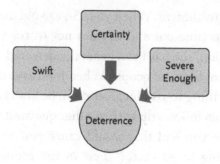

Figure 1.1. Components Necessary for Effective Deterrence.
Source: Bentham ([1789] 1970).

tend to drive fast frequently, you have learned that most of the time you will not be caught and punished. The efficacy of deterrence is limited to how certain the person is that they will get caught.

Third, and finally, Bentham suggests that deterrence will work only if the punishment is severe enough that someone would not want to risk getting caught. If all the mother does is scold her son, he will likely get used to the tongue lashings and not be deterred by them. Conversely, if the punishment is too severe, the person is unlikely to learn from that either. The child who is placed in time-out for an entire day would likely see the punishment as unjust and therefore not accept its moral message. In other words, people who believe they have been singled out and harmed for no good reason are unlikely to learn deterrence from their punishment.

Since punishment rarely meets these three criteria, a person's ability to make a purely rational choice related to the potential risks of his or her behavior seems unlikely (Beccaria, [1764] 1963). Although punishment may be one of the tools we use to deter bad behavior, it is, according to Bentham, an evil to be used cautiously.

Another reason for punishing individuals is grounded in moral reformation. Many early punishments in Europe had their roots in the Judaic Christian tradition. The belief was that crime is a moral problem and therefore moral training is essential. Simply put, if people learn right from wrong, then they will make good choices and avoid crime. Hard labor was frequently the method for moral training.

Hard labor as a method to teach values might seem odd. However, the current boot-camp prison movement is not really that different.

Inmates, usually young, are sent to quasi-military-style prisons where their heads are shaved, they exercise regularly, and correctional officers act like drill sergeants. They work long hours under the rationale that these wrongdoers will learn from iron discipline and carry this discipline out into the world upon their release.

Perhaps the most important reason for incarceration is to *protect society*. By protecting innocent people from those who would harm them, prisons serve society well. When a serial killer or rapist is sent to prison, everyone is safer. As we will show, however, truly dangerous people make up a small percentage of those in prison in the United States.

As we will discuss, modern societies have determined that incapacitating those whom we fear is the best way to keep society safe. If we simply lock up offenders, we will all be more secure. In our work, we both have met people in prisons who should be incarcerated. They are dangerous people. However, our experiences have shown that these offenders are the minority of prisoners.

The United States, at one point or another in its history, has used virtually all the theories of punishment we just discussed. Frequently the religious, political, and economic forces of the nation have influenced our history of prisons and punishment.

Early settlers from Great Britain brought to the colonies attitudes toward punishment that were like those they had left behind in England. Begging and theft had become a problem in England, and so workhouses were instituted to keep potential troublemakers off the streets. Workhouses were essentially factory-style prisons that produced a source of cheap labor for the emerging capitalist class. Exploitation of these workers was common. It was hoped that through work these criminally minded people would be taught the importance of "proper" living.

Troublemakers might also become indentured servants. Rather than be sent to filthy dungeons, offenders would sign on to work for a craftsman. Their contract typically lasted 7 years. In exchange for their labor, they received housing and vocational training. Many chose this path to escape the poverty and overcrowding of England and make passage to the New World, later called the "Americas." However, indentured servitude was often as bad as slavery.

Slavery was instituted in the New World almost from the colonies' inception. Africans were taken from their homeland and forced to work, enriching the landed classes, particularly in the South. Until the Civil War, it was a criminal act if a slave endeavored to extricate him- or herself from slavery. During the Civil War, the U.S. Congress passed the Confiscation Act of 1862, which declared that all slaves who took refuge behind Union lines were free.

The slaves' new liberty was not long enjoyed, as homeless ex-slaves fleeing from their southern masters found themselves in poverty and frequently dependent on the federal government for sustenance (Freedmen, 2013). Many ex-slaves, then referred to as "freedmen," were sent to refugee camps where they were hired out to loyal Unionist plantation owners for low wages. Many died in the deplorable conditions of the camps. After the Civil War, some freedmen voluntarily returned to their former masters as sharecroppers.

Racial inequality is clearly a part of U.S. history. As it applies to incarceration, we see a link between the way we treated slaves and former slaves, as well as Native Americans, and the disproportionate rates of incarceration of these two groups. Table 1.2 shows the rate of incarceration by race and ethnicity as reported by the Federal Bureau of Prisons. It also provides the percentage of each racial and ethnic group in the U.S. population. The numbers are staggering. Although mass incarceration is detrimental to the American way of life for all citizens, many researchers believe it to be catastrophic for ethnic minority populations (M. Alexander & West, 2012; Wilson, 1987). Asian Americans and Caucasians are underrepresented in prison in proportion to their population, but African Americans are overrepresented

Table 1.2. PERCENTAGE OF INMATES BY ETHNICITY

Ethnicity	Percentage of Inmates	Percentage of U.S. Population
Asian	1.4%	6.3%
Black	38.6%	13.6%
Native American	2.6%	1.3%
White (non-Hispanic)	27.5%	58.9%
Hispanic	29.8%	19.1%

Source: Federal Bureau of Prisons (2023).

by a factor of almost three, while Hispanics and Native populations are also overrepresented.

This reality has led some to think of the prison system as a new form of slavery because either the state or private corporations are making money at the expense of African Americans and Indigenous populations. This prompted civil rights lawyer, advocate, and legal scholar Michelle Alexander to suggest that we are living in a new Jim Crow era. Her well-researched book *New Jim Crow* points to this hypothesis and the damage that it inflicts on families and communities (M. Alexander & West, 2012). This injustice is one of the reasons we decided to write this book.

In the past, researchers focused on those incarcerated, those released from prison, and those who returned to prison. However, over the past 10 years, researchers have begun to look at the collateral effects of incarceration—the cost to society due to loss of wage earners and the disruption to families and communities caused by incarcerated members. Additionally, the correlation between the formerly incarcerated and rising homeless populations in many metropolitan areas is also being noted. While being homeless does not in and of itself increase the odds of incarceration, having been incarcerated clearly increases the chances of being homeless (Moschion & Johnson, 2019). This is in large part due to a lack of postrelease programs and support for those released from prison.

This connection is particularly related to the age at which an individual is incarcerated. In short, the younger a person is when they are incarcerated, the greater the odds of experiencing homelessness, and the greater the length of time they remain unhoused. Research shows that the effect of juvenile incarceration and being unhoused is even stronger for women when compared to their male counterparts (Cox, 2021; Metraux & Culhane, 2023). Imprisonment of nearly three-quarters of a million parents disrupts family life, a critical foundation of any society. It also affects the network of familial support and places new burdens on government services, such as schools, foster care, adoption agencies, and youth-serving organizations (Travis, 2005; Wakefield & Wildeman, 2014; Patterson, Talbert, & Brown, 2020).

Although recidivism of over half a million offenders annually has been the primary concern, an equally important focus should be on preventing disruption to social networks. This disruption results when a significant number of offenders are in concentrated areas, such as inner-city neighborhoods. There is almost a revolving door of people in many of these neighborhoods, with some leaving for prison just as others are returning. This cycle leaves family and neighborhood life significantly disrupted and economically devastated (Rose & Clear, 2001).

When you think of a *criminal*, do you think of a father, mother, sister, or brother? It is easier to think about criminals as statistics. However, they are people—people with families and human needs and desires. After all, they were not born in prison. They usually had jobs before they became inmates. Most have families, children, and friends. Once released from prison, former inmates need food, clothing, and shelter, which they often cannot pay for. Jobs are hard to get, and bills are hard to pay. They need medical care, which they cannot pay for. They also age, with all the extra needs that come with being elderly. Since many have not worked steadily over their lifetimes, their Social Security retirement income will be low, if it exists at all.

Very few researchers have studied the tsunami of children who are likely to head to adult prisons. In 2006, nearly 300 juvenile detention and correctional facilities housed about 93,000 teens, many of whom will eventually find their way to adult prisons (Davis, 2008). In 2000, 14,500 minors were in adult jails and prisons (Austin, 2000a), and in 2013, 3,000 were serving life sentences (Equal Justice Initiative, 2013).

According to the National Center for Children in Poverty, about 16 million U.S. children, or one in five, live below the poverty level, and 32.4 million are members of low-income families. These are important statistics, as research has shown that many people in prison were raised in poverty (Clear, 2007). Impoverished children are seven times more likely to be abused and neglected (Payne, 2005), which can lead to the development of serious mental disorders (American Psychiatric Association, 2013). If left untreated, these disorders can eventually develop into severe, chronic mental disorders in adulthood, thereby increasing the likelihood that those affected will end up in prison, since community mental health resources are inadequate.

The bottom line is that we have a huge problem that costs states more than $50 billion a year, with budget increases for prisons over

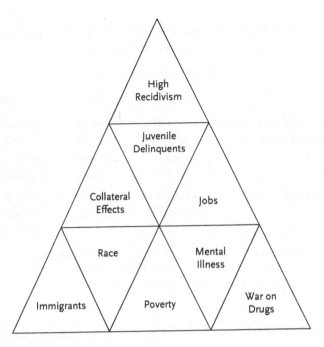

Figure 1.2. The Mass Incarceration Mountain.

the past 20 years outpacing increases in other essential government services such as transportation, education, and public assistance (Petersilia, 2011). Figure 1.2 shows the elements that make up this mountain of a problem. Throughout our history, we have built this mountain based on values and beliefs about punishment and morality. Even if we stop incarcerating people tomorrow, millions of prisoners will be discharged from prisons over the next 10 years. Many will leave with untreated substance addictions, posttraumatic stress, limited work skills, medical problems, and poor social skills. How many of them will be able to productively contribute to U.S. society?

The millions of U.S. children now growing up in poverty will reach adulthood over the next 20 years, and a portion of them will not function well as adults or productively contribute to society. Certainly not all impoverished children will end up in prison. In fact, most will turn out to be hard-working Americans. However, too many of them will cross the border into the Country Called Prison, condemning them to a life of poverty and stigmatization. This should be a major concern of anyone interested in shrinking the prison population.

Table 1.3. COMPARISON OF CORRECTIONS POPULATIONS
BY CATEGORY, 2011 AND 2021

Item	Bureau of Justice Statistics		
	2011	2021	Change
Total federal and state corrections	6,994,500	5,444,900	22.2% decrease
Community supervision[a]	4,818,300	3,745,000	22.3% decrease
Probation	3,973,800	2,963,000	25.4% decrease
Parole	855,500	803,200	6.1% decrease
Incarceration total[a]	2,252,500	1,775,300	21.2% decrease
Prison	1,599,000	1,204,300	24.7% decrease
Detention/jail	735,600	636,300	13.5% decrease

[a] Some totals slightly affected by numerical rounding by the Bureau of Justice Statistics and instances in which offenders were counted in two different populations, such as probation and parole.

Sources: Carson (2022); Carson and Kluckow (2023); Carson and Sabol (2012).

Since the first edition of our book, de-incarceration efforts around the United States have grown more popular. Stakeholders and concerned citizens have unified with political leaders who are looking to cut budgets, which requires reducing the number of prisoners and offenders supervised on probation and parole. Since the writing of our first edition, this trend has generally been consistent in most states. As has been shown with the previously cited research on homeless populations and incarceration, the issue then becomes what resources exist to help those who are being released from prison adapt and be reinstituted into American society.

Table 1.3 provides a 10-year analysis of the corrections population in the United States. Note that across all levels of supervision, we are incarcerating and supervising fewer people.

What these data show is that across the board, at both the state and federal level, we are seeing a marked decrease in the incarceration of individuals in the United States. Table 1.4 shows the relationship of these decreases as they relate to issues of race and gender. Here too we see that the declines are relatively consistent between these demographic categories.

These trends represent a movement away from mass incarceration and toward alternatives to incarceration that, if given time, should eliminate some of the issues created by mass incarceration. However,

Table 1.4. 10-YEAR PRISONER POPULATIONS BY
GENDER AND RACE

Criteria[a]	Bureau of Justice Statistics		
	2011	2021	Change
Male	5,712,900	4,488,200	24% decrease
Female	1,218,600	956,700	24% decrease
White	3,243,100	2,606,000	22% decrease
Black	2,356,000	1,704,000	32% decrease
Hispanic	1,904,000	861,000	75% decrease

[a] Some totals slightly affected by numerical rounding by the Bureau of Justice Statistics and instances in which offenders were counted in two different populations, such as probation and parole.

Sources: Carson (2022); Carson and Kluckow (2023); Carson and Sabol (2012).

unless the latent effects of these changes are considered and anticipated, it is unlikely that this transition will come with no costs to society. We will address this more specifically in the final chapter of the book, where we outline our plan to hopefully continue to decrease the unnecessary use of prisons while at the same time avoiding some of the unintended consequences of such a decision.

Since prisons have become de facto mental health lockdown units, exactly what will we do with all the people suffering from mental illness? This is a primary question because it is the main negative consequence of mass incarceration and the creation of a new nation within the United States. This issue must be addressed soon, particularly since prisons are not designed to be the place for people with chronic and persistent mental illness. The incarceration mountain is not only built on a foundation of criminality, but also one of mental illness. This means a Country Called Prison, exists both inside the fences of correctional facilities and in neighborhoods throughout America.

To put into context the reality of incarceration in the United States, it is always a good idea to look at the data in comparison to other countries. While our country is decreasing its prison population significantly, it also had a rather profound head start in both its number and rate of incarcerations (Sawyer & Wagner, 2023).

There are more than 2 million prisoners in the United States, 1.69 million in China (plus unknown numbers in pretrial detention and

Table 1.5. TOP 10 PRISON POPULATIONS BY COUNTRY

Prison Population Rank	Country	Total Prison Population	World Population Rank
1	United States	2,068,800	3
2	China	1,690,000	1
3	Brazil	478,000	7
4	India	471,000	2
5	Russia	309,000	9
6	Thailand	291,000	20
7	Turkey	266,000	18
8	Mexico	189,000	10
9	Iran	189,000	17
10	Philippines	165,000	13

Source: Fair and Walmsley (2021).

other forms of detention), 478,000 in Brazil, 471,00 in India, 309,000 in the Russian Federation, 291,000 in Thailand, 266,000 in Turkey, 189,000 in Mexico, 189,000 in Iran, and 165,000 in the Philippines (see Table 1.5). Of course, one may rightly question the numbers in authoritarian regimes as to their accuracy. Other definitional issues may apply as well. For example, China does not include in their official number those in pretrial detention or other forms of detention.

The total number of inmates in a country could certainly be affected by its size. The total number could also be misleading because some countries may not have the same level of economic development and quality of law enforcement that the United States does. For example, if a country has few high-value, lightweight items, like laptop computers, there is less to steal. In this imaginary country, because everyone is poor, it seems unlikely that such a nation would have high crime rates. A more important question is, how does the United States compare to other countries of all sizes?

Using rates of incarceration allows for a fair comparison. The rates in Table 1.6 represent the number of incarcerated people per every 100,000 members of the population. Table 1.7 shows the prison population rates for the world's 10 richest countries according to the World Prison Brief (2022) and the population size ranking of those countries according to the U.S. Census. According to these data, the United States ranks first in the rate of incarceration for every 100,000 people

Table 1.6. COUNTRIES RANKED BY RATE OF
INCARCERATION PER 100,000

Country	Rate of Incarceration per 100,000
United States	629
Rwanda	580
El Salvador	564
Cuba	510
Palau	478
Virgin Islands, United Kingdom	477
Panama	435
St. Kitts and Nevis	423
Grenada	413
Virgin Islands, United States	394

Source: Fair and Walmsley (2021).

Table 1.7. INCARCERATION RATES OF THE RICHEST COUNTRIES

GDP Rank	Country	GDP 2022	Incarceration Rate per 100,000
1	United States	25,462,700	629
2	China	17,963,171	119
3	Japan	4,231,141	37
4	Germany	4,072,192	70
5	India	3,385,090	35
6	United Kingdom—England, Wales	3,070,668	131
7	France	2,782,905	119
8	Russian Federation	2,240,422	326
9	Canada	2,139,840	104
10	Italy	2,010,432	91

Sources: World Economic Outlook Database (2023); World Prison Brief (2022).

of the population. You will note that most of the countries listed are relatively small and, with three exceptions, island nations. None of these nations, except the United States, would be considered an economic leader in the world.

Table 1.6 orders the countries by their rate of incarceration. The United States is the most populated country on this list. Comparing the United States to these nations may seem unfair and perhaps misleading, because we are not like most of them. Nearly all of them are underdeveloped or are small island nations and/or emerging economies.

Since the countries that report high rates of incarceration are so different from the United States, another question comes to mind. How does the U.S. incarceration rate stack up against similarly wealthy countries? The 10 largest economies in the world in gross domestic product (GDP), according to the International Monetary Fund, are listed in Table 1.7. The table ranks the countries by size of GDP and shows their value in trillions of dollars. The table also ranks the countries by prison population per 100,000 people, as well as their rate of incarceration.

As is commonly known, the United States has the largest economy on the planet. As Table 1.7 shows, except for Russia and the United States, there seems to be almost an inverse relationship between wealth and incarceration rates. Wealthy countries, except the United States and Russia, generally have low rates of incarceration, suggesting that wealth does not inherently increase incarceration rates. So, the claim that the United States is wealthy and so naturally has a high crime rate does not seem to fit international comparisons.

To illustrate this point further, as you consider the data, you will notice some interesting facts. Japan, the third-richest country in the world, is about a quarter of the economic size of the United States but has an incarceration rate approximately 13 times lower than ours. Germany's incarceration rate is about nine times lower, while France is about seven times lower.

These data seem to raise more questions than they answer. Wealth and incarceration rates do not seem to be obviously related. Perhaps the answer is that the United States simply has more crime. After all, if we incarcerate more of our citizens than our wealthy industrialized counterparts, perhaps it is because our citizens are more criminal than theirs. Just as with incarceration rates, international data tell the story (Crime Rate by Country, 2020).

Table 1.8 provides comparison data for the United States and a few other wealthy industrialized democracies in relationship to their crime rates. It is important to note that many of the countries listed in the table are likely to keep good records and openly report all of their incarcerated citizens. One can certainly point to the nondemocratic

Table 1.8. COMPARISON OF CRIME RATES
FOR INDUSTRIALIZED NATIONS

Country	Crime Rate
United States	47.7
China	30.14
Japan	22.19
Germany	35.79
India	44.43
United Kingdom—England, Wales	46.07
France	51.99
Russian Federation	39.99
Canada	41.87
Italy	44.85

Source: World Population Review (2023).

countries of Russia and China and argue that this is not true for these nations, a statement with which the authors would not quibble. For example, China does not include detainees in its official data, whereas people awaiting trial in the United States are included.

Excluding Russia and China, the others listed in Table 1.8 all provide an accurate snapshot of reported crimes in 2022. These data show some surprising results. Contrary to what many think, the United States does not have the highest crime rates in the world. Of course, it is important to remember that exactly what constitutes a specific crime may vary by country, and these data do not differentiate violent from nonviolent offenses. Nevertheless, these data do indicate a simple reality—that the United States does not have substantially MORE crime than, say, the United Kingdom, France, or even Italy, and yet our incarceration rates are substantially higher.

So, the clear connection between rates of crime and incarceration is not present. One reason for this is related to the issue of drug crimes. When looked at separately, we can see a bit more of the story. As opposed to most other developed nations, the United States has decided to criminalize drug use, and in many states punish it quite harshly. Table 1.9 provides the rate of drug arrests in the largest-GDP countries ranked by the size of their economies. We will address the issue of the War on Drugs in many locations in this book, but for those

Table 1.9. COMPARISON OF DRUG CRIME RATES
FOR INDUSTRIALIZED NATIONS

Country	Drug Arrests per 100,000
United States	503
China	12
Japan	10
Germany	346
India	2
United Kingdom—England, Wales	234
France	348
Russian Federation	140
Canada	247
Italy	58

Source: United Nations (2018).

who are unaware, President Nixon began a policy of drug interdiction and harsh punishment in the 1970s that became known as the War on Drugs. However, this "war" ramped up Nixon's power, as well as that of Ronald Reagan during his 8 years as president. Few presidents since then have been willing to do much to change the policies of punishment for addiction.

While criminality may be part of the reason for the high rates of U.S. incarcerations, it is also important to note that the rates of incarceration do not match up perfectly with these differences. For example, the United States incarcerates at a rate of 629 per 100,000 people, while France incarcerates at a rate of 119 per 100,000. But France's crime rate is not five times lower than that of the United States; in fact, France's crime rate is only slightly lower than the United States'. A quick review of Table 1.8 may partially explain this. France and most European nations see drug use and addiction as health issues and allow their medical systems to address them first. Certainly, they have illegal drugs, but they generally do not lock up first-time drug users for possession of a controlled substance.

A simple review of these nations' data and total crime rates shows one thing clearly. While some of these nations may have lower total crime rates, the rates seem to be minimally related to these nations' incarceration rates. Therefore, proclaiming that "the United States must incarcerate more people because there are more criminals" is not supported by the data. The data do point to the United States incarcerating more drug criminals as part of its answer.

If these countries have similar rates of crime, why do they have lower rates of incarceration? The simple answer is that these countries have different social policies and cultural attitudes about incarceration. The United States decided that prison is the best, and frequently the only, way to control people who do things most citizens do not like.

Put another way, the United States incarcerates those who frighten society, as well as those whom society is mad at for their irresponsible lifestyles. No one questions the wisdom of incarcerating violent offenders—those we fear. Most of the nations listed in the tables do just that. The difference in incarceration rates between the United States and other countries is often the way in which these other countries punish people who do things their societies do not like. For example, no one likes to see someone drunk or high on drugs in public. It is unpleasant to see an addict in the subway. However, should we really spend millions of dollars incarcerating these people?

Prisons are ubiquitous in the United States. They have become a part of life for many. Almost everyone knows someone who has either been to prison or works in one. Prisons are not just centers for punishment; they are also places to work.

The Bureau of Labor Statistics (2022) reports that prisons always need workers. The bureau reports that the median annual salary for a correctional officer is $49,610 a year, or $23.85 an hour. Compare that to the current minimum federal hourly wage of $7.25, and you can see why working in a prison might be a pretty good job. The job requires no advanced training or certification, since on-the-job training is provided. It is no wonder that in 2022 more than 395,000 people in the United States worked in correctional jobs. Of course, correctional officers are the tip of the proverbial prison employment iceberg. There are more than 90,000 probation officers and correctional treatment specialists. In addition, literally millions of people work in prison-related businesses. Criminal justice has become not only a way of life for many in the United States but also a way to make money.

A report on prisons by the Pew Charitable Trusts (2013) identifies that, from 1977 to 2003, state and local expenditures on prisons increased by over 1,100%. Meanwhile, spending for education and health care grew by less than 600%, and public welfare expenditures grew by a little over 700%. Spending on prisons has continued to grow at significantly higher rates than other important human services. This diversion of money from public or social goods to prisons raises an interesting question. Are we spending tax money wisely when we spend it on prisons?

Data from the Prison Policy Initiative (Sawyer & Wagner, 2023) show that in 2017, the United States spent approximately $80.7 billion on public prisons and jails, and another $3.9 billion on private prison facilities. However, this does not include all the other components of the criminal justice system. When adding in the budgets of all criminal justice entities, the cost is about $182 billion a year. In later chapters, we will discuss in more detail the costs of prisons, but suffice it to say, prisons are a costly social program.

The government funds social services for the public good to improve the lives of America's citizens. Generally, this spending is intended to benefit large numbers of people. If your town is building a new park, then the government is spending that money on the justification that the park will be a public good. Defining what is and is not a public good is the source of great political debate. Those on the far political left suggest that almost all public services should be deemed public goods, while those on the far political right suggest that almost nothing, other than military protection, should be viewed as such. We cannot hope to resolve this debate in our book, but we do raise the question: Is spending money on prisons really a social good, or are we inadvertently developing a new nation inside U.S. borders?

As you read this book, we hope to take you on a journey of understanding that will provide you with up-to-date facts, figures, theories, and research, as well as human stories of life in the Country Called Prison. Max Weber (1968) challenged researchers to practice *Verstehen*, to attempt to understand the actions of an actor from the actor's point of view. This is what we attempt to do in this book. We want to move you, the reader, beyond the mere facts and figures that you can find in any textbook. Through the anecdotes in this book, we want you to see the lives behind the data.

We are not prison abolitionists. Having both worked inside prison walls, we are aware that all societies will have some need to control the behavior of people who seem bent on harming others. However, the decision of who to incarcerate and what to do with them while they are incarcerated deserves serious consideration.

We are not the first researchers to argue that prisons function like a community. Nearly 80 years ago, Donald Clemmer (1940) studied various prison communities and identified something called the *convict code* that existed alongside, and sometimes in opposition to, prison policy and procedures. He outlined a process by which prisoners were socialized into the prison community, which he referred to as *prisonization*.

But we are perhaps the first to take the theory further—that prison culture is no longer contained within the walls of correctional facilities but now exhibits the characteristics of a country with provinces both inside and outside the razor-wire fences. Citizens of the Country Called Prison live all over the United States, adversely influencing the next generation and draining resources that could be spent on more socially progressive endeavors. How did we arrive at this new perspective? We are both mental health professionals and university professors with education and training in criminology and business. With more than 30 years of combined experience working in prisons and with marginalized citizens in the community, we have witnessed some of the history that you just read about. As social science researchers, we are curious about the ways humans interact with each other and are interested in the ways people excel and at the same time fail. Thus, we view human problems from a wide angle.

We are also not the first to suggest the U.S. criminal justice system needs reform. Over the last decade or so there have been attempts to reform the system, and yet little has changed. Good books with good ideas on ways to improve the system have been written, not only on prisons and reentry programs, but also on crime and sentencing policies and educational programs in poor communities (Reiman, 1979).

In 2007, President George W. Bush signed into law the $330 million Second Chance Act, which gives government and community service agencies funds to initiate best-practice reentry strategies for people being released from prison. These programs may be part of the reason the incarceration rate is slowing. Additionally, more and more states are experimenting with prison diversion programs like drug courts and alternative sentencing. These too could decrease the rate of incarceration. Slowing the rate is good, and declining rates are even better, but to shrink the Country Called Prison will take a concerted effort.

As if mass incarceration is not trouble enough, another crisis is heading our way. The event horizon—the point of no return—that makes this problem imperative to address is the aging of the baby boomers, those born between 1946 and 1964. Over the next 20 years, an average of 10,000 people per day will reach the age of retirement eligibility (Snyder, 2013). Who will pay into the Social Security system to fund the baby boomers' retirement? Since the correctional system is not, in fact, about correcting behavior and is more about containment and control, the millions of offenders and ex-offenders are unlikely to be part of the employment pool (Solomon, 2012). Eliminating millions of potential workers from the tax pool certainly does not help solve this problem.

When a problem is framed through an inaccurate paradigm, solutions grounded in that paradigm do not correct the problem. Rather than shifting the paradigm, however, those invested in the current system often just blame the offenders. Although William Ryan (1971) in his famous book *Blaming the Victim* first described this rationale for justifying racism and social injustice against African Americans, the phenomenon of victim blaming is well established in human psychology. "She was asking for it" is said of a victim of domestic violence. For years, the "ex-con" has been blamed for returning to prison, not trying hard enough, or just going back to his or her old ways—"once a crook, always a crook." Regardless of why a person returns to prison, the reality is that we are all worse off when it happens. It's bad for the public, bad for the taxpayers, and bad for the offender.

Our intention in writing this book is to share with you a new perspective of the mass incarceration epidemic and the latent effects that are threatening America's prosperity and potential. We use the word *epidemic* as a metaphor for the U.S. incarceration problem because it is used in public health whenever there are significantly more people sick than would normally be expected from a specific disease in a specific area during a specific time. We believe, as our earlier data demonstrated, that there are far too many people in prison than crime rates suggest there should be. We hope our perspective will shift the paradigm so that new solutions can be developed that address the foundation of the problem, not the structure.

CHAPTER 2

Prison History and Private Prisons

The purpose of punishment is not to inflict revenge, but to prevent crime.

Cesare Beccaria

In the first chapter we considered the justifications for punishment and some of the more ancient forms of punishment tried by human society. Eventually, humans settled on using a method of restricting the movements of the offender, which we call imprisonment.

Prisons have been around for a long time. They've existed since the first millennium BC, as evidenced by archeologists digging up ruins in Mesopotamia (http://www.prisonhistory.net). They were at first holding cells for people awaiting execution or awaiting some other form of punishment, like becoming a galley slave who would row ships for naval vessels. However, as societies became larger, they had to decide what to do with those considered to be dangerous and destructive. In this chapter you will discover that the Country Called Prison did not appear overnight, and its history involves both public and private mechanisms to use prisoners for profit.

There is nothing new about individuals making money off the criminal justice system, and particularly those involved in it. In England as far back as the Middle Ages there are records of jails owned by private citizens. In fact, as far back as the 1200s there are records of jails being used by private citizens and charging the Crown for their services. Jailers would charge fees to the inmates for almost anything, and if the jailed person could not pay, the jailer would go to the magistrate to

A Country Called Prison, Second Edition. John D. Carl and Mary D. Looman, Oxford University Press.
© Oxford University Press 2024. DOI: 10.1093/oso/9780197768310.003.0002

raise the funds. In addition, jail keepers could sell products to inmates with impunity; if a person had means, they could get a better cell, alcohol, or better food. Since there were no governmental controls at this time, running a jail came under the supervision of the local sheriff; therefore, jail characteristics could be quite diverse. Regardless, jails became a rather profitable business and were often passed down to family members or sold to investors (Shichor, 1995).

Workhouses and houses of correction were the ancestors of modern prisons. In 1557, the first workhouse was in London, England. The jailer managed to take care of and discipline the vagrants, debtors, and undesirable people in their care. Soon workhouses spread throughout all of Europe with the fundamental concept that those housed in the workhouse were there to work. Workhouses were owned by individuals, and often the contract for the labor was held by private companies that paid them low rates for the labor. This allowed profits to rise for both the contracting company and the workhouse owner. While labor was needed, workhouses were not very lucrative compared to the jails, primarily because the workers were often less than motivated and required heavy supervision to ensure quality work (Shichor, 1995).

The story of the settlement of the "Americas" is the story of legends that generally suggest that individuals seeking freedom, fame, and fortune risked their lives to "tame" a new and undeveloped world. However, it was not long after the first settlers began arriving that they experienced a labor shortage and requested more labor from the home country for their enterprises. One solution was to import indentured servants who sold themselves into a period of bondage for a trip to the Americas. They hoped for long-term freedom but often found they were little more than forced-labor prisoners (Christian, 1998).

"Transportation" was also another source of labor for the growing colonies. In England, transportation to the colonies became the most common punishment used by the courts, with the lion's share of convicts being sent to Australia. However, the Americas would later receive their fair share as well. Those transported would be sold as slaves to landowners and businesspeople when they arrived. Convicts were cheaper to buy than African slaves, in part because they were less desirable, but also because their sentence of "ownership" was limited to a set number of years (Ekirch, 1985).

Nearly 50,000 British prisoners were transported to America between 1717 and 1775, with most finding their way to Maryland and Virginia. Since convicts were less desirable, many would be sold to traders, who would take them farther into the frontiers for sale to smaller landowners as a source of cheap labor. It is important to note that at this time England controlled what today is known as Ireland and so the bulk of those transported were Irish. The crimes committed by those transported ranged from serious violent crimes to almost any minor type of crime like nonpayment of a debt. However, most were sentenced for minor crimes. For example, in Ireland (at this time a part of England), the most common charge for which people were transported was vagrancy. The idea of transportation was clear to England: Ship away any of its troublemakers by sending them to the colonies (Smith, 1934).

At the same time, the population of the Americas was growing, and cities began to expand. Along with this growth came increases in crime and the societal responses to it. As cities grew in America, jails were often among the first structures erected by local governments. Public education did not exist in the same way it does today, and so quickly there were more jails than schools or even hospitals. The irony of a country being founded on "freedom" is simply that it has a long history of limiting the freedom of certain groups, such as criminals, the transported, indentured servants, slaves, and Native Americas (Christian, 1998).

After the Revolutionary War ended in 1783, America was in an era of political turmoil until the signing of the U.S. Constitution on September 17, 1787. By 1800, 11 states had built state prisons, suggesting that this new country had a crime problem. States called these prisons "penitentiaries." They were named as such because crime was considered a sin, and the criminal should learn to be penitent. The notion of penitence has deep roots in Puritan religious traditions, in which many of the colonists believed. You may recall Nathaniel Hawthorn's novel *The Scarlet Letter*, which details the punishment of an adulterous woman who is forced to wear a scarlet "A" on her clothes as part of her penance. Prisons at this time were philosophically designed to be the place where offenders would become "right" with God through their penance.

These centers of punishment did little to rehabilitate offenders and mostly were built as they had been in England, as large holding cells with few amenities. These prisons were little more than dungeons where a large group would be held together with no privacy. Cells were cold and filled with filth and disease. In fact, more people died not from the punishment, but from diseases contracted in the squalor (Johnston, 2000). As prisons continued to be built, the architecture would change a great deal as philosophies about the role of prisons changed.

In the early 1800s, Pennsylvania built one of the first prisons that took on the philosophy that prisons should not be "schools for crime." The new philosophy called for isolation of inmates as a better source of control while also allowing more time for reflection and penance, based on the monastic tradition where monks live a life of solitude and reflection. Furthermore, there was an increasing belief that criminality was like a "disease" and so isolating prisoners would keep the disease of criminality from spreading to others. These types of prisons are often termed the Pennsylvania system.

Auburn, New York, built a prison under a different philosophy, which became known as the Auburn system. The primary difference from the Pennsylvania system was the inclusion of work as an expectation of incarceration. Groups performed work silently, with no communication allowed between the inmates. The Auburn system aimed to keep the strengths of the Pennsylvania system while at the same time trying to make the prisons "self-sufficient." It was not long before prisons in New York were able to not only break even but also become profitable (Shichor, 1995).

Profitability began when New York State contracted prison labor for the production of goods. It was not long before the Auburn system swept throughout the country, becoming the dominant system in most states. State legislatures passed laws requiring inmates to work and labor to be "sold." For example, in 1838 New Jersey passed an act requiring all prisoners to be kept at "hard labor," with profits being used to offset costs. Inmates were paid for their labor, but the cost of supporting them was deducted from their wages, thus allowing prisons to profit (Sellars, 1993).

California became one of the first states to allow prisoners to be sent to outside contractors who provided them with food, clothing, and shelter while detaining them in exchange for their labor. The California Prison Act of 1851 allowed this to occur until escapes became so common that the state allowed its first private prison to be built in San Quentin in 1852. Inmate labor built the prison; the design had inmates always staying within the walls. However, shortly after the prison was completed, the company managing it went bankrupt. The prison management returned to the state, where it has remained (Sellars, 1993).

Before the Civil War began, many states and territories investigated having private prisons. In the southern states these private prisons were often used to hold escaped slaves. Louisiana's first private prison dates to 1844, where inmates had to make clothing. Torture and abuse of inmates were common. This carried over after the Civil War as states often used private prisons filled with incarcerated former slaves for what amounted to forced labor camps (Bauer, 2018).

In the 1800s a lease system for prisons appeared. Private owners took over complete control of the prison, including the maintenance and discipline of the inmates. Prison operations were effectively leased to private contractors who charged the state a flat fee to run the prison. If the contractor made a profit from running the prison, either through inmate labor or the fees, they were free to keep the profit. In other locations inmates themselves were leased for their labor while prisons remained under the control of the state. For example, one prison in Missouri leased inmates to a company to build houses in the community. Throughout the country prisons were built next to factories or factories were built inside prisons so that labor could be leased (Shichor, 1995).

In the North, the Civil War decreased inmate contract labor as male inmates were sent to the war and incarceration rates dropped. After the war, in the North particularly, the labor movement was just beginning to take root. Labor unions argued that selling prison labor was tantamount to slavery, and courts and legislatures started to agree. In 1871, the Virginia Supreme Court outlawed forced prison labor on the grounds that it was no different than slave labor. In New Jersey, unions argued that prison contract labor was a threat to regular workers seeking employment, and by 1891, the state abolished contract prison labor. These ideas spread throughout the country and most states passed laws stopping the practice of contract prison labor (Sellars, 1993).

After the war, southern states were struggling with how to rebuild their infrastructure while at the same time experiencing a massive labor shortage as freed slaves now could leave plantation life. In the South specifically, incarceration rates began to rise, driven by large numbers of former slaves being detained on oftentimes trumped-up charges. These incarcerated men were then leased to rebuild the South during Reconstruction. This eventually became an extremely profitable source of cheap labor to rebuild the southern states. Convicts were regularly abused, suffering more than they did during slavery. However, profits were high, and the forced labor of convicts replaced the forced labor of slaves in many parts of the South (Shichor, 1995).

Following the years of Reconstruction, U.S. attitudes toward many social issues began to change. By the end of the 19th century, America entered what is known by historians as the Progressive Era. Progressives looked to improve society for everyone, and so laws to control business and deal with social ills began to emerge. Prior to the Progressive Era, the United States was generally an open society when it came to drug and alcohol use. The thinking was simply that individuals should have the freedom to put into their bodies whatever they wished. However, this thinking began to change as thousands of Civil War veterans returned home and were suffering from addiction to alcohol and morphine. Soldiers were known to take an injection before battle to calm their nerves, and the injured were prescribed opium for their pain. The rampant use of morphine led to a massive addiction issue and a huge social problem after the war, as addicted veterans were lethargic, unable to work, and often dying of emaciation caused by their lack of hunger. This has been called America's first opioid crisis. And it was not only a problem for veterans; opium was one of the most prescribed drugs by doctors in the 1800s. Women would receive it for their "nerves," and since drugs at this time were not controlled substances, many in society would self-medicate with opiates (J. S. Jones, 2020).

At the same time, America was experiencing a growing rate of alcoholism, which led to increased political lobbying by temperance societies, with the goal of ending addiction in the country. Social policy debates raged as to whether addiction was a moral failure or a disease. As this related to the issue of crime, the question arose, was the cause of crime rooted in addiction or personal choice? Those who saw addiction as the cause proposed the elimination of intoxicating substances from society. Eventually those who championed temperance would "win the day," expanding temperance laws that ultimately led to the passage of the 18th Amendment, in 1919, which criminalized alcohol in the United States (Achenbaum et al., 1993).

During this time, policymakers began debating the ethics of using prison labor contracts, and in 1887, Congress passed a law restricting the interstate transfer of prison-made goods, effectively limiting prison contract labor. Shortly after this, New Jersey stopped all prison labor contracts, and it was not long before other states did the same, effectively ending the lease and contract systems (Sellars, 1993).

In the late 1800s and early 1900s, the United States was also experiencing a period of intense immigration, particularly from Central and Eastern Europe. These immigrants settled in major cities of the country, which eventually led to turf wars between immigrant groups. In New York City, ethnic queues restricted what areas of the economy individuals could work in; for example, Italians worked on the docks, while the Chinese worked in restaurants and laundries (Zhou, 1992).

The rehabilitation movement began during this time with the creation of the school reform movement of the early 1900s. As cities continued to grow and immigration increased, crime in cities became even worse, particularly as it related to young men wandering the streets of major cities in the United States. The central question became how best to combat violence, crime, and youth gangs.

At this time, there were no programs such as foster care or child welfare services. Children who were abandoned, orphaned, or abused were left with two choices, appeal to a church for aid or join a gang. The first youth gangs appeared in the late 1800s and grew into bigger problems by the early 1900s. In response to this, states started to use "reform schools" for young men who had shown a proclivity to violate the law. The concept of the state taking control of children was at this time quite controversial. Governmental officials and progressive activists argued that the government had a right under the common law principle of *parens patriae* to assume guardianship over youth.

In these reform schools young men were to be treated and released back into society once reformed. The juvenile justice system of the United States appeared at this time, with the hope to prevent criminality via early intervention in the lives of delinquent youth. Of course, the inhumane and abusive treatment occurring in these reform schools would take decades to correct. However, accusations of frequent beatings and abuse didn't change the practice of placing young men in reform schools. Many thought children were malleable and so transformation was possible with the right intervention (Pisciotta, 1994).

People were committing crimes at an earlier age, so policymakers tried to institute reforms early in the lives of young people to curb this disease that was affecting society. This led to the rehabilitation movement in prisons, built on the premise that prisons should help eradicate crime by giving criminals the skills they need to avoid future offenses (Blomberg & Lucken, 2010). As a result, the states began to increase their efforts in rehabilitation. Criminals were seen as "sick" and in need of some "correction." If a criminal could be rehabilitated, then it was good for both society and the offender. Society was freed of the criminal act, and the criminal was no longer in need of supervision. The proponents of the rehabilitation model argued that this was a "win-win" outcome (Christian, 1998).

This meant that prisons would soon become more than holding cells for inmates or locations from which cheap labor could be sold. Instead, they became the place to try to "fix" the ills of a crime-filled society. Prisons began to offer vocational training programs to supply released offenders with job opportunities. The task of the prison was to educate the inmate, change their predispositions, and release them into society as a person ready to reintegrate. This model peaked in the 1950s as all sorts of educational and vocation programs found their ways into American prisons (Testa & West, 2010).

Until the 1970s, the United States had two separate systems: The criminal justice system dealt with the criminals, and the asylum system dealt with those struggling with mental illness. Asylums, like prisons, have a long history. Prior to the advent of modern psychiatric medications, asylums were often filled with a variety of individuals, some who had serious psychosis, and others who had experienced a short-term "breakdown." Prior to the 1970s, a suicide attempt would likely land a person in an asylum, from which they might never be freed (Jencks, 1994).

State asylums varied greatly and often did little more than tranquilize patients with the latest medications designed to keep them calm. Treatments such as we have today did not exist, and so asylums were filled with people who had dementia, seizures, and psychological problems, which could have resulted from diseases like syphilis. With one visit to a judge, an individual could be civilly committed for the rest of their life.

By the 1960s, many saw the U.S. civil commitment laws as too easily accessible, and legal battles emerged to free individuals who were perceived to be unlawfully detained. Through a long series of legal battles, laws began to change. Fiscal conservatives, who were weary of expanding government funding, joined forces with civil libertarians to end the expansive asylum system. This is often called the deinstitutionalization era (Jencks, 1994).

Ideally, those released from asylums were supposed to be supplied community-based mental health care under a law from 1963, the Community Mental Health Centers Act. While deinstitutionalization was an exceptionally positive thing for many who had been unnecessarily detained, it did not prevent the possibility of being charged with a criminal act. Those who were released from mental health hospitals now found themselves in prison for behaving in ways that previously would have landed them in an asylum (Testa & West, 2010). The end of the asylum system certainly contributed to the growth of prisons. The U.S. prison system became the system of last resort for many with mental health problems as states reduced the number of long-term commitment beds (Jencks, 1994).

Criminological studies suggest that deinstitutionalization did little to alleviate the actual root cause of crime and in fact transferred individuals out of a medical-type setting into one that was created for social control and public safety. The prison system became the final stop for many with serious mental health problems. This became known in the literature as "transinstitutionalization" since many who suffered persistent psychiatric disorders found themselves jumping from one short-term mental health center to another, and eventually into the prison system (Lamb & Weinberger, 2005; Prins, 2011).

Both authors have experience working inside prisons trying to supply mental health treatment to individuals who live there. However, the challenge of this work is great, particularly since prisons are set up to ensure security, while mental health centers are set up for treatment. Data from the Bureau of Justice Statistics shows that between 14% and 26% of inmates in American prisons showed signs of serious psychological distress in the previous 30 days. Twenty-four percent of all inmates had been diagnosed with a mental disorder at some point in their lives. By comparison, only 5% of the general population meet this standard. Transinstitutionalization has made the prison system the largest mental health provider in the United States (Bronson & Berzofsky, 2017; Prins, 2014).

Deinstitutionalization led to the end of the asylum system and, in part, to the growth of the prison system, which transitioned the United States away from the rehabilitation model toward a warehouse model. Two important characters to push this transition were President Ronald Reagan and sociologist Robert Martinson.

Ronald Reagan was a former actor and governor of California who was elected president in 1980. He entered the presidency during the era of deinstitutionalization. He faced increasing rates of self-medicating mentally ill people living on American streets and often engaging in crime. Reagan inherited Nixon's War on Drugs policy and set about treating the drug problem as a crime problem. Reagan and his Republican-controlled Congress pushed through laws making punishments harsher while expanding enforcement efforts that started the United States on the road to mass incarceration. From 1980 through 1996, the U.S. prison population grew by over 200%, in large part due to the policies put in place during the eight years of the Reagan administration. The Sentencing Project (2020) shows that from 1980 to 2020, the U.S. prison population grew by over 500%.

At this time, the United States was also embroiled in a media-induced fear known as "stranger danger." In the 1980s, a few well-published horrific crimes dominated the U.S. news. They all involved innocent children being abducted by strangers, brutalized, and usually murdered. Both political parties jumped on board to protect the children of the country. Despite the actual criminological evidence that these crimes were rare and, in fact, no more frequent in their occurrence than earlier times, fear and mass hysteria seemed to rule the day. Task forces to sort out these crimes were established and get-tough laws were passed by both Republican- and Democrat-controlled legislatures across the country, which increased the penalties for people who hurt children (Renfro, 2020).

By the 1990s, the United States was under the control of President Bill Clinton, who continued the rhetoric of the Reagan years. States began to memorialize child victims by passing legislation using the dead child's name. The Wetterling Act, in Minnesota, was named for a boy who was kidnapped and murdered. Megan Kanka, 7 years old at the time of her death, was murdered by a neighbor who was a discharged sex offender, which fostered amendments to the Wetterling Act to create a national sex offender registry to protect parents and allow anyone to track the movements of a released inmate who had been convicted of a sexual offense. Quickly, all states would follow suit while at the same time extending the severity of punishments for a host of crimes (Renfro, 2020).

During this same time, Robert Martinson, a sociologist, became a focal point for many who wanted more severe punishments. Martinson had been involved in social activism most of his life while at the same time researching what "worked" in prisons. After a review of recidivism data and program efficacy, he published a brief article entitled "What Works? Questions and Answers About Prison Reform" (Martinson, 1974). In the article, he argued that rehabilitation efforts had largely failed and were not successful in curbing criminality. Martinson's article, which was published initially in a relatively obscure source, would be discovered by politicians and the media, leading to a firestorm of articles, television appearances, and reports that "nothing works" when you're dealing with criminals (Lipton et al., 1975). This began a movement to effectively end the rehabilitation model of incarceration as it was a waste of time. After all, if "nothing works," then why pay to have rehabilitation programs in prisons? The incapacitation model, locking people up with few if any rehabilitation efforts, appeared as the dominant model for prisons in the United States in large part because of the work of Martinson (Cullen, 2013).

Many later investigations of the success or failure of rehabilitation appeared to contradict Martinson's claim. He eventually retracted his first article for methodological flaws, citing a host of programs that in fact did "work." These included but were not limited to family therapy, higher education, development of critical thinking skills, and psychological interventions, all of which either "worked" or "showed promise." However, this did not change the minds of politicians, social activists, and stakeholders, all of whom favored mass incarceration (Gendreau & Ross, 1987).

At this same time, legislatures began to pass what criminologists often call "get tough" laws, which all had the effect of keeping people in prison for longer and longer periods of time. Legislators who fought for increasing the severity of punishment often cited the work of Albert Blumstein and colleagues (1986), who coined the phrase "career criminal." Blumstein published research suggesting that most offenders were "repeat" offenders and that many did not particularly specialize in one type of crime. In other words, car thieves might be just as likely to rob you as take your car. Blumstein argued that small numbers of career criminals managed the lion's share of all crime. Logically, then, if you could simply incapacitate these "bad apples," crime would decrease.

As was the case with Martinson, Blumstein's research method was widely debated and doubted; researchers questioned his conclusions. Blumstein and his associates later agreed with those who questioned his research, but that did not change the minds of those who had decided that locking up "bad seeds" would stop crime (Piquero et al., 2003). This led to the rates of incarceration growing even more, not just because of an increasing number of people being incarcerated, but because those same people were kept in prison for longer and longer periods of time. It is important to note that much of the justification for these decisions was based on research that was questionable and that would later be criticized by the original authors of the studies, but that didn't change the trajectory of incarceration.

James Austin and Irwin (2001) note that from 1980 to 1998, the number of people incarcerated in the United States rose by over 200%, and this was predominately driven by "nonviolent" offenders. In 10 more years, the U.S. incarceration rate was so high that one out of every 48 adults was in prison.

This massive increase in incarceration had no quantifiable effect on the level of crime but certainly had an impact on spending on prisons

(Schmitt, 2010). The Pew Charitable Trusts report that spending on prisons increased by over 1,100% from 1977 to 2003. Meanwhile, spending on health and education programs grew by less than 600%, and public welfare spending increased by about 766% (Pew Charitable Trusts, 2007, 2013).

With states increasingly struggling to fund their growing prison systems, old ideas became new again. The job of a prison was simple—protect the public from "bad apples"—and it did that simply by keeping them locked up. Soon, the prison industry began to propose private prisons that could do the job of incarceration cheaper and better. Since rehabilitation programs were a minor concern and many felt that little could be done to change offenders, cheaper was better (Hallett, 2006).

Recall the model from the Middle Ages, where jails were owned by individuals and the state paid fees to house criminals. In 1983, the Corrections Corporation of America was formed and quickly grew into one of the largest and most lucrative prison companies in the United States. They built and operated prisons, claiming they could supply the same quality at a lower price (Gotsch & Basti, 2018). This appealed to state legislators who were struggling with overcrowded prisons and the need to use public funding to build more space to house the millions of people their policies had placed in the prison system (Hallett, 2006).

Private prisons quickly spread across the nation to meet the need for prison bedspace, resulting in 34 of the 50 states utilizing private prisons as a means to deal with their growing prison populations. In just 17 years, from 2000 to 2017, the private prison population grew by more than 70,000 inmates (Gotch & Basti, 2018).

Few seemed to question the morality of turning incarcerated people into profit centers for private enterprise, and since the majority of states were using private prisons, it became a normal part of the U.S. prison system. Table 2.1 shows the percentage change in the use of private prisons by state from 2000 to 2017. Seven states that were using private prisons in 2000 completely stopped using them by 2017. Meanwhile, other states, like Arizona, increased their use of private prisons by over 479% (Gotsch & Basti, 2018).

During the Obama administration, the use of private prisons was called into question. The Obama administration ceased using private

Table 2.1. PRIVATE PRISON USE BY STATE

Jurisdiction	% Change 2000–2017
Arkansas	−100
Kentucky	−100
Louisiana	−100
Maine	−100
Michigan	−100
North Dakota	−100
Utah	−100
Wisconsin	−100
North Carolina	−90.9
Alaska	−82.1
Maryland	−74.8
Idaho	−62.8
South Dakota	−24.4
Wyoming	−13.8
Texas	−9
Mississippi	−3.4
Virginia	−1.1
Oklahoma	6.1
New Jersey	6.4
Nevada	13.2
Hawaii	35
California	39.9
Montana	42.9
New Mexico	72.3
Federal System	77.6
Colorado	79.1
Georgia	110.4
Tennessee	116.8
Florida	198.5
Ohio	276.6
Indiana	309.8
Arizona	479.2

Source: Gotsch and Basti (2018).

prisons in the federal prison system, but that all changed with the election of Donald Trump. Trump reversed Obama's decision, and stock prices for the two largest prison corporations rose by about 100% (Long, 2017).

M. Alexander and West (2012) argue that public belief about the costs of incarceration goes largely unquestioned, indicating that most people feel their tax money is well spent on prisons. However, we are faced with the question as to whether or not this is actually true. As the reader progresses through this book, we will discuss many of the latent consequences of mass incarceration, and whether or not it is wise that we have created a Country Called Prison within our nation. We will argue that these policies have inadvertently created a country that we call Prison, which affects not only this generation but also future generations. One might question if the privatization movement has performed at the level it had promised. Is it, in fact, doing the job better and cheaper?

In a meta-analysis of 12 large studies on the efficacy of private prisons, Lundahl et al. (2009) found that the cost savings promised did not occur, at least not in all settings. At the same time, the outcome data for inmates did show some differences. For example, publicly managed prisons supplied better training programs and had fewer inmate complaints. Overall, the results promised by private prisons appear mixed. Private investment allowed states to continue to incarcerate larger and larger percentages of their populations without having to incur the infrastructure costs of building prisons. However, data on the cost per inmate is variable depending on the studies, suggesting that privatization has not yielded the promised results in all settings.

As a criminologist who has spent a career reviewing societal attempts to curb miscreant behavior, it is abundantly clear to me that no society has been able to end crime. In fact, the only way to successfully carry out that task would be the elimination of all laws. But that solution would clearly create more problems than it would solve.

Prisons have become the solution to the crime problem used by most of the Western world, not necessarily because they ever "worked," but perhaps because we cannot think of anything else to do with the people who break the rules of society.

Recidivism refers to an inmate returning to prison after incarceration. Studies on recidivism show that approximately two out of every three inmates released from prison will return within 3 years, and about three out of four will return within 5 years (Durose et al., 2014). However, it is important to note that a substantial number of those who returned to prison did not commit a new crime but violated their parole. Studies of the U.S. prison system show that about one in five people who enter prison in any given year is returning due to their parole being revoked, which can happen for technical violations such as missing a meeting, having a bad drug test, or not completing a required training in a prescribed period (P. Burke & Tonry, 2006; Grattet et al., 2008, 2009; Petersilia et al., 2007).

This chapter has tried to lead the reader through the history of incarceration in the United States, tracing its roots to a European system predominantly based in England. Even a cursory review of history will show that inmates have almost always been used as a profit center, and while it is no longer legal to force them to work as part of their incarceration, their presence in the prison results in public costs to care for them. Incarcerating anyone moves a person from a taxpayer to a tax user, and public policy should be reviewed to assure the public that their monies are being spent in the most effective, efficient, and humane manner.

CHAPTER 3

What Makes Prisons a Country?

Facts do not cease to exist because they are ignored.

Aldous Huxley

James was a young man from a troubled home, not that much different from millions of other troubled youth in America. His father was a high school dropout, frequently absent, occasionally abusive, always addicted. His mother, who was in a codependent relationship with James's father, prided herself on keeping a job. Each night she worked stocking shelves at a local Walmart, leaving James home alone with his drunken father.

Along with absent parents, James's siblings abandoned him as well. His older sister left the house when she was 16, and his brother died in a gang shootout at 18. Thus, James, the youngest, spent a great deal of time by himself. He ventured out of his home to enter a dilapidated neighborhood where his friends all had similar backgrounds. As he aged, James joined the family business—addiction. By the time he was 14, he was using and selling marijuana and methamphetamine to his friends. Frequent run-ins with the law led him to juvenile court and repeated trips to a variety of programs, all poorly funded and all optimistically promising to provide hope to the hopeless.

At 17, James was arrested during a drug sting; his prior juvenile record and age landed him in adult court. He pled guilty and accepted a 3-year sentence for selling drugs on school property to avoid the 10-year sentence for trafficking.

A Country Called Prison, Second Edition. John D. Carl and Mary D. Looman, Oxford University Press.
© Oxford University Press 2024. DOI: 10.1093/oso/9780197768310.003.0003

James had been in prison for about a month when John met with him to provide crisis counseling. The morning John met him, he found James in the shower, bleeding from his anus, after having been repeatedly raped by an undetermined number of prison inmates. While John addressed his mental health needs, a nurse provided emergency care. Later prison officers drove him to a hospital, where he had surgery to correct the physical damage from the rapes. When the hospital released James from the hospital, he was sent to a different prison for his own protection; officers placed him in seclusion for the remainder of his sentence. James wisely never revealed who had raped him. In prison, ratting out your fellow inmates could be grounds for murder.

James's story is like those of thousands of people who have been sent to America's prisons. A young man or woman with a troubled background commits a minor crime. They are incarcerated in an unsafe situation for a lengthy period. For many, that first incarceration puts them on the road to a lifetime of trouble. The options for life outside of prison for someone like James are quite limited. When he returned home, he reentered a community similar to prison because it too had few jobs. In addition, the neighborhood had limited social resources such as educational opportunities, mass transit, and social welfare agencies designed to help former inmates reenter society. Add to this the fact that when the Jameses of the world return home, they often reintegrate with the same unreliable, addicted, and criminal social networks they had left and you can see why this community, and many more like it across the United States, are merely provinces of the Country Called Prison.

Prison changes a person, and it certainly changed James. In our careers we have met many people like him. They come from dysfunctional families and end up in prison for minor drug offenses. Then they leave prison after a few years, only to return a few months or a few years later. This is the cycle of their lives. People just like James made us realize that when a person enters prison in the United States, they, in effect, cease to be American citizens. Instead, they become citizens of a Country Called Prison.

Inmates enter a country with its own culture, language, rules, and regulations that they learn. Once they are released from prison, their original homeland rarely welcomes them back. In fact, prisoners are like the millions of undocumented immigrants who enter the United States each year, people who live in plain sight but are not a viable part of American society.

James and those like him are members of a foreign country, living not on foreign land but within the borders of the United States. Of course, they are different from the thousands who cross U.S. borders illegally each year because they were born here. Now they are citizens of another country but live in America as *legal aliens*. In this chapter, we discuss the elements that make a group of people *a country* (or nation) and why the U.S. prison system fits those characteristics.

WHAT MAKES A COUNTRY A NATION?

According to the Oxford Dictionaries online (http://www.oxfordd ictionaries.com), a *nation* is a "large body of people united by a common descent, history, culture and language, inhabiting a particular state or territory." While on the surface this description does not seem to apply to prisoners and prisons, we believe that each of these characteristics is present in the current prison system of the United States. Residents of a Country Called Prison form a national identity and develop a social personality that stems from shared experiences, which suggest that they have a shared culture. Therefore, to understand what makes prison a country, we must first understand the concept of *culture*.

Animals are born with instincts to survive. While humans are born with a basic survival instinct, we have something better than instinct to help ensure our survival. We have culture, and cultures can evolve just like animal species. The 1981 film *Escape From New York* depicts a culture that evolved from a prison environment (Carpenter, 1981). The movie depicts a future where the United States has turned New York City into one large maximum security prison. A large wall surrounding the city creates a fortified prison. The courts send the worst of the worst antisocial citizens to the city for the rest of their lives, and prisoners run the city as they see fit.

In the movie, the president of the United States ejects from a damaged *Air Force One* and lands in the middle of New York City. Through a series of plot twists, Snake Plissken (Kurt Russell), a prisoner held in a "regular" U.S. prison, is offered freedom if he can rescue the president from New York City. Of course, the prison lord of the city, known as the Duke of New York (Isaac Hayes), runs the city with his own gang of thugs who control every aspect of life there. This group, left to its own devices, created a culture with political, economic, and social norms. The film shows that in the absence of prescribed rules and roles, humans will band together to survive. Out of this process society members create a culture.

Culture is composed of material and nonmaterial components. The material aspects of culture involve the physical stuff you can taste, touch, and feel. When you visit a prison, you experience an unfamiliar material culture. You enter through a "sally port," which is a secure sliding door. In prison, you become accustomed to locking doors, small windows, and bars. Razor-wire fencing becomes something through which you view the outside world. All shirts worn have "inmate" or "corrections" stenciled on the back. All these aspects, and many more, make up the material culture of a Country Called Prison. The nonmaterial aspects of culture include the shared knowledge of the customs and the way members of society do things. We will discuss nonmaterial culture further in later chapters.

Without culture, we cannot survive physically or psychologically. Culture serves some essential functions. It teaches us values and beliefs. It gives us a language. It organizes our lives and helps us make sense of the world around us. Most of the time we take culture for granted, giving it little thought.

When John teaches about culture, he asks his students to name the core components of U.S. culture. The students write a list of values, beliefs, and expected norms or behaviors that are unique to America. It usually takes some time to compile the list. Once completed, and the students agree that the list accurately represents U.S. culture, the class has something to bind the members together. Culture does much more than tell us what to believe, how to talk, and how we should behave. It binds us to other people from the same culture. In short, it creates a blueprint for social solidarity.

Culture, in any society, is not static. It is adaptive, meaning that it changes with the times. Since culture provides us with social norms and notions of acceptable behavior, it must be fluid. Social situations are always changing.

Culture teaches us the acceptable and unacceptable ways to behave in certain situations. For example, if you are at a football game, it is normal to yell. If you are at a funeral, it is not acceptable. The setting determines the appropriate behavior. As an intake psychologist, Mary meets adults as they are entering into prison. First-timers are always frightened and unsure of what they are supposed to do. Some hide their fear, acting calmer than anyone should upon entering prison. Others show their distress with an angry tone and derogatory statements. Occasionally someone breaks down and cries in Mary's office. She always tries to help new prisoners deal with their feelings, but she also teaches them that crying and showing fear and excessive anger will likely cause them trouble in prison.

A culture is like a stream that meanders around rocks and erodes soft riverbanks. The stream never flows the same way year after year. Culture works in the same way. Think about how Americans have changed the way they socially interact with each other since the invention of the computer and mobile phones compared to 30 years ago. At one time we called people to see how they were. Today if we use a phone, we normally text. More frequently we use social media to catch up with old friends. All cultures change. What is the point of this discussion? Prison is a culture, and culture changes over time. Therefore, prisons have changed a great deal in the past 30 years, yet many are still operating with 30-year-old standards.

Culture is not innate in human beings; we are not born with an instinct for a specific culture. We learn culture through interactions with others and from adults, especially parents and teachers. Infants begin learning language and facial expressions the minute they are born. By age 2, children have learned the language, gestures, voice tones, and symbolic meanings of their world and readily understand if mom is mad about the crayon marks on the wall. By middle school, preteens have learned the subtleties of flirting and the hurt of sarcastic snubbing. If we were to move to another country, we would need to adapt to that culture to survive socially and psychologically, and sometimes even physically. As we move forward, let us review the characteristics of the Country Called Prison.

Land, in and of itself, does not a country make. If it did, Antarctica would be a country. People create a country. Even people living as a group do not always make a country. Many U.S. universities with 20,000 students or more might be considered small countries. So why are we claiming that criminals and prisoners, as a group, are a country?

First, let us look at the demographic characteristics of those in prison in the United States. Table 3.1 shows the ages of male and female prison inmates sentenced in 2019 in the United States (Carson, 2020). These data combine both state and federal prison data and follow a predictable pattern. Males and females enter prison at higher percentages in their 20s and lower 30s. The largest percentage for reception of both groups is in their early 30s, with the late 30s and late 20s following. More than 56% of new receptions in 2019 were under the age of 40. This follows a historically predictable pattern over the past several years. Simply put, nothing curbs incarceration odds like a 40th birthday. Notice how the percentage of receptions of both men

Table 3.1. PERCENTAGE OF SENTENCED PRISONERS IN U.S. STATE AND FEDERAL CORRECTIONAL FACILITIES AS OF DECEMBER 31, 2019, BY AGE AND GENDER

Age Group	Total	Male	Female
	100	100	100
18–19	**0.7**	0.7	0.4
20–24	**8.1**	8.2	7.4
25–29	**15.4**	15.2	16.9
30–34	**16.2**	15.9	19.6
35–39	**15.8**	15.6	18.1
40–44	**12.4**	12.4	12.5
45–49	**10.1**	10.1	9.6
50–54	**8.1**	8.2	7.1
55–59	**6.3**	6.4	4.6
60–64	**3.6**	3.7	2.1
65 or older	**3.2**	3.4	1.6
Number of sentenced	**1,380,427**	1,279,079	101,348

Source: Bureau of Justice Statistics. National Prisoner Statistics, 2019.

and women consistently drops with age. Thus, the population of the Country Called Prison is young. Demographically speaking, young adults contribute more to the welfare of society than do older adults because they are at their peak economic production years. This loss of potential income for this group is difficult to measure but important to note (Ogunwole et al., 2021, August).

As discussed previously, Black people are overrepresented in the prison population. The data suggest however, that this is more pronounced in the young. A review of Table 3.2 shows that overrepresentation of both Black and Hispanics is most pronounced with individuals under the age of 34. Data from the Bureau of Justice Statistics show minimal variability between age group and the race of offenders (Carson, 2020). Thus, regardless of racial category, the rate of incarceration follows the same percentages for the total age groups shown in Table 3.2.

Table 3.3 provides racial data on admission to prisons of the three largest racial/ethnic groups in the federal prison system. Only 7.7% of

Table 3.2. PERCENTAGE OF SENTENCED PRISONERS IN U.S. STATE AND FEDERAL PRISONS AS OF DECEMBER 31, 2019, BY AGE, GENDER, AND RACE

Age Group	Male				Female			
	White	Black	Hispanic	Other	White	Black	Hispanic	Other
	100	100	100	100	100	100	100	100
18–19	0.3	1	0.6	0.5	0.2	0.6	0.5	0
20–24	5.5	9.8	9.1	7.4	5.6	9.6	9.5	7.8
25–29	12.1	16.7	16.7	15.1	15.4	18	18.9	17.5
30–34	15.1	15.7	17.4	16.5	20.3	17.4	20.5	20.5
35–39	15.8	14.8	17	16.9	18.8	15.2	18.9	18.7
40–44	12.5	12.1	13.4	12.9	12.9	11.2	12.1	12.7
45–49	11.1	9.7	9.6	10.6	10.2	9.6	8.4	8.4
50–54	9.6	8.1	6.8	7.8	7.3	8.4	5.8	6.6
55–59	8.1	6.2	4.6	5.7	5	5.6	3.2	4.2
60–64	4.8	3.5	2.6	3.4	2.3	2.2	1.1	2.4
65 or older	5.1	2.3	2.2	3.2	1.9	1.7	1.1	1.8
Number of sentenced	374,900	435,000	301,700	167,400	47,900	17,800	19,000	16,600

Sources: Bureau of Justice Statistics, Federal Justice Statistics Program, 2019 (preliminary); National Corrections Reporting Program, 2018; National Prisoner Statistics, 2009–2019; Survey of Inmates in State and Federal Correctional Facilities, 2004; and Survey of Prison Inmates, 2016.

Table 3.3. PERCENT OF SENTENCED PRISONERS IN THE CUSTODY OF FEDERAL PRISONS, 2019

		All Prisoners	Male	Female	White	Black	Hispanic
	Total	100	100	100	100	100	100
Violent Crimes		7.7	8	4.1	6.4	10.2	2.7
	Homicide	1.7	1.7	1.3	0.7	2.6	0.4
	Robbery	3.5	3.6	1.4	3.9	5.4	1
	Sexual abuse	0.8	0.9	0.1	0.7	0.4	0.2
	Other	1.7	1.7	1.4	1.1	1.8	1
Property		5.3	4.7	14.1	7.2	5.5	3
	Burglary	0.2	0.2	0.1	0.1	0.3	0
	Fraud	4.2	3.6	11.9	5.7	4.3	2.6
	Other	0.9	0.8	2.1	1.4	0.9	0.4
Drug		46.3	45.3	59.2	38.1	43.3	59.8
Public Order		40.3	41.6	22.1	47.6	40.8	34.3
	Immigration	5.3	5.4	3.3	0.5	0.3	16.1
	Weapons	18.5	19.6	4.7	14.6	30.1	9.3
	Other	16.5	16.6	14.1	32.4	10.4	8.8
Unspecified		0.4	0.4	0.4	0.6	0.3	0.2
	Total number of sentenced prisoners	158,107	147,100	11,000	45,900	57,900	48,800

Sources: Bureau of Justice Statistics, Federal Justice Statistics Program, 2019 (preliminary); National Corrections Reporting Program, 2018; National Prisoner Statistics, 2009–2019; Survey of Inmates in State and Federal Correctional Facilities, 2004; and Survey of Prison Inmates, 2016.

all prisoners in the federal system are in for violent offenses. However, almost half the prisoners (46.3%) have drug offenses. This is in keeping with the federal emphasis on enforcing the War on Drugs.

The second largest category in the federal system is classified as public order crimes (40.3%), which include weapons violations, immigration violations, and the catch-all "other" category, which encompasses a host of violations including human trafficking. Violent crime admissions to federal prisons are higher for Black people than any other category, other than sexual offenses, which is dominated by Whites.

Table 3.4 details state-level incarceration rates for the year 2020. A quick review shows a stark difference between the percentages of those incarcerated in the state prison system versus the federal system, with most male offenders being incarcerated for violent offenses

Table 3.4. PERCENT OF SENTENCED PRISONERS UNDER THE JURISDICTION OF STATE CORRECTIONAL AUTHORITIES, 2020

Most Serious Offense	All	Male	Female	White	Black	Hispanic
	100	100	100	100	100	100
Violent	62.4	63.9	45	54.6	67.9	79.2
Murder	15	15.2	14.3	11.5	18.2	17.2
Negligent manslaughter	1.8	1.6	3.8	1.6	1	1.3
Rape/sexual assault	15.5	16.4	3.1	19.6	9.7	15.9
Robbery	12.5	12.9	7.7	6.7	19.3	11.7
Aggravated/simple assault	13.9	14.1	11.5	11.5	15.4	28.8
Other	3.8	3.7	4.7	3.7	4.1	4.3
Property	13.5	13.1	19.3	18.5	10.9	8
Burglary	7.6	7.8	6	9.3	7	5.4
Larceny/theft	2.5	2.3	6	4.2	2	1
Motor vehicle theft	0.7	0.7	0.9	0.8	0.4	0.4
Fraud	1.2	1	4.5	2.1	0.8	0.4
Other	1.4	1.4	2	2.1	0.8	0.8
Drug	12.6	11.8	24.7	15.1	10.8	6.4
Possession	3.2	2.9	7.6	4.5	2.3	1.3
Other	9.4	8.8	17.1	10.6	8.5	5.1
Public Order	10.5	10.5	9.9	11	10	6.1
Weapons	3.7	3.9	1.3	2.2	4.9	2.9
DUI/DWI	1.4	1.4	2.2	2.1	0.6	0.8
Other	5.3	5.3	6.3	6.7	4.5	2.5
Unspecified	0.7	0.6	1.1	0.8	0.4	0.3
Total of inmates	1,043,705	973,343	70,362	327,300	345,500	226,800

Sources: Bureau of Justice Statistics, National Corrections Reporting Program, 2018; National Prisoner Statistics, 2018; and Survey of Prison Inmates, 2016.

and drug offenses accounting for 12.6% of all offenders. Regarding the racial data, there is consistency with the federal system, with White people having higher rates of rape and sexual assault crimes and Black people and Hispanics having higher rates of murder.

Depending on the group, drug and property crimes account for almost half of those going to prison in the federal system, but this is not so in the state system, which houses mostly violent offenders. It is important to note that 3.8% of the violent offenses are under the category "other," which frequently can include selling certain types of drugs in large enough amounts to be considered by a court as "violent." Additionally, violent offenses carry a longer sentence than nonviolent

Table 3.5. PERCENTAGE OF CRIME BY MALES AND FEMALES

Offense	Percentage by Male	Percentage by Female
Total Violent	31.5	18.4
Murder	2.4	1.7
Negligent manslaughter	0.8	1.1
Rape/sexual assault	6.3	1.0
Robbery	8.3	6.9
Assault	11.2	6.9
Other violent	2.4	2.8
Total Property	26.4	36.0
Burglary	12.6	8.0
Larceny	5.3	10.6
Motor vehicle theft	1.7	1.5
Fraud	3.1	11.7
Other property	3.7	4.1
Total Drug	23.9	32.5
Possession	7.2	11.7
Other drug	16.7	.08
Public Order	17.4	12.0
Other	0.7	1.1
New Court Commitments	351,326	47,383

Source: Carson and Golinelli (2013).

ones, and so while it is certainly true that in the state system we have more offenders imprisoned for violent crimes, this does not necessarily tell the whole story.

Table 3.5 provides data on new prison commitments in 2011, breaking them down by offense and gender. One can see that reception data are different from incarceration data in that they are dominated by nonviolent offenders who commit drug or property crimes. The discrepancy in the data can be attributed to the reality that violent offenders serve longer sentences, and so while the prison populations, particularly in state prisons, are dominated by violent offenders, the individuals who enter prison in any given year are less likely to be violent offenders.

These commitment data also show some variation, particularly as it applies to gender differences. For example, women are more likely to commit property offenses, with fraud (usually writing a bad check or using someone else's credit card) and larceny (usually shoplifting) leading the way. Furthermore, women who enter prison for drug possession do so at a higher rate than men. A third of new female commitments to prison were for drug offenses, compared to 23.9% for their male counterparts. For comparison purposes, 68.5% of men versus 81.6% of women enter prison for nonviolent offenses. So, depending on how you want to review the data, you can tell different stories. What all the data do show is that prisons, whether federal or state, have a substantial representation of drug offenders.

Next, Table 3.6 tells the tale of who is in prison. Many have addiction problems. The table provides trend data on offenders in the years 1991, 2001, and 2011, taken from statistics gathered by the Bureau of Justice Statistics. It breaks these data into two groups, first for new

Table 3.6. TRENDS IN FIRST COMMITMENT AND PAROLE VIOLATIONS

Offense	1991		2001		2011	
	First Commitment	Parole Violation	First Commitment	Parole Violation	First Commitment	Parole Violation
All Violent	28.7	23.7	29.4	23.9	30.0	27.4
Murder	3.0	1.7	2.5	1.3	2.4	1.2
Negligent	1.3	0.5	1.0	0.4	0.8	.3
Rape/sex assault	5.6	3.6	6.3	3.4	5.7	4.8
Robbery	9.9	11.6	8.1	9.2	7.9	8.4
Assault	7.5	5.5	9.2	7.9	10.7	10.5
Other violent	1.4	0.7	2.3	1.8	2.5	2.2
All Property	31.4	42.4	27.4	32.5	27.5	32.4
Burglary	13.5	20.8	10.4	12.9	12.1	13.1
Larceny	8.1	11.7	6.6	8.8	5.9	6.6
Motor vehicle theft	2.4	4.1	2.0	3.9	1.7	4.9
Fraud	3.8	1.8	4.7	3.3	4.1	3.4
Other property	3.6	1.8	3.7	3.5	3.8	4.4
All Drug	29.9	25.5	30.5	35.1	24.9	26.2
Possession	6.9	7.0	8.7	9.1	7.8	8.7
Other drug	23.0	18.5	21.8	26.0	17.2	17.5
Public Order	8.9	6.1	12.1	8.0	16.8	13.2
Other	1.1	2.3	0.6	0.5	0.8	0.8
Number of Admissions	317,237	142,100	365,229	215,344	398.709	200,481

Source: Carson and Golinelli (2013).

commitments that year, and second for those who violated parole and returned to prison. The parole violator data are categorized by the offense that initially sent the criminals to prison, not by the offense that returned them to prison. Therefore, one should not conclude that the same type of crime returned the offender to prison—the data do not provide that level of accuracy. But the data do show that over this 20-year period, the percentage of violent offenses remained stable.

The last row shows the number of admissions for each category. You can see that the group returning to prison via parole violation is half the size of the group entering prison for the first time. Therefore, in general terms, about a third of those who went to prison in the years listed were parole violators. Across the board, the ratio of violent criminals to property criminals varies. In some years first-time offenders are more likely to be property criminals instead of violent offenders, and in others it is just the opposite. The point is that these rates have not changed a great deal. The percentages of who goes to prison and for what crimes remain stable over time.

While data on parole violations do not show us why the individual returned to prison, they do illustrate the prison population further. Many of those currently in prison had been released after serving their time but now have returned for some reason. We will discuss technical violations of parole in subsequent chapters. It is important to note that violating parole may or may not mean that another crime has been committed. Missing a meeting with the parole officer is enough to send a person back to prison under the right circumstances.

We talked a bit about who lives or has lived in prison. But how many people are in prison? This question should be easy to answer. After all, inmates are counted every night. However, the answer is more complex than you might think.

To curb crime, the United States began experimenting with large-scale incarceration. In the late 1970s the total prison population (state and federal) was approximately 300,000. Now, the number has soared to well over 1.5 million prison inmates (Glaze & Parks, 2012). However, if all individuals who are currently under some form of government supervision—via parole, probation, prison, and local jails—are included, that number explodes to more than 6.9 million. We suggest that everyone who is under supervision by the criminal justice

Table 3.7. U.S. PRISON POPULATION COMPARED TO
THAT OF SELECTED COUNTRIES

Population Rank	Country	Population
101	Bulgaria	6,924,716
	A Country Called Prison	6,900,000
102	Laos	6,803,699

Source: Central Intelligence Agency (2013).

system is a citizen of the Country Called Prison. Table 3.7 provides some comparisons for you to consider related to countries and their size relative to 6.9 million.

When one compares the number of people under supervision by the criminal justice system to the population estimates of countries around the world, relative to country size, the U.S. correctional system ranks 101st out of 239 countries in population size. It is larger than many countries, including New Zealand (which is 125th), Norway (119th), and Denmark (113th; Central Intelligence Agency, 2013). The fact is that one out of every 33 people, or about 3% of the U.S. population, is under some form of supervision for criminal activity at any given time (Glaze & Parks, 2012).

Despite recent small declines in prison populations, the total number of individuals who inhabit the Country Called Prison is larger than the populations of half of the countries in the world. And this number does not include the millions who have been arrested and convicted of a felony but have not gone to prison. We suggest that once you are arrested and convicted of a crime, regardless of whether you go to prison or not, you become a legal alien in the United States as you cross the border into the Country Called Prison.

Estimates suggest that 65 million Americans have criminal records by the time they are 23 years of age. Having a criminal record can lead to employment problems and a host of other social ills (Glaze & Parks, 2012). At the same time, only 14% of the arrests are for violent or simple assault crimes (Solomon, 2012). Data show that those 65 million who have an an arrest record by the age of 23 make up a country with a slightly lower population than France but higher than Great Britain, making it the 22nd largest country on the planet (Central Intelligence

Agency, 2013). We suggest that once an individual enters into the world of criminal records, they being begin the process of joining a country called prison.

This does not tell the whole story though. What about those who have been released from prison? In 2001, 4.3 million of the 5.6 million adults who had been incarcerated previously were no longer in prison. In other words, a vast majority of those we had previously sent to prison had been released. However, that does not mean they reassimilate to the U.S. culture. In fact, former prisoners account for 77% of all adult residents who had ever been confined in prison (Bonczar, 2003).

Research completed by the Bureau of Justice Statistics estimated that 5.1% of all Americans will go to prison in their lifetime (Bonczar & Beck, 1997). So, using current population numbers, we can estimate the current population who have been or will be in prison. In 2023 the U.S. population was calculated to be approximately 339,996,563. If we take 5.1% of that number, we get 17,339,825. This number would rank as the 73rd largest country in the world (Table 3.8), just slightly smaller

Table 3.8. WORLD POPULATION REVIEW OF CRIMES BY COUNTRY

Rank	Country	Population (2023)
1	India	1,428,627,663
2	China	1,425,671,352
3	United States	339,996,563
10	Mexico	128,455,567
19	Germany	83,294,633
38	Canada	38,781,291
55	Australia	26,439,111
72	Netherlands	17,618,299
	U.S. Prison Population	17,045,927
82	Belgium	11,686,140
100	Austria	8,958,960
115	Denmark	5,910,913
139	Jamaica	2,825,544
179	Iceland	375,318
216	Liechtenstein	39,584

Source: World Population Review (2023).

than the Netherlands and slightly larger than Senegal. Seventeen million people would be a country approximately twice the size of Austria and half the size of Peru. These data certainly support the notion that the U.S. prison population is sufficiently large enough to be considered a nation (World Population Review, 2023).

But let us consider one more comparison for the prison population. If the total population of those incarcerated, as well as those who have been or will be incarcerated, were considered as a whole, that number of 17,045,927 would rank as the fifth largest state in the nation (Table 3.9). Imagine if these people were collectively treated the same as nonoffender citizens and had political representation like a state. Prison would become a "swing state" in any presidential election and have more representatives in Congress than 45 other jurisdictions. Of course, this does not happen, but the power of these numbers certainly identifies a large enough population of incarcerated people to be considered a country.

We present these numbers to give you a perspective on the size of the Country Called Prison. They paint a picture of a large population of people who share similar cultural experiences. Their crimes are nonviolent, and they are disproportionately people of color.

So how many citizens make up the Country Called Prison? Conservatively, we believe 17 million, since that is a statistical estimate built on firm research. However, since one does not actually

Table 3.9. STATE RANKING BY OFFENDER POPULATION

State Ranking	Population (2022)
California	39,029,342
Texas	30,029,572
Florida	22,244,823
New York	19,677,151
U.S. Prison Population	17,045,927
Pennsylvania	12,972,008
Illinois	12,582,032
Ohio	11,756,058
Georgia	10,912,876
North Carolina	10,698,973

Source: World Population Review (2023). U.S. Census. (2020).

have to go to prison to be a citizen of the Country Called Prison (they need only be convicted of a felony), we believe the population is much larger. When you add in the families and friends of inmates, this number becomes even larger.

Being convicted of a felony changes lives permanently. Jobs, housing, and many career paths are limited for most felons. If someone is convicted of a drug felony, certain college funding sources become unavailable. Furthermore, once convicted of a felony, not only you but also your entire family are more likely to suffer. For example, children whose fathers go to prison are at increased risk of incarceration themselves (Wakefield & Wildeman, 2014).

However, even at the more conservative number of 17 million, which is based on empirical data, we are talking about a population that is greater than that of the fifth largest state in the nation and a country bigger than many of our allies. For this reason, we believe that the U.S. prison system can be considered a country with its own culture that exists within the borders of American society.

Regardless of its exact size, the population of the Country Called Prison is considerable. As we demonstrated earlier, about half of those who go to prison do so for nonviolent offenses, offenses that do not scare us but only make us mad. This raises many questions about social policies and the use of tax dollars. However, at this point, let us look further into why we consider the prison system to have its own culture, which makes it a country and not just a large group of people.

COMMON HISTORY

People from a country share a common history, which usually means, at least from a nation-state point of view, that they share experiences and historical connections to similar events. Americans all share a common history when we celebrate the Fourth of July or Thanksgiving. Clearly people in the Country Called Prison share these common historical events with all Americans. The question is, do they share other aspects of a common history that noncriminals do not share?

Although most people in prison do not know each other prior to entering, many share a common history—that of poverty, abuse, and alienation from the U.S. culture. Research has clearly demonstrated that prisons in the United States are disproportionately filled with people from lower-income homes (Reiman, 1998; Western & Pettit, 2010). Poverty, as we will discuss later in this section, is common to the lives of many who end up in prison.

In 1940 Donald Clemmer published the first research to suggest that prisons have a common culture. Working in a penitentiary in Illinois, Clemmer suggested that inmates create a culture and society with different values and norms. He termed the process by which prisoners learn these norms and values *prisonization*. With so many returning year in and year out, prison becomes a part of the common history all felons and inmates share. Many prison inmates are parents, and their children will also adopt this prison culture as normative. In many respects, the normalization of prison is a travesty of the modern age. Normalizing children's visits to see their incarcerated parents seems particularly problematic if our goal is to decrease criminality and incarceration.

Following the work of Clemmer, Gresham Sykes (1958) suggested that prison culture originates from the deprivation that the offender experiences in prison. Sykes identified five types of deprivation: loss of liberty, loss of goods and services that one is used to in the free world, loss of autonomy, loss of heterosexual relationships, and loss of safety. Since material goods are culturally important to Americans, the inability of inmates to acquire material possessions in prison is quite damaging to their self-worth and self-esteem. Based on our observation, deprivation of material goods is one of the main reasons that the predatory milieu and contraband exist in most prisons.

Another question to ask is, are the individuals who go to prison generally surprised by deprivation? Jeffrey Reiman's book *The Rich Get Richer, and the Poor Get Prison* (1998) provides ample evidence to support the claim that the poor are disproportionately represented in the prison population. While the poor may or may not be more criminal, they certainly are more likely to go to prison. Since social class differences permeate the prison system, many who enter prison are already set up for the deprivation that Sykes describes.

In her transformational book *A Framework for Understanding Poverty*, Ruby Payne (2005) identifies the differences between those who grow up poor and those who grow up in the middle and upper classes. Her description of individuals growing up in poverty mirrors Sykes's deprivation model in many ways. People who are poor struggle to obtain needed goods. They frequently must live in substandard housing in dangerous neighborhoods. Therefore, they suffer the deprivation of safety just as they would in prison. In addition, many suffer a loss of personal autonomy, primarily due to the poverty in which they live. Without expendable cash, individuals struggle to be independent and have limited choices.

When we add Payne's ideas to the work of others, we find it hard to deny that many in prison, particularly those who come from poverty, enter with an ingrained perspective of deprivation. As many have pointed out, when one lives in poverty, goods, freedom, and autonomy are difficult to obtain, which resembles the prison experience (Brooks-Gunn et al., 1993; Edin & Lein, 1997; W. Wilson, 1987).

The Brookings Institute found that almost half of incarcerated men were employed in the 3 years prior to their incarceration (Looney & Turner, 2018). Their median income during that time was around $6,250, and less than 14% earned more than $15,000 a year in any of these years. The study also found that the individuals not only were poor but also came from poor neighborhoods and poor families. A boy from a family in the bottom 10% of incomes in a country was 20 times more likely to end up in prison than someone from a more affluent background in the top 10%. Single-parent households were found to increase the odds of incarceration by a factor of two.

A common history is the way a group of people thinks, perceives themselves, and believes about themselves in relation to other groups. While all people in the United States are free to choose, the choices are not always as plentiful as people might think. Choices are made in the context in which one lives. If, for example, you ask yourself why you married the person you did, you may find that a social context was involved. Most people marry someone who is geographically close to them. If you grow up in Montana, you are likely to marry someone from Montana. If geography is strongly linked to marriage, is your choice of a marriage partner really "your choice"?

Many life choices work that way. Instead of making choices using an objective thought process, people choose because of a complex series of social accidents. Put another way, the way we make choices is often influenced by the way we see the world, something that is often unconsciously and culturally learned (Edin & Kefalas, 2005).

For example, the university where we teach has a rival university in another part of the state. Students say they "hate" our rival. We ask our students, "If you happened to have been raised in the town of that rival university, and if you happened to have had a parent who worked there, would you feel differently about that institution? Would you hate it as vehemently?" The honest answer for most is "probably not." So why did they choose our university? For most of them, the university is geographically close to their home or they received a scholarship. Like the decision to select a life partner, selecting a school is hardly a free, unrestricted choice.

The poor in America make choices that many in the middle and upper classes may not understand. In the book *Promises I Can Keep*, Edin and Kefalas (2005) suggest that many poor women make the decision to become mothers in a social context that is often difficult for those who are not poor to understand. For some women, the decision to become a mother is made because it is an event that they believe they can control. In a world where they have so little power, poor women believe that parenting is a promise they can keep. Therefore, many young, single women growing up in poverty choose to get pregnant, which does not always make sense to the middle and upper classes.

Most of our decisions occur in a context that is beyond others' experience. We both have taught at the community-college level and have known poor students who often miss class because they have childcare responsibilities. Others miss because their cars break down or their ride to school does not show up. Their childhoods were not filled with Little League baseball and summer camps. Their choices occur in a context that many "traditional" college students can barely understand. If you are a poor mother and your child is sick, you are going to miss an exam, even if it means you fail the course.

Conversely, the complications of choice are not all that influence the lives of those who may become citizens of the Country Called Prison. As previously mentioned, poor neighborhoods in America also tend to experience more violence. If you are poor and you live in a dangerous neighborhood, you do not have the financial resources to move. You are trapped. And sometimes protecting yourself means you end up committing a crime that lands you in prison.

Children growing up in such neighborhoods share similar disadvantages. When you are surrounded by drug abuse, violence, and underperforming schools, you are disadvantaged in the U.S. society. When you know nothing else, you are truly disadvantaged. The limited availability of role models to teach children another way of life places limits on their potential, as well as their freedom and autonomy. Since inmates are more likely to be from poor backgrounds, many share this common history of disadvantage (W. Wilson, 1987).

Not only are poor people deprived of autonomy by their economic situation, but also they lack autonomy because of their limited opportunities. Nowhere is this more pronounced than in education. Numerous studies show that educationally the poor are underserved. The schools they attend are often poorly funded and the quality of public education they receive is not equivalent to that of their middle- and upper-class counterparts (Kozol, 1991; Roscigno et al., 2006).

The same holds true for higher education. The poorer that people are, the more difficulty they have in completing a college degree (K. Alexander et al., 1987; Dynarski, 2003; Haveman & Smeeding, 2007). Inmate populations reflect these educational differences. Data previously published in our first edition mimic more recent data showing the educational disadvantage of those who are incarcerated. In 2003 data showed that slightly more than 41% of inmates had only attended some high school or less, compared to 18% of the general population (Harlow, 2003). Data from the National Center for Educational Statistics updated the review of the prison population in 2016 and found similar trends (Rampey et al., 2016). Table 3.10 presents the data discovered in their research. Note that the data represent the

Table 3.10. COMPARISON OF EDUCATION LEVEL OF PRISON POPULATION AND U.S. HOUSEHOLDS, 2016

Highest Level of Education	Percentage in Prison	Percentage in U.S. Households
Graduate/professional	1%	13%
Bachelor's degree	1%	12%
Associate's degree	4%	9%
High school credentials	64%	50%
Below high school	30%	14%

Source: Rampey et al. (2016).

highest level of education for each group. Sixty-four percent of U.S. households have educational attainment of high school or lower, while 94% of inmates have that characteristic. Most of our students see education as a way to financial success. However, these data show that those who enter the Country Called Prison are likely to be some of the least educated people in America and, therefore, the least successful.

Economic deprivation greatly complicates people's lives. American culture is dominated by materialism and equates wealth with success, thus making the poor the least valued. We often link self-esteem and definitions of success to wealth in the United States. In fact, economic success dominates the American scene. Some have argued that the disadvantages of the poor, coupled with the dominant cultural value of wealth and success, may be the reason some turn to criminal behavior (Messner & Rosenfield, 2008). While this may or may not be true, one thing is certain: The Country Called Prison is filled with residents who come from disadvantaged backgrounds.

Having worked in corrections, psychiatric centers, and hospitals for years, we have witnessed a striking reality. Many people have never really been taught how to act properly in society. This is especially true of offenders. Many were never actually socialized into U.S. culture before they came to prison. Since many come from deprived backgrounds, it is not surprising that the rules they learned growing up hinder their success. Recall that James followed in his family's footsteps and embraced the addict lifestyle.

Rather than receive *re*habilitation in prison, many of the people with whom we have worked need "habilitation." Why would we say this? Because many offenders were never educated in American social norms and citizenship standards of the United States in the first place. Not only do offenders find themselves excluded from U.S. culture while they are in prison, but also, once they are released, opting back into society is extremely difficult for most.

NATIONAL IDENTITY

As both Clemmer and Sykes showed in their research, inmates maintain a separate identity from American society. Accepting a national identity is part of being a citizen of a country. Respecting the flag and watching fireworks on the Fourth of July are part of U.S. national identity. Most citizens of a country take pride in their national identity and believe their nation is number one.

For citizens of the Country Called Prison, national identity is a little different. First, inmates know they hold an identity that few want. In fact, most people, including those who go to prison, want to avoid this identity. However, there is no avoiding the distinctiveness that is associated with the Country Called Prison. Inmates have their own body language, slang, and dress. Just like America is known for cowboys, jeans, McDonald's, and Disney World, prisons are known for shanks, cellies, contraband, canteen, and pulling chain. We will address prison jargon and cultural symbols in subsequent chapters. However, it is important to discuss these social elements now, since they clearly demonstrate that the Country Called Prison has its own unique national identity. Anyone who has ever worked in prison will agree that it is another land and that there is nothing like it elsewhere.

It is important to note that a person immediately gains a new identity when they enter prison. Those who move to another country often retain their citizenship from their birth country and never change their national identity; they merely adapt to the new nation's customs. People who enter prison accept their new national identity quickly because they are immediately given a DOC (Department of Corrections) number. This small and seemingly insignificant act immediately strips them of their American name and immediately brands them as citizens of the Country Called Prison. A new prisoner's given name is no longer relevant to anyone. Inmates are told to memorize their DOC number because they may be asked for it at any time. In addition, they must always have their DOC identification card clipped to their shirt.

Furthermore, new inmates experience "welcome" rituals when they enter prison, such as having their heads shaved, being strip-searched, or donning an orange jumpsuit. Gone are their old clothes and looks. New identities result from these rituals, which are meant to inform new arrivals that they are no longer a person but an inmate (Garfinkel, 1956). As they cross this border into the Country Called Prison, they are also no longer an American citizen. They have been cast out of their country of origin and forced to accept the customs, language, and roles of their new nation.

National identity can often be subtle. When Mary's daughters were preteens, the family moved from a metropolitan northern city to a rural area of Oklahoma. As a child, Mary frequently visited her grandparents, who lived in a small rural town in western Kansas. So she was aware that customary dress was different in rural areas. Before her daughters attended their first day of school, she bought them clothes that she thought would be appropriate—jeans, t-shirts, and cowgirl boots. However, they were upset when they came home after school because Mary had bought them Levi jeans instead of Wranglers. As a result, their peers made fun of them all day. The same is true for the Country Called Prison, where national identity shows up in subtle ways, such as prison tattoos, one long fingernail on one hand, or starching and ironing prison-issued, elastic, pull-on pants.

From the outside, one might suspect that no one would be proud to have an identity of "incarcerated felon." We believe that this is mostly true, but we think it is a more complex issue than observation would suggest. We have observed that when a new inmate enters a prison yard, another inmate might yell out a welcome such as, "Hey, Big Mike, whatcha doin' back? How's Becka? Meet ya at the place later," as if they just saw each other at a football game or the mall. Inmates have specific tattoos that designate the number of times they have been to prison and in which prisons they have lived. Prison gang tattoos designate leadership levels and special honors. We have often observed a group of offenders visiting with others while waiting in medical for their appointments. They share stories of the various experiences they have had, the different prisons they have been to, and their opinions regarding different officers and staff and boast about the various crimes they have committed without getting caught.

At least at times, a country's citizens see each other as something more than a group of individuals who happen to live in the same area. When the United States was attacked on 9/11, Democrats and Republicans, rich and poor, northerners and southerners all rallied together to support their country. Students left college to enlist in the military to defend "the homeland." External attacks—or the threat of them—tend to unite people.

This is true in prison as well. Behind bars, threats are both internal and external. Inside prison, security and staff have almost unlimited power over inmates, who as a result see them as threats. Prisoners know that these people can search them at any time, ask them to do things they do not want to do, take away their few belongings, lock them in solitary confinement, or disallow visitors. Internal threats from peers are numerous in prison. Prison gangs maintain a great deal of power regarding prison activities, including who is accepted and who might be targeted for violence. In addition, some extremely violent prisoners prey on the weak because their sentences are so long that they have nothing to lose if they get in trouble. Some are severely mentally ill and can attack based on delusions that other prisoners are devils or monsters. Prisoners often find themselves in a catch-22 situation, since one way to protect themselves is to get in good with the prison staff and security. Of course, if one gets too chummy with prison staff, other inmates are likely to view this with hostility.

In prison, privacy and private property do not exist. Security personnel can search a prisoner's cell at any time and confiscate anything they want. They can stop a prisoner at any time to perform a strip search. Prisoners con each other out of items and steal from each other almost every hour of the day. The national identity that pervades the Country Called Prison is built on fear and mistrust. Americans proudly speak of their country as "the land of the free and the home of the brave." In prison, inmates derisively say, "Get what you can and don't get caught."

When someone, such as a missionary, has been living in another country for many years and returns to the United States, they are usually welcomed home with open arms by family and friends with whom they have stayed in contact. While it may take them a few months to get reacquainted with the society they left behind many years ago, they usually adapt with little stress or difficulty. Not so for inmates leaving prison and returning to American society. They often seem to experience the same trouble reassimilating as veterans who are returning from years of wartime deployment. Just putting a person back in a familiar environment does not necessarily mean they can blend back into what they left behind.

Once inmates leave prison, their identity is connected to having been "inside." Former inmates have a shared experience. In overhearing inmate conversations throughout the years, we have found that inmates and former inmates see themselves as alike in many ways and not like Americans who have not been "inside." The threats from within prison itself strengthen this sense of group identity in much the same way that military war veterans are bonded for life due to the shared dangerous experience they survived.

Upon release, threats come from outside. These threats may be from the public, which does not want former prisoners living in their neighborhoods, or from law enforcement, who keep track of their movements. Some police officers believe that they have probable cause to pull over a car driven by a former inmate. Threats may come from family members and former friends who now see an ex-con who is undeserving of attention and acceptance. In addition, employers are often resistant to hiring former prisoners. These threats unify citizens of the Country Called Prison, which in turn strengthens their national identity.

COMMON TERRITORY

A country is more than just people. There is a geography that separates one country from another. The Country Called Prison has millions of acres of land, with millions of miles of razor-wire fencing. These acres contain hundreds of millions of dollars of buildings. Its geography includes everything from maximum security prisons to halfway houses to parole offices.

In school, when children are studying geography, they learn about various places around the world and the conditions people live in. Often children have discussions about places where it would be "cool" to live or places where it would be "horrible" to live. When Mary was growing up, she thought that Calcutta, India, would be a terrible place to live. Interestingly, she has worked in prisons most of her adult life and found many of them to be rather wretched indeed. While they are not as wretched as the slums of Calcutta, prisons are still dismal places to be.

Yet, in the United States, the courts send thousands of citizens to these wretched and dismal places every day. Prisoners live in small cells with people they do not choose as roommates. The prisons at which we have both worked are in southern states. The cells have small windows on their doors, no windows that can open to the outside, and no air conditioner. In the heat of the summer, with temperatures rising to well over 100 degrees for weeks, these cells quickly become like ovens. Locked in a sweatbox with someone who may be your enemy is most definitely not fun. In the winter, our prisons are frequently cold, with cells heated only to a minimal temperature, but at least the stench of body odor declines. All of this is a part of the geography of the Country Called Prison.

Of course, the geography of prisons involves more than cells and bars. The government secures millions of acres of land and adds new buildings every year. From June 2000 to December 2005, state and federal prisons increased in number by 9% (from 1,668 to 1,821; Stephan, 2005). But this increase does not tell the whole story.

During these same years, private, for-profit prisons increased from 16% (264) to 23% (415) of the total prison bed space (Stephan, 2005). Private prisons accounted for the highest percentage growth in adult prisons, with the number almost doubling in a 5-year period. Government leaders know that new prisons will fill quickly; many take new prisoners before the construction stage finishes. The remaining one-third were under federal contract.

Prison geography involves more than just the sheer number of prisons; it also includes the size of prisons. During this same period, from 2000 to 2005, prisons housing fewer than 500 inmates increased by 86 prisons (Stephan, 2005). The number of moderately sized prisons, housing between 500 and 999 inmates, remained unchanged. However, the number of large prisons, housing from 1,000 to 2,499 inmates, grew by 57. Mega-prisons, those holding more than 2,500 inmates, increased by 11 (Jonson, Eck, & Cullen, 2014).

In other words, during a 5-year period, the United States increased the number of prisons by more than 200. Of these, most were built at the minimum security level (a total of 155). Minimum security prisons are just as you would expect from their name, minimally secure. Usually, these prisons do not even have a fence around them. Prison staff assign people to minimum security when they are not likely to escape. Oftentimes prisoners at minimum security facilities are nearing their discharge date and so would be unlikely to attempt to escape, which would earn them more time in prison. Yet, low-security inmates do not have the rights of American citizenship, the opportunity for work, post–high school education and training, and their families. Most important, these low-risk inmates are tax users, not taxpayers.

During this same period, maximum security prisons increased by a count of 40, while medium security prisons decreased in number by 42. Many of these became maximum security institutions. What does this mean? Maximum security prisons house inmates that are the most dangerous. This is the prison you have seen on television and in the movies. Razor wire, guard towers, and lockdown units are all a part of a maximum security prison. These prisons often lock down offenders for 23 hours a day and allow them out only 1 hour a day for court-ordered recreation, which usually involves standing in a small cage alone with a basketball hoop, with or without a ball.

The decline of medium security prisons may be of concern. Frequently medium security prisons provide meaningful jobs and job training for inmates. Inmates in these prisons, circled by razor wire, have highly restricted lives, but less so than would be the case in a maximum security environment. Therefore, these prisons can offer rehabilitation programs, educational opportunities, and other activities that maximum security prisons generally do not.

The decline in medium security prisons could be the result of the courts convicting more people with less serious crimes and shorter sentences and thus sentencing them at increasing rates to either minimum or maximum security institutions. If this is true, this means the population of a Country Called Prison is stable. The data available are not completely clear. Certainly, we have more minimum security beds than we had in the past, but we also have increased maximum security bed space as well. When prison administrators assign more inmates to maximum or minimum security prisons, then medium security prisons decline, along with a significant loss of rehabilitation programs (Stephan, 2005).

If you drive across America, you may see other communities that create citizens for the Country Called Prison. These are the communities where you see bars on store windows, broken-down houses and cars, and yards filled with weeds and debris. These are the communities of the poor and the working poor, which society ignores.

COMMON LANGUAGE

Language is a system of combining sounds, hand gestures, and/or symbols to communicate meaning. Language is not just for communication but also provides an internal organizational system for thinking. Languages all over the world share common characteristics: grammar (rules about word structure and use), syntax (grammatical correctness), morphemes (smallest unit of language meaning), phonemes (basic language sounds), and practical aspects such as tone, inflection, etiquette, and slang (Chomsky, 1975).

The Country Called Prison has its own language. It includes terms like "shipping" and "the wire" that do not mean the same thing in American society. In America, shipping is when you send a package; in prison, it is when you send a person to another prison. Bars in American society are places where you meet friends to socialize. In prison, bars are on all the windows, reminding inmates that they are captives. In American society, if you are "shaken down," you are being swindled. In prison, it means correctional officers are tearing up your cell, looking for contraband.

As Clemmer suggested long ago, the language and gestures that are part of prison life create a separate culture. When individuals enter such a setting, they must learn a new language and understand its importance. When they return to American society, they must leave that culture behind. This bouncing back and forth between cultures is part of the reason that many former prisoners find it difficult to reintegrate into American society.

SHARED VALUES, BELIEFS, AND SOCIAL BEHAVIOR

In a Country Called Prison, people have fewer choices. An "us versus them" mindset becomes dominant. Prisoners know that no matter to what degree a therapist, officer, or warden may be friendly, there will never be a genuine relationship. These people have power, and prisoners do not.

The few choices prisoners have are not the choices that Americans have. This lesson can be hard to learn and harder still to forget. Lengthy prison sentences can create inmates who become institutionalized and thus find it hard to live in American society. As one man on parole whom John knew stated, "Prison has become my home. I do not know how to make it on the outside."

Trust also has a different meaning in American society and in a Country Called Prison. In most neighborhoods in America, we trust our neighbors. Trust is not likely in the Country Called Prison. In prison, friendship is tenuous. There can never be trust when there is no freedom of choice. While offenders may play a friendly card game with others in their unit in the evening, they each know that sharing personal confidences during the game will set them up for a swindle later. Although offenders form groups, much like civic clubs on the outside, these are really gangs that offer protection rather than friendships. No one in prison wants to become a victim like James.

Another value is the ability to manipulate staff. In one prison in which John worked, an inmate who worked in the kitchen would tip off the support staff he liked when they should skip lunch. The directive to avoid lunch usually meant that an inmate put glass, human waste, or some other nonfood substance into the food that they prepared. While on the surface this seemed like a respectful act of kindness, the prisoner used this "friendship" as a means for obtaining favors. He gained the trust of staff this way and would occasionally get extra privileges that his fellow inmates did not. Of course, no one ever really checked the food when the worker warned the staff, so it may have all been a con. Either way, John learned quickly to bring his own lunch to work.

Once offenders receive their prison birth name in the form of their DOC identification number, clothes and social roles quickly follow. Offenders are not "guests" or "clients." They are not people. They are "convicts," "inmates," "the chomo" (child molester) whose lives are no longer their own. When James transferred to another prison after his surgery, officers said he "shipped," as if he were a UPS package. James became little more than an object to the Country Called Prison.

COMMON POLITICAL SYSTEM

A great deal of the literature relating to the culture of prisons supports the idea that inmates connect to others for a variety of reasons, but chief among them are status and self-interest. In every prison, there are security personnel who are friendly to inmates and some who are hostile; each of these relationships affects an inmate's level of status as well as comfort. At the same time, leaders of gangs call the shots in the inmate world. In some cases, the gang leader helps to determine who gets the best work detail or who gets beat up.

When you work and live in prison, you quickly learn that the political environment is clearly different than in the free world. While on the surface prison life seems very structured by pages and pages of policies and procedures, there are no clear-cut rules. For example, prisoners often assault child molesters. However, child molesters with marketable skills may achieve high status. An attorney has a valuable role in prison, even if he committed a sex offense, because he can file legal papers for inmates.

Although security staff appear to oversee prison operations, with an average officer-to-inmate ratio of 1 to 7 (American Society of Correctional Administrators, 2010), a small subset of inmates is really in charge. In some prisons, inmate gang leaders possess a great deal of informal power, and inmates follow their rules or end up dead. We have observed officers meeting with prisoner-leaders to arrive at a solution to calm a facility down when too many fights start breaking out among rival gangs.

MATERIAL CULTURE AND ECONOMY

In every country, members value material items or work positions more than others. The items that are important to citizens of one country are often different from that of another. When you travel outside the United States, you need to exchange your U.S. dollars to the currency of the country you have entered. You will not get far in France with dollars, but a euro can take you anywhere.

Prisons have currency as well. In the movie *The Shawshank Redemption* (1994), the inmates trade cigarettes as currency. Increasingly, U.S. prisons are becoming nonsmoking facilities. So what do prisoners use instead? Drugs are an obvious item of value. However, inmates can trade services, both sexual and personal. Inmates can legally purchase candy, gum, and aspirin and then use them as a means of barter. Illegal cell phones may have the most value in prisons today. Smuggled in or thrown over the fence, these phones open the world outside of prison to the inmate; therefore, their economic value is high.

The material items you see in prison are different from those in the outside world. We have both traveled outside the United States and continue to be fascinated by items in other countries that are not available in America, such as a different type of light switch or a toilet that you stand over instead of sitting on. The material culture of the Country Called Prison includes bars, jumpsuits, cells, trays, and razor wire. A billion-dollar prison industrial complex produces items made only for prisons. For example, prison televisions must be securely built so that the electrical wiring cannot be taken out and used to open security gates.

Prisons do not allow most items from the outside world to come into the prison environment. Why? Security always comes first. Everything must pass the security test to avoid the likelihood that it could be taken apart and *weaponized*. We have seen "shanks" (homemade knives) in prison made from soap and rolled-up newspapers. Imagine what a prison inmate could do with the metal box that surrounds an old radio.

Just as there are illegal materials in America, there are illegal materials in prison. In prison, correctional staff regularly search housing units to uncover contraband and find everything from homemade beer to heroin; cell phones are the most common commodity found during cell searches. Prison inmates have an amazing ability to find a way to get what they need. In one prison in which John worked, correctional staff discovered that a prison inmate was editing a pornographic magazine using a contraband word processor. Inmates are also skilled at conning people into helping them get whatever they want—another unique aspect of prison culture. For many inmates, the "con game" is as entertaining as watching a sporting match.

There is no doubt in our minds that prison is another country. It has a large and growing population with its own geographic location. It has separate rules and roles for citizens. It has a unique set of values and language. Former and current inmates frequently feel a sense of camaraderie because they share a national identity. While it is certainly true that prison inmates frequently fight for control over material items and power in prison, at the end of the day they all realize one thing. Once they were convicted and sent to prison, they became members of a new nation that they will continue to belong to even after discharge.

Offenders who enter this country are left out of the free world while in prison and have difficulty reintegrating into American society after release because of the cultural and identity issues we have discussed. After a stint in the "joint," ex-cons assume the identity of *legal alien* when they return to America.

We have coined the word *legal alien* to describe convicted offenders who are legally members of American society because they were born in the United States. However, once courts convict someone of a crime, that person officially enters the Country Called Prison, where they assume a different social status and, we think, a new national identity. Once convicted, that person is also excluded from many of the privileges afforded to Americans. In most states, a convicted offender will lose their right to vote. Depending on the crime, they may lose access to their children. They obtain a negative social status that they will carry with them throughout their lives, even after they leave prison, probation, or parole.

For this reason, we consider the elimination of the Country Called Prison to be a challenge to more than just prisons. In this book, we will suggest ways in which a warden can change a prison and the way policy decision-makers can change the entire criminal justice system. We first want to discuss the philosophy behind our ideas.

The first thing to consider is the way society views crime. Is crime a matter of social control or a matter of public health? The answer may depend on the type of crime committed.

As we discussed in the preface, the United States has the second-highest incarceration rate in the world. Furthermore, drug crime is one area in which we tend to incarcerate at much higher rates than our counterparts that are also wealthy, industrialized, and democratic nations. So what do these other countries do about the drug problem that the United States does not?

In short, most of America's peer countries view drug addiction not as a matter of social control but as a matter of public health. Societies cannot punish away social control problems, whereas public health matters can be diagnosed and treated. We would never consider incarcerating someone who goes to the county health department for a measles, mumps, and rubella vaccine. Free inoculations are a matter of public health. If we keep disease at bay, then we will all be better off. Most of America's counterparts throughout the world, who have lower incarceration rates of drug offenders, do just that. They believe that addiction is a disease and should be treated as a public health matter.

Another way to reduce criminality is to divide up the types of interventions we are going to use. Social workers understand that in any social setting there are levels of intervention. If we want to eliminate a problem, we will need a combination of efforts. The levels of interventions we will address are primary, secondary, and tertiary.

Primary approaches address the firsthand actions that people can take to bring about change. Frequently these include the organizational practices of prison. It could also include the use of nongovernmental means to address some of the social ills that set people up to enter the Country Called Prison. If you live in a neighborhood of inferior-quality housing, then a primary approach might be to make residences more livable. In subsequent chapters, we will discuss ways that prisons can function more efficiently, less expensively, and more humanely by addressing some policy and procedure changes.

Secondary approaches deal with sociological and psychological factors that influence the way people live. As we have already discussed, poverty is a problem for many who end up in prison. Programs that address poverty would be considered secondary, because although it is related to incarceration, it is not clearly linked to it. One program that seems to have had a significant impact on reducing incarceration rates is the famous Perry Preschool project.

The Perry Preschool program began at Perry Elementary School in Ypsilanti, Michigan (1962–1967). It measured the efficacy of early childhood intervention on the long-term ability of children to escape poverty and many of the problems associated with it, such as criminality.

Each week children attended 12.5 hours of school, and they were visited at their homes once a week. During home visits, parents were taught parenting skills, which mostly involved telling them what was effective from a developmental point of view (something we will discuss later).

The results from this research project support the notion that high-quality, early childhood education improves the chances of long-term positive outcomes (Weikart, 1985). Most of the children in the project were poor and from single-parent homes. In addressing many of these children's structural problems, the project had amazing results.

Schweinhart (2002) did a follow-up study with these children after they had reached 40 years of age. They had improved educational outcomes and income and much lower rates of arrest than one might have expected. In comparing two groups, one in the program and the other not, Schweinhart's study shows the positive benefits of early intervention on not just income and education but also on crime. In short, these children outperformed their counterparts and are taxpayers in the United States, rather than people in the Country Called Prison, who drain taxes from the U.S. economy.

Tertiary approaches address large system problems associated with incarceration. All of Chapter 6 is devoted to these issues. We will provide a road map that we think will assist in changing the mindset of most Americans who believe that high rates of incarceration are acceptable. These tertiary approaches are usually structural and will require legal action to implement them.

We believe that the metaphor of the Country Called Prison clearly fits the current situation in the United States. We spend billions of dollars each year to support this new nation growing in America and get little in return. As we have noted, at least half of those we send to prison have not committed a violent offense, and yet we treat them as if they had killed or raped someone. In so doing, we turn taxpayers into tax users and expand a nation within America's borders.

The last time John saw James he was headed back to prison. He had once again fallen off the proverbial wagon and this time created mayhem with his car. Luckily, no one died in the accident, but James's life was once again spent idling away in a prison. Many think this place will correct his behavior, but instead it will merely integrate him even more into a country that is growing ever bigger within America's borders, a Country Called Prison. In the next three chapters, we will discuss the social and psychological realities of the Country Called Prison in the hope that you will come to understand how this new nation within America was formed.

CHAPTER 4

Who Are the People of a Country Called Prison?

In matters of truth and justice, there is no difference between large and small problems, for issues concerning the treatment of people are all the same.

Albert Einstein

O ver the years, whenever we told someone that we worked in a prison, we invariably received one of two reactions. One had to do with the perception that prison is a dangerous environment, which then led the person to wonder about the way we managed our fears and protected ourselves. The other reaction was curiosity regarding the "evil" and "mentally deranged" inmates who live there. As we responded to people's reactions, we discovered that most really did not want to hear about our jobs. They didn't want to contend with the reality of who lives in prison. Television is filled with crime dramas that nearly always result in the "good guys" capturing the "bad guys." Therefore, society has been trained to believe that the good guys win and the bad guys go to prison. However, the line in prison between who is "good" and who is "bad" is not always clear.

We have met some extremely dangerous people while working in prison. However, most prisoners are not frightening. They are like the people we discuss throughout the rest of the book—men and women incarcerated for nonviolent crimes and serving sentences that are less than 5 years. Although these men and women are not scary, they are frequently psychologically and socially impaired. This perception of

A Country Called Prison, Second Edition. John D. Carl and Mary D.Looman, Oxford University Press.
© Oxford University Press 2024. DOI: 10.1093/oso/9780197768310.003.0004

the criminal mind came about suddenly for Mary. Early in her career, an event occurred when she was working at a medium security men's prison that caused her to question her own thinking about criminals. Until then, she had believed that most criminals were self-centered people who deliberately broke the law and should be feared.

At this prison, the men were allowed to move about the compound unrestricted throughout the day but had to be in their dormitories right after dinner. Many of the men worked during the day and in the evening watched television, played cards or board games, read books, or worked on art projects. One late afternoon, she was in the case manager's office in the dormitory, informing a prisoner that his mother died. Afterward, as she tried to leave, she discovered that the front door was locked. The unit officer was in another part of the building doing her required population count. So Mary, an attractive young woman, found herself in a room with about 50 male criminals. Her heart quickened a bit and she found herself momentarily afraid, although she kept her happy, confident face on. Interestingly, though, when she turned around to make a joke to the men about her predicament, they were all staring at her, tense and afraid as well. They certainly were not afraid of Mary. But they did seem afraid of this out-of-the-ordinary situation. They obviously did not know how to react and froze in whatever activity they had been doing. An unlikely hero came to everyone's rescue. Jim was a middle-aged resident in prison for growing marijuana in his backyard. He was playing dominoes with three peers and called out, "Hey, Doc, you're just in time to sit in for me. I've got to use the facilities. Me and my partner here have the highest score and I don't want to leave him hanging. I figure an educated lady such as yourself surely can keep us in the lead. You feel up to helping us out till the officer gets back?" Just as a clear, blue sky appears after a storm passes, the tension in the room abated as Mary sat down to save the team.

These men were not that much different than Mary. They were not the bad men she expected. Everyone makes mistakes in life. While she had not violated the law, she nonetheless had hurt others and felt remorse for her actions. In her years of working with prison residents, she discovered that many also felt remorse for their criminal behavior. Yet her regret for having hurt someone in the past prompted her to not make the same hurtful mistake twice, whereas many prisoners seem unable to learn from their mistakes. What is different about those who live in the Country Called Prison and those who do not?

On the surface, many of the prison residents we have met seem to have had ordinary lives. They had jobs before they were arrested and lived with a spouse (or significant other) and their children in a home or apartment. Based on their own belief system, they tried to be good spouses and parents. They had active lives with friends and family. Beneath the surface, however, they frequently were addicted to drugs and/or alcohol. They had difficulty maintaining employment. Their relationships with their spouses and children were tenuous at best. They had poor grooming habits, their command of the English language was poor, and they generally used profanity as adjectives. They lived in the moment, with little thought regarding their future. They rarely had plans for ways their lives could be different. Most of them didn't even understand that their lives *could* be different.

Although prosocial people commit crimes, such as lying on tax returns or using their company laptop for personal business, they are rarely caught in the act. Some may feel guilty, but many excuse their behaviors with claims like "the government takes too much for taxes already" or "I don't get paid enough so using the copy machine at work for my home business is only fair." Even if they get caught committing these types of crimes, society often excuses them. People often rationalize that "everyone does it once in a while." Considering that nearly everyone does a wrong deed in their lifetime, one is left with a question: Why do some people cross the line of criminality and move past the socially acceptable crimes to those that can land them in prison?

Over the years, criminologists have proposed different theories regarding the ways people develop prosocial or criminal behavior patterns. Differential association theory, developed by Edwin Sutherland (1947), suggests that we learn to deviate from society's norms from the close relationships we build with others. This is particularly true as we reach our teenage years, when we quite literally adapt the behaviors of the different groups with which we associate. We learn different rules and norms depending on the group with which we interact, which suggests that values and attitudes learned by members of street gangs and church groups are different. This difference leads to deviance for some and conformity for others.

In his containment theory, Walter Reckless (1970) suggested that all human behavior is contained by both internal and external forces. In childhood we develop internalized control mechanisms, such as a sense of morality or conscience, a fear of getting caught, guilt, and self-esteem. These mechanisms lead to our *internal control* later in life. Strong internal control corresponds with low levels of criminality. We are also surrounded by external controls, such as the presence of the police, a teacher, or a parent. These external influences may control behavior immediately, but they cannot control us all the time. Why? Because police, teachers, and parents cannot be everywhere. Our internal desire to get our own way is only contained by our internal controls.

Travis Hirschi's (1969) social bond theory postulates that children develop internal control because of the bonds they make. He agrees with Reckless that internal control is the key variable in predicting criminality. Internal controls are directed by the social bonds we formulate. Four key bonds—attachment, commitment, involvement, and belief—work against our self-centered desires to get our own way. According to social bond theory, weak bonds lead to criminality, while strong bonds lead to conformity and prosocial behavior.

Attachment refers to the people we value in our life. In short, if you bond with conformists, you are unlikely to become deviant. *Commitment* refers to the goals and aspirations that you may have related to living a prosocial life. If you are committed to becoming a doctor, you are unlikely to skip school. *Involvement* suggests that if we are active in prosocial events, like student government, we are unlikely to have the inclination to join a gang. Finally, if we *believe* that the rules of society are fair and applied fairly, then we are unlikely to break them. Our belief will direct our behavior. For Hirschi, the strength of these bonds determines who will and who will not commit crimes.

Michael Gottfredson joined Hirschi to develop the general theory of crime (Gottfredson & Hirschi, 1990). They hypothesized that lack of self-control—the ability to delay gratification—is a key element in criminal behavior in that it affects the bonds we create. People with a lot of self-control gravitate to others like them. Conversely, those who cannot put off short-term rewards in the hope of a better long-term consequence find others who are spur-of-the-moment types as well.

People with high levels of self-control are unlikely to commit crimes because they consider the long-term consequences of their actions before they act. When individuals repeatedly commit crimes and don't seem to learn from their behavior, they do so because they lack self-control. The general theory of crime hypothesizes that self-control, learned early in life, is resistant to any significant change throughout a lifetime. Here is where we disagree. We have seen many deviant people make significant changes later in their lives to become prosocial.

The common element in these theories is *childhood*. How do we grow up? With whom do we grow up? The way adults model behavior and teach children directly affects their perceptions of right and wrong. Psychologist Albert Bandura's (1963) theory about social learning integrates behavioral and cognitive theories into a comprehensive model of ways we learn information and behavior. His concepts of vicarious reinforcement, modeling, and reciprocal determinism show that children learn in a social context through observation, imitation, and reinforcement, as well as direct instruction.

As shown in Table 4.1, Bandura identified four ways that we learn while interacting with others. We learn by watching other people's behaviors and learning from their consequences. As an example, a younger child might see her older sibling being prevented from watching television because a chore was not completed; the younger child learns to complete her chores so she isn't punished. When the younger child obeys her parents because she has witnessed her sibling being punished, this is *vicarious reinforcement*. When the older child is prevented from watching television, this is *reinforcement* that misbehavior

Table 4.1. SOCIAL LEARNING THEORY

Element	How Learning Takes Place
Vicarious reinforcement	Observe consequences of the actions of others
Modeling	Observe and extract information from observation and decide to use it or not; learning something does not mean change occurs
Reciprocal Determinism	Own thoughts, the environment, and own/others' actions influence each other
Reinforcement	Assists in learning but is not always effective

Source: Bandura (1963).

is not accepted. However, if reinforcement (either negative or positive) is too little, too harsh, or not immediate, reinforcement does not usually work.

A similar learning strategy is *reciprocal determinism*, which takes place through interactions with others and the environment. Here each person involved in the interaction learns from the other, as well as the environment. Following the previous example, if when a parent confronts the older sibling about not completing the chore the older sibling lies and tells the parent that she was helping her younger sibling with homework, she may receive a compliment instead of a punishment. The negative behavior is reinforced and is produced by the child herself. By lying, she manipulates her mother and receives a reward for antisocial behavior. Such behavior sows the seeds of criminal thinking.

For the past 20 years or so, children and teens have been watching and interacting with electronic media more and more hours per day (Legner, 2022). Today, children (ages 8 to 10) watch or use electronic media about 6 hours a day, tweens (ages 11 to 14) about 9 hours, and teens (ages 15 to 18) about 7.5 hours. Although this e-media can entertain, educate, and keep children occupied on long car trips, they can also watch the wrong shows, such as one containing violence and risk-taking behaviors, sexual content, substance use, negative stereotypes, and misleading information. Excessive screen time affects physical and mental health issues, such as obesity, depression, behavioral issues, and anxiety. Electronic media games provide instant gratification while real-world interactions with people do not, leading to temper tantrums, disrespect, and violence.

In the past 20 years, there has also been an increasing number of latchkey children—children at home before and after school without adult supervision. Research by Rajalakshmi and Thanasekaran (2015) indicates there are as many as 10 million children caring for themselves before or after school. Their research also suggests that these children face many challenges, such as physical and sexual abuse, crime and delinquency, depression and suicide, drug and alcohol abuse, emotional and behavioral problems, learning difficulties, school attendance problems, domestic violence, pregnancy, abortion, and venereal disease. Many children and teens experience dangerous situations without ready access to adult guidance and support.

The wealth of information obtained from social science research regarding the way children learn appropriate social and interpersonal behavior from adults is inconsequential if there are no prosocial adults interacting with children, according to William Golding's classic novel *The Lord of the Flies* (1954). In the story, preadolescent boys are stranded on an island. At first the boys are excited about the adventure and the lack of adult supervision. But the fun soon wears off, and savagery begins to take over. The story ends with one of the boys being murdered just before they are all rescued, and the boys realize the horror of their actions. The story is a timeless metaphor of the conflict between our need for group survival through a cooperative, civilized society and our desire to satisfy our selfish needs through power.

As what you have just read suggests and research has proven (Marquis, 1992), delinquent teenagers and antisocial adults likely come from chaotic, neglectful, and abusive families. Why? What happens in early childhood that is so important in the development of prosocial behavior? All animals need attention at birth; however, in comparison to most animals, humans come into the world and need adult guidance for nearly 20 years. Most animals can walk rather quickly after birth, while humans take at least a year before they walk without assistance. Humans need a great deal of care in the first years of their lives. Therefore, parental caregiving is paramount if a child is going to reach adulthood with positive characteristics, attitudes, and social morality.

We will continue to use the word *parent* for ease of discussion. However, we are aware that many adults in a Country Called Prison had different types of primary caregivers. Most people don't think of parenting as a job with goals and an outcome that can be measured. From a species-survival point of view, parenting is a job, a very important job, one that produces the next generation of adults who will further the human species. Research by Looman (2010) identifies three tasks (competencies) of effective parenting: nurturance, regulation, and attachment. These are summarized in Box 4.1. *Nurturance* is the ability to provide children unconditional love, demonstrated by acceptance, support, and encouragement. *Regulation* is the ability to protect children from harm as they learn and explore their environment, as well as help them learn important social skills so that they fit into the culture in which they were born. *Attachment* is the ability to form an endearing bond with a significant adult whereby the child feels wanted and valued.

Research by Christopher Mruk (2006), a leading expert in self-esteem development, suggests a way that we can identify the goals of parenting. As summarized in Box 4.2, Mruk's research indicates that competent parents help infants grow into adulthood with the ability to (a) sustain their own lives, (b) be autonomous yet connected to others, (c) control their responses to environmental stimuli, (d) accept responsibility for their actions, (e) have a sense of purpose, and (f) contribute toward humankind in some meaningful way. We believe that most of the teenagers and adults in homeless shelters, juvenile detention centers, jails, prisons, crisis centers, and inpatient mental health facilities have not developed these skills. This might be the reason offenders have higher suicide rates and lower levels of educational attainment than the general population.

In 2019, state and federal prisons had 340 persons commit suicide, and in local jails, 355 persons died by suicide (Carson, 2021), while the rate for the general population was about 14.1 per 100,000 (Garnett & Curtin, 2023). In 2018, about 80% of prisoners did not complete high school (Choudry, 2018), while 5.2% of students (2 million) in the general population did not complete high school (National Center for Education Statistics, 2023). As you will read more later, offenders have poor relationships skills, tend to blame others for their problems, and have developed impaired thinking strategies, referred to as *criminal thinking*. Frequently this appears to stem from poor modeling of appropriate behavior.

Just as studies have identified different management styles and their influence on organizational outcomes, research by Diana Baumrind (1967, 1991) identified different parenting styles that significantly affect childhood development. According to Baumrind's research, summarized in Table 4.2, authoritative parents can establish rules as guidelines but take a more egalitarian approach to enforcing them. When their children make mistakes, these parents tend to be more nurturing and guiding rather than strictly punishing. Other types of parents tend to either harshly enforce rules, disregard rules altogether, or be psychologically absent in the child's life. The thousands of prison residents we have met over the years were not usually raised by authoritative parents.

To become well-functioning adults, children must progress through a variety of developmental stages under the guidance of their parents and teachers. According to Eric Erikson's life-span model of psychosocial development (1959) and Stanley Greenspan's emotional development model (1997), the first 7 years of life lay the foundation for healthy adult functioning. Table 4.3 provides a description of these stages.

Table 4.2. PARENTING STYLES AND CHILDHOOD DEVELOPMENT

Style	Rule Orientation	Effect on Child Development
Authoritarian	Follow all rules	Obedient but lack social competence
Authoritative	Rules are responsive to child needs	Obedient and socially competent
Permissive	Very few rules	Antisocial and do poorly in school
Uninvolved	Few rules, low responsiveness	Poor self-control, socially incompetent

Source: Baumrind (1991).

Table 4.3. STAGES OF EARLY CHILDHOOD DEVELOPMENT

Age	Psychosocial	Emotional	Outcome
0–1	Trust versus mistrust	Making sense of sensations; relating to others	Hope
1–4	Autonomy versus shame	Intentionality	Will
2–5	Initiative versus guilt	Purposeful interaction; symbolic meaning, language	Purpose
5 +	Industry versus inferiority	Emotional reasoning	Confidence

Sources: Erikson (1959); Greenspan (1997).

Within the first month of life an infant must be able to decipher sensations, organize stimuli, and maintain a minimum level of calm to survive (feeding, sleeping, and so on). Infants must learn to trust the world is safe and caregivers will provide for their needs. Within the first 3 months of life, an infant must bond with a primary human and be able to understand the caregiver's voice tone, expressions, and basic actions, and then correlate sensation and emotions to decide intentional actions (e.g., a smile response). With a sense of safety in place, infants can explore their environment and attend to important patterning, such as speech and emotional cueing. Within a year, infants begin to crawl, then walk, and learn they are separate from their caregivers. By age 2, toddlers begin to separate from caregivers, becoming more autonomous and independent, thus developing a sense of self-identity. Competent parents provide a safe environment from which children can independently explore their social world. Parents also instruct children in appropriate behavior, model appropriate behavior and play with them, and talk with them so that sounds become words with meanings.

As young children begin to interact with peers in play, they develop skills for planning, organizing, and initiating their own goals. By age 4, children develop a sense of purpose and understand, through play, that one thing can represent another. They learn moral reasoning when they break a sibling's favorite toy or cause a peer to cry. Competent parents are actively involved with their children, listening to their stories, validating their feelings, answering their questions, and helping them solve problems.

By age 7, children begin to take pride in their ability to finish homework assignments, participate in sports, draw a picture, or play a musical instrument. They learn about the joy of working with others to accomplish a goal and sharing their accomplishments with others. Children are generally able to identify their strengths and weaknesses, share in peer group identity, recognize adults whom they like and admire, and take pride in obeying rules and participating in group and solo activities. They now have the foundation for their self-ego, which will continue to grow and carry them through life. Children raised by competent parents can form bridges between their own thoughts and feelings and those of others and begin to construct a cohesive internal reality that will develop into their sense of purpose in the world.

How does all this apply to those who live in the Country Called Prison? In our experiences, most criminals do not grow up with proper nurturance, regulation, and attachment. They report that their parents were either excessively strict or overly indulgent. In addition, they report their parents were uninvolved in their lives and unresponsive to their psychosocial needs, and that there was no routine or consistency in their daily lives. In short, they never knew what was going to happen next. Offenders report that they never could trust their parents because their parents would say one thing and do another. They often made promises they never kept. When people grow up this way, they develop sensory distortions regarding reality, often misinterpreting emotional and interpersonal cues. They tend to be impulsive and believe that there are no predictable consequences for actions. They get mad when someone "does them wrong" yet steal from others if they need something. They tend to be vindictive and malicious, as Tammy's story demonstrates.

Tammy had been in prison for about 17 years when Mary met her. Tammy began attending meetings of Mary's Lifers' Club. The women who came to the meetings made items such as quilts or sweaters for elderly people who lived in the nursing home near the prison. As attendees worked on projects, they talked about issues in their lives, supporting each other much the way sisters do. Tammy had been sexually abused by her father, her brothers, and two of her uncles. By age 13 she was addicted to cocaine and began selling her body to get money to buy drugs. As an adult, she became a stripper and a prostitute. She lived with a man she had met at the strip club. He was an unemployed addict who beat her often. By age 25, she had given birth to two children who were taken from her at birth because they tested positive for drugs. After her seventh trip to the emergency room for another broken bone, she went home and burned up the man who abused her while he slept in their bed.

Why didn't she go to a battered women's shelter? Why didn't she call a women's hotline? Why did she endure abuse year after year until that moment when she threw the burning cigarette lighter on the bed? Children who grow up abused come to think of abuse as a normal family function and are likely to repeat the cycle when they grow up because it is all they know (Keeshin et al., 2011). A person's view of the world begins in infancy. The reality of right and wrong, normal and abnormal, develops in childhood. All future decisions and a sense of reality stem from this foundation. The Country Called Prison begins here, not at the prison gate.

Children growing up surrounded by chaos, abuse, and neglect generally develop poor self-esteem and have difficulty managing emotions (Greenspan, 1997; Mruk, 2006). They also tend to have poor relationships with authority figures, so they have difficulty in school and often drop out. As adults, they often suffer from chronic depression or personality disorders and have addictive personalities. They usually have difficulty maintaining employment and relationships, focusing on their own needs without understanding that their behaviors affect others. In a chaotic or abusive environment, children learn to tell stories to fit the reality they want or think their parents want, which might not always fit the true reality of the situation. When adults do this, prosocial citizens call it "lying." Psychologists call it "living in denial or fantasy." In the Country Called Prison, citizens call it "the truth, honest to God." Ineffective parenting practices teach children to habitually break the law (Moffitt & Caspi, 2001).

When Steve entered prison, he was a young adult and single. He had been raised in a family where his parents were often absent. When they were home, there was usually a lot of yelling and drinking and occasionally some beatings, if either parent got drunk. By the time he arrived in prison, he had a 5-year-old child in foster care because the child's mother was in prison for prostitution and possession of cocaine. Child protective services terminated the parental rights of both Steve and his girlfriend. Steve was in prison because he had gone out with friends to celebrate completing drug court, with which he had been involved for the past 3 years. After leaving the bar, he was arrested for driving under the influence, possession of drugs, and illegal possession of a firearm. For 3 years, Steve had followed the rules of the drug court and remained substance free; yet the very day that he was released from supervision he returned to his previous lifestyle. Why did he not integrate the lessons he learned from drug court?

Steve was motivated to leave drug court as soon as possible so he could "get on with his life." He learned in childhood to tell his parents and teachers what they wanted to hear so that he would get what he wanted. So he put on the show of being the recovered addict. However, as soon as he was released, he "got on with his life" of getting what he wanted regardless of the cost to others. Society calls this antisocial behavior; Steve calls his behavior normal. Sociologists Gresham Sykes and David Matza (1957) studied ways people learn to rationalize their self-interested behavior to avoid following social norms. Criminals tend to use these neutralizing techniques to protect themselves from self-blame (guilt and remorse) and to deflect the condemnation of others. Thus, they do not learn from their mistakes. Box 4.3 provides a list of the techniques most used by rule breakers.

Following Sykes and Matza's research, Stanton Samenow has studied criminal behavior for over four decades. He ardently argues that abuse, poverty, and media violence do not cause criminality. Instead,

---

Box 4.3. TECHNIQUES TO NEUTRALIZE DISTRESS CAUSED BY ANTISOCIAL BEHAVIOR

Denial of responsibility
- "It wasn't my fault."

Denial of injury
- "It is not a big deal. They can afford the loss."

Denial of the victim
- "After what he did to my friend, he deserved it."

Condemnation of the condemners
- "Like you've never done anything wrong before."

Appeal to higher loyalties
- "My sister needed help with her rent. What else could I do?"

Source: Sykes and Matza (1957).

he believes *criminal thinking* causes crime. In the second edition of his book *Inside the Criminal Mind*, Samenow (2004) identified at least 36 thinking errors that characterize the thought processes of criminals. His research indicates that all criminals view people as objects that can be used to satisfy their needs. While at times they seem to have a conscience and behave in a prosocial manner, they can turn this behavior off without feeling guilt or remorse. For a quick review of his thesis related to these characteristics, see Box 4.4.

Most criminals view themselves as decent people and their lives as exciting. They often think people who obey social norms are boring and unfulfilled. When you listen to their life histories, it is easy to see why they are in prison. When you know about their childhoods, you might feel sorry for offenders who return to prison for a second or third time. Samenow does not deny this reality but suggests that if we wish to stop criminal behavior, we need to improve the criminal's cognitive reasoning.

Competent parenting is only one aspect of child development. Genetics, the environment, and the child's own temperament are also important components. At birth, the human brain weighs about 10 ounces and needs to add another 38 ounces by age 20 to fully develop (Dawson & Guare, 2010). From their first breath after delivery, infants

---

Box 4.4. TWELVE COMMON CHARACTERISTICS OF CRIMINAL THINKING

Extremely energetic yet lazy

Chronically fearful

Periods of absolute worthiness and hopelessness

Chronic state of anger used to control others

Grandiose; better and more deserving than others

Absolute need to control others

Concrete; very black-and-white thinking

Fragmented personality and rapid shifts in personality

Belief that person is unique, not like others

Habitual lying; do not know how to tell the truth

Victim stance; blames others

Lack of empathy for others

Source: Samenow (2004).

---

begin to absorb and assimilate millions of stimuli from their environment. The brain builds neurons and synapses as learning takes place yet periodically prunes them as skills and information are consolidated into concepts. Consolidation stages occur at ages 5, 12, 20, and 40. At each stage, crucial pathways must be able to lock into place for the next neurological stage to occur properly.

A good metaphor for brain development is the construction of a roadway. Generally, the width of the roadway is prepared first, then the bridges go up, and finally the roadway. Many years ago, Mary discovered a bridge that had been put in the wrong location. As she approached the correct bridge, she saw a sign by the wrong bridge that humorously stated, "The McDonald County Bridge to Nowhere." Some offenders seem to have a bridge to nowhere in their own minds.

Although the brain takes nearly 20 years to fully develop, the most crucial of all neurological abilities, executive functioning, develops by age 7. Executive functioning, which assists in healthy adult functioning, is described in full in Box 4.5. It is like the foundation of a building. Mary once commuted to work on a busy highway and frequently had to stop because of a car accident further up the road. The stoppage usually occurred at about the same place a 16-story building was being built. Since there was a tall fence around the construction site,

---

Box 4.5. EXECUTIVE FUNCTIONING CHARACTERISTICS

Definition of executive functioning
- The ability to manage emotions and monitor thoughts to regulate actions

Skills of executive functioning that help achieve goals
- Planning
- Time management
- Organization
- Working memory
- Awareness of own thinking processes (metacognition)

Actions of executive functioning that lead to achieving goals
- Inhibit responses (delayed gratification)
- Manage emotional responses
- Be able to adapt to changes in the environment
- Persistence (manage frustrations)

Source: Dawson & Guare (2010).

for about 4 months no building grew above the fence line. Mary mentioned this to an engineer at work who taught her about foundations. A foundation needs to be strong enough to support the building, as well as manage the structural stresses caused by the earth shifting. The taller and larger the building, the deeper and more structurally reinforced the foundation needs to be. It is the same with humans, who must cope with challenges and stressors throughout their lifetimes.

After observing and visiting with hundreds of people who live in the Country Called Prison, we believe that many offenders have poor executive functioning skills because of ineffective parenting (Greenspan, 1997; Moffitt & Caspi, 2001) and/or impaired brain development due to childhood abuse and neglect (Tarullo, 2012), parental drug and alcohol use while pregnant, or secondhand smoke from recreational drugs and cigarettes (Blackburn et al., 2004; Frank et al., 2001; Zukerman et al., 1989). We have observed that offenders do not know ways to think about the pros and cons of choices. They do not understand their emotions and why they are feeling them. They are not able to incorporate emotional reasoning into their problem-solving process and tend to be impulsive and have difficulty delaying gratification. They do not understand that their behaviors affect others. If they do, they tend to minimize their own responsibility by blaming their behavior on someone or something else. Since many dropped out of high school, they failed to go through the American socialization process that naturally occurs in high school. Most are governed by a deep underlying shame and sense of unworthiness that they frequently numb with drugs and alcohol. They know at some psychological level that they were outcasts in U.S. society long before they came to prison.

Ted's story illustrates the way poor executive functioning tends to make someone reckless and imprudent. Ted is a tall, middle-aged man with a weathered face that makes him appear much older than he is. He came into Mary's office to receive his new arrival assessment. After welcoming him, she mentioned that he looked familiar. He shook his head, turned his eyes toward the floor, and stated, "Yeah, I was here last fall [about 7 months ago]." Mary asked him what brought him back. He looked up with tears welling in his eyes and said, "Oh, I got out about 2 months ago and even had a job in construction; my brother helped me get it. But I needed gas to get to work and hadn't gotten my paycheck, so I broke into a vending machine to get some money. I was going to leave the guy a note that I would pay him back, but wouldn't you know, the cops were just coming out of the restaurant across the street and caught me." Since Ted was out on parole, his parole officer brought him back to prison the next day.

Ted was not able to plan for his future needs. He was not able to think about what he would need to maintain employment. He was not able to organize and execute plans to be prepared for the next day. He was not able to manage his impulsivity in solving problems. He was not able to identify resources available to him, including supportive people who could help him with issues and problems. He more than likely had not had breakfast and had not prepared any food for lunch; obviously he did not have money to go out for lunch. He did not have water, and he was probably not dressed appropriately for construction work. Along with poor executive functioning skills, Ted also had a second problem. He had become *prisonized*. For the last 3 years, prison had given him everything he needed. Now, on his own, he was supposed to suddenly figure out what he needed, where to get it, how to get it, and when to get it.

Throughout this book we refer to the problems associated with mass incarceration as an *epidemic*. We think this is a good metaphor. Ted was infected with the "unsocialized virus," for which the prison system has not cured him. Like many others, he keeps getting reinfected. Ted's unsocialized virus flares up now and again and he finds himself back in prison. He also infects other people, such as his children or friends he convinces to use drugs and commit petty crimes with him. In epidemiology, medical personnel label a disease or illness as an epidemic when the number of people who become ill significantly exceeds an expected base rate. Epidemics happen when the ecology of a given population changes or a new parasite enters a population for which there is no natural immunity. America's incarceration rate certainly meets this condition. Although illegal drugs were in use prior to the 1970s, the punishments for their use increased a great deal. Instead of treating illegal drug use and addiction as a public health issue, policymakers made it a criminal issue. The main goals of federal and state public health departments are (a) to prevent epidemics by monitoring the community; (b) to investigate and identify health hazards; (c) to inform, educate, and empower people about health issues; and

(d) to mobilize community partnerships to identify and solve health problems (Office of Disease Prevention and Health Promotion, 2014). Many of the changes we propose in this book are patterned after these public health goals.

We have also met nonviolent offenders who are shunned and outcast like lepers in ancient times. In medieval Europe, the nobles had infected people isolated against their will and they had to wear a bell in public to identify their presence (Rodrigues & Lockwood, 2011). When you consider the plight of the mentally ill whom we incarcerate, the analogy of modern-day lepers certainly holds true. Although we have known for more than 50 years that mental illness is caused by chemical imbalances in the brain and have developed effective medications and therapeutic rehabilitation protocols, society continues to fear the mentally ill. Health insurance companies, both private and public, fail to reimburse for services as adequately as they do for treatment of physical conditions. Consider the data from the Bureau of Justice Statistics in Table 4.4 showing comparisons between 2005 and 2016 (James & Glaze, 2006; Maruschak & Bronson, 2021). Although there was a decrease in the number of prisoners with mental illness (due to overall reduction in corrections populations), the percentage of prisoners with mental illness remains significantly high compared to the 18.9% rate of people in the general population with mental illness (Substance Abuse and Mental Heath Services Administration, 2018). Is incarceration really the best way to deal with people with mental illness?

History shows that when the United States had fewer jails and prisons, the mentally ill were admitted to psychiatric hospitals. As the number of prison facilities began increasing nearly 50 years ago with *get tough on crime* legislation, social control agents (legislators, police, district attorneys, and judges) began to impose criminal rather than psychiatric definitions on people's behavior, thus shifting the management of mental illness to the criminal justice system (Fisher et al., 2006). As we have already mentioned, the buildup of prisons coincided perfectly with the deinstitutionalization of those with severe and persistent mental illnesses.

For many years social constructionists have argued that criminalizing mental illness has created a social response that no longer views mental illness as a medical issue but as a public safety issue (Erickson

Table 4.4. PERCENTAGE OF PRISONERS WITH MENTAL ILLNESS: COMPARISON OF 2005 AND 2016 STATE DATA FROM THE BUREAU OF JUSTICE STATISTICS

Data Category	2005 State Data	2016 State Data	% Change
Life History of Mental Illness	56%	43%	13% decrease
Females	73%	69%	4% decrease
Males	55%	41%	14% decrease
White	62%	53%	9% decrease
Black	55%	33%	22% decrease
Hispanic	46%	36%	10% decrease
Severe Symptoms Last 30 days	24%	14%	10% decrease
Disorders			
Depression	33%	27%	6% decrease
Bipolar disorder	43%	23%	20% decrease
Psychosis	16%	9%	7% decrease
Anxiety	NA	22%	NA
PTSD	NA	14%	NA
Personality	NA	11%	NA
Received Treatment	38%	60%	22% increase
Mental Illness & Addiction	74%	49%	25% decrease

Sources: James and Glaze (2006); Maruschak and Bronson (2021).

& Erickson, 2008). According to social constructionists, by identifying mental illness as a crime, society no longer needs to view people with mental illness as sick and in need of compassion. Society no longer needs to *feel guilty* about failing to provide adequate treatment and care. Likely you noticed that the statistical data for Table 4.4 came from a Bureau of Justice Statistics report written by Maruschak and Bronson in 2021. They used research data from a prisoner survey conducted in 2016. We searched for hours trying to find comparable data from research projects conducted around 2020 with no success. This one small factor significantly demonstrates that people from the Country Called Prison are not valued as members of American society. Their health is not even worth investigating, let alone treating.

However, we did find one recent research project regarding factors that predict jail population sizes in relation to individuals with behavioral health issues. In 2019, jails—the front door to the Country Called Prison—admitted more than 10.3 million individuals. Researchers for BMC Health Services Research (http://bmchealthserv res.biomedcentral.com) decided to examine community public health services and the local legal system to determine if there were factors that might predict jail population sizes and consequentially prison population sizes (Ramezani et al., 2022). The research project identified that counties with greater resources, including mental health treatment, had smaller jail populations per capita. This is in part, because community service access is a potential driver of incarceration. Counties with smaller adult populations, a significant percentage of individuals without a high school diploma, a higher number of health-related issues, and a higher rate of mental illness and addiction had larger jail populations per capita. The study also showed that counties with a higher citizen-to-police ratio had a higher jail population for nonviolent crimes. The violent crime rate did not predict a significant jail admission rate. As one might expect, the researchers concluded that better access to and more community-based services for individuals in poverty, with mental illness and addiction, and with chronic severe health issues would prevent increases in incarceration rates as well as improve the health and welfare of the county.

In Table 4.4, note the decrease in the percentage of prisoners with mental illness and the 22% increase in treatment. We believe these are the result of two additional changes within the criminal justice system, as well as the increase in community services suggested by the previous research project. The first is the decrease in the number of arrests and convictions due to changes in the *get tough on crime* philosophy, especially regarding the decriminalization of marijuana. The second is the increase in the use of specialty courts, which are diversionary treatment programs. Specialty courts focus on reducing the criminalization of mental illness by addressing the treatment needs of individuals rather than incarceration. Table 4.5 identifies the number of specialty courts in the United States. The National Drug Court Resource Center (2021) reports that every state has drug courts operating in local court systems, and most large cities have drug courts, mental health courts, co-occurring mental illness/addiction courts, and family courts. These changes show that the criminal justice system

Table 4.5. SPECIALTY COURTS IN THE
UNITED STATES, 2020

Type of Court	Total Number in U.S.
Drug and opioid courts	Adult 1,771; juvenile 308
DWI/DUI/hybrid	300
Co-occurring mental illness/addiction	74
Family	317
Mental illness	469
Reentry	64
Veterans	476
Specialty juvenile courts	69
Total	3,848

Source: Devall, K., Lanier, C., & Baker, L. J. (2022). Painting the Current Picture:
A National Report on Treatment Courts in the United States – Highlights &
Insights. National Treatment Court Resource Center, https://ntcrc.org/pcp/.

is capable of transformation. We will talk more about this in Chapter 7,
"Decarceration: Emigrating From the Country Called Prison."

What is the cost, in lives and money, for our lack of empathy for
the poor and the mentally ill? Between 55% and 65% of people living
in jails and state prisons in the United States have a mental illness,
nearly four times the number for the general population (Maruschak
& Bronson, 2021). A quarter of this group reported that they had been
to prison three or more times. Over half of the inmates with mental illness reported that a family member had been incarcerated, and 15% to
19% lived in foster care at some point in their childhood. Nearly 40%
reported that their parents abused drugs and alcohol, and 27% had
been physically and/or sexually abused prior to arrest. Approximately
15% had been homeless the year before they were arrested, and half
reported that they had previously received public assistance. These figures reinforce our earlier discussion of the chaotic lives lived by many
of those who live in the Country Called Prison.

Sam's story demonstrates the criminalizing of mental illness. Sam
entered prison when he was 52 years old. His developmental age was
about 7, and he had been living with his parents in a small rural community. His parents, now in their 80s, had difficulty caring for themselves, let alone their son. One afternoon, Sam found a pellet rifle and
shot out the lights in an abandoned warehouse. Arrested and charged

with destruction of property, Sam received a sentence of 5 years in prison.

Culpability for criminal acts is touchy. People like Sam with cognitive deficits find their way to prison with regularity. Often, these individuals are well known to the police for committing petty crimes. Because of their cognitive deficits, they struggle with issues of cause and effect and have trouble learning from their experiences. They can become frustrated easily and sometimes turn to violence as a result. John's experience as a social worker taught him an important lesson. People with cognitive delays are frequently not physically impaired at all. If their delays lead to aggression and frustration, they may be bound for prison because few states provide residential treatment for those with intellectual but not physical disabilities. At one prison where Mary worked, 168 men (an entire unit) all tested below the normal range on their intelligence test. The staff and mental health professionals on this special unit attempted to provide the care that a community residential treatment facility could have done more easily and less expensively. While they were successful in keeping these fragile inmates from being abused by others, the long-term effects of incarceration on those with intellectual disabilities leave them with the same stigma attached to anyone who goes to prison. Is prison really the place to care for people with cognitive impairments?

Our second story is about Shamika, who not only had a mental illness but also was poor and Black. She had trouble all through school and was finally suspended. Afterward, the school counselor referred her to the community mental health center. But her mother was unable to take time away from her job to drive Shamika to appointments. At age 19, Shamika was caught shoplifting from a convenience store. When the police came, she thought they were demons coming to kill her, so she fought them. The court charged and convicted her of assault and battery of a police officer and sentenced her to 7 years in prison.

During Shamika's intake, Mary diagnosed her with severe mental illness, referred her to the psychiatrist for appropriate medication, and recommended placement in the prison's mental health unit. There Shamika learned about her illness and ways to manage her symptoms as well as a few life skills. By the time she left prison, she had already been approved for Social Security disability and Medicaid assistance.

She left prison with a future appointment with the community mental health facility.

Fourteen months later Mary conducted yet another intake interview with her. Why did this happen? Mary had done all the right things to set her up for success after her release—or so she thought. Shamika had been through one of the best treatment programs the prison had. She had been housed in a mental health unit, where she learned effective coping and living skills. She had funding for housing and food on the outside, and she had been referred for follow-up services in the community. Unfortunately, the community mental health center rescheduled her appointment for a later time, and Shamika ran out of medication. She relapsed into self-medicating with drugs and alcohol. Based on our experience, we believe Shamika returned to prison because the services in prison for the mentally ill were better than those in the community. But this is a costly way to take care of someone with a mental illness.

A recent meta-analysis of international articles discussing mental health issues in prison found that across multiple countries and studies, incarcerated women had higher rates of substance abuse disorders than incarcerated men or the general population. The rate of substance abuse for incarcerated women was 51%, while it was only 30% for men (Hidayati et al., 2023).

In a study of U.S. jails, Green et al. (2016) found that incarcerated women who were suffering from mental health problems were statistically more likely to have suffered from trauma as children or as adults. Women who were in these facilities were disproportionately victims of severe abuse in their past.

Likewise, Patterson et al. (2020) discusses the relationship between mental health issues, and incarceration. They found that women who had family members incarcerated were more likely to suffer from mental health challenges. This was found to be particularly true for African American women; however, disproportionate percentages of women, regardless of race, who are incarcerated suffer from mental health disorders.

Many women in prison are victims of heinous violent crimes but are nonviolent criminals themselves. However, a greater impact to society is that many female prisoners suffer from a serious mental disorder that for many will go untreated in prison, setting them up for failure when they are discharged. They also are likely to have children who are in foster care or living with relatives, and they often regain custody of their children after release. These children have a 25% greater chance of ending up in prison than children whose parents have not been in prison (Wakefield & Wildeman, 2014), and these children often have mental illnesses requiring inpatient care. So the generational mental illness and imprisonment cycle of the Country Called Prison continues.

Since mental illness is treated like a crime in America, we now tell the story of the growing number of veterans who have found their way into prisons instead of treatment centers. Devon grew up poor in a family where many of his relatives had been to prison. His neighborhood was a battlefield for gangs. By the time he turned 17, he had witnessed the deaths of two of his friends. He managed to make it through high school because he was a good athlete, playing starter positions on both the football and basketball teams. Teachers encouraged him to join the army when he graduated. Unfortunately, Devon ended up in a war zone during Operation Desert Storm, where he experienced many horrors. After 4 years, he was medically discharged due to post-traumatic stress disorder (PTSD). He began working for a construction company and married his high school sweetheart. It seemed that everything was falling into place. However, as nightmares and flashbacks of the war worsened, he began using drugs and alcohol to try to make them go away. Driving home from work one evening high on drugs, he ran a red light and hit another car, injuring three people. The court sentenced him to prison for 10 years for DUI, drug possession, and assault with a dangerous weapon via his car.

According to a report from the National Criminal Justice Association (2022), one in three veterans reported being arrested and booked into jail at least once, compared to one in five civilians. Of these veterans, many reported that they had difficulty getting treatment for depression, anxiety, and/or PTSD, and they compounded their problems by self-medicating with alcohol and drugs. From our experiences, there are many nonviolent offenders who also suffer from PTSD resulting from years spent living in neighborhood "war zones," where they never knew when the "bombs" of gang violence were going to explode. These nonviolent offenders reported having no access to treatment and used drugs to self-medicate. They often sold drugs to pay for their drug habits. Prison will not help these people. Prison time will only increase the tax burden by making them permanent citizens of the Country Called Prison.

Research in the past two decades has shown that Moral Reconation Treatment (MRT) cohorts have proven to be successful for incarcerated offenders (Blonigen, 2021). MRT is a cognitive-behavioral treatment process lasting about 2 years that increases moral reasoning, leads to better decision-making, and increases prosocial behavior. It began in the 1980s for prison-based therapeutic communities and expanded to general inmate populations both in and outside of jails and prisons; objective measurements continue to show consistent success outcomes. In 2019, the U.S. Veterans Health Administration (VHA) surveyed 66 VHA facilities that provided MRT therapeutic cohort programs. Seventy-nine percent of the facilities reported that they had been sustaining active programs for about 3 years, with strong intrafacility (veterans' justice and behavioral health services) and interagency collaborations (VHA and criminal justice system stakeholders) that generated referrals for cohort groups, external incentives for client engagement, and staffing to maintain group coherence. This demonstrates an effective, evidence-based treatment and habilitation process that could be used in all types of specialty courts and reentry programs. We will talk more about this in Chapter 7.

As the stories in this chapter demonstrate, many criminals are poorly educated, poorly socialized, often addicted, and frequently mentally ill. Many believe that fear of imprisonment prevents crime. However, for many criminals, prison is not that much different from life at home. Many think that if prison were more punitive, people would never want to return. For some, prison life is less harsh than their lives in the neighborhoods in which they grew up or the box under the bridge in which they lived before they were arrested. We acknowledge that Ted, Shamika, and Devon committed crimes. But do they need to be in prison? And if they do need to be in prison, what kind of prison should it be? If we, as a society, can help them change, all of us would be better off—prisoners as well as taxpayers. Why? Society would not have to pay to send offenders to expensive prisons, and offenders can get treatment and rehabilitation. To accomplish this, society must stop criminalizing mental illness, gender orientation, and physical and mental disabilities.

One of the reasons social change agents have not addressed the problem of mass incarceration is that they do not realize (or acknowledge) the long-term consequences of the numbers they see in criminal justice reports. Although we have already provided some general numbers, we now want to focus on some rarely discussed statistics that highlight underlying issues, which, if not addressed, will continue to increase the population of the Country Called Prison.

From 2011 to 2021 is the first time the Bureau of Justice Statistics compiled data for one decade regarding prisoner crime statistics (see Table 4.6; Carson, 2022; Carson & Sabol, 2012). During this same period, the U.S. Census completed its 2020 census survey (N. Jones et al., 2021). The survey identified that the White population decreased by 8.6% yet remains the largest population in the United States. A new race category—mixed race—increased by 129% (33.8 million) compared to Black only (46.9 million), making mixed race the second largest population. The Bureau of Justice Statistics has not yet compiled data for the new mixed-race category, so comparison of corrections data and census data should be done with caution.

Now let's look at some specific prisoner crime characteristics presented in Table 4.6. From 2011 to 2021, total crimes for incarcerated offenders decreased by 27%. There were several events that led to this decrease. The 2020 census showed fewer teenagers and young adults in the general population. For several past decades, this age group had been the largest age group in prison. Decriminalization of marijuana in most states in the past decade significantly decreased arrests of drug users and increased the release of incarcerated offenders who had previously been incarcerated. Interestingly, the number of females incarcerated for drug crimes increased from 6% in 2011 to 13% in 2021. This suggests that more women may have become drug dealers in their prison communities over the past 10 years to increase their income as social services were disrupted during the pandemic and changes in presidential and congressional leadership.

Although the percentage of violent crimes decreased by 11% from 2011 to 2021, the percentage of violent crimes compared to all crimes increased to 62% from 53% in 2011. This is the first time since the 1970s that the violent crime population exceeded the nonviolent one. During this decade several social and political situations

Table 4.6. COMPARISON OF PRISONERS BY CRIME CATEGORIES IN 2011 AND 2021 BY BUREAU OF JUSTICE STATISTICS

Item	2011	% of Total	2021	% of Total	% Change
Crime Type Federal and State Incarceration	Total All Crime Types 1,362,028	1st Line = % of 1,362,028 2nd and 3rd Lines = % of Crime Category	Total All Crime Types 1,043,705	1st Line = % of 1,043,705 2nd and 3rd Lines = % of Crime Category	27% decrease
Violent[a]	Total = 725,000	53%	Total = 651,800	62%	11% decrease
	Male = 683,700	94%	Male = 622,200	95%	
	Female = 33,700	6%	Female = 31,700	5%	
Nonviolent[b]	Total = 629,000	46%	Total = 382,200	37%	49% decrease
Property	Total = 249,500	18%	Total = 141,500	14%	55% decrease
	Male = 224,800	90%	Male = 127,900	90%	
	Female = 26,900	10%	Female = 13,600	10%	
Drug	Total = 237,000	17%	Total = 131,600	13%	57% decrease
	Male = 224,500	94%	Male = 114,600	87%	
	Female = 24,600	6%	Female = 17,400	13%	
Public Disorder	Total = 142,500	10%	Total = 109,100	10%	27% decrease
	Male = 135,375	95%	Male = 102,554	94%	
	Female = 7,125	5%	Female = 6,546	6%	

[a] "Other" crime type not included, minimal percentage.
[b] Some totals are affected by numerical rounding by the Bureau of Justice Statistics and instances in which offenders were counted in two different populations, such as probation and parole.
Sources: Carson (2022); Carson and Kluckow (2023); Carson and Sabol (2012).

influenced this increase in violent behaviors, such as protests occurring around the country regarding the 2016 election process; police brutality against Black people and subsequent Black Lives Matters protests; the January 6, 2021, insurrection riot in which 2,000 people attempted to take over the U.S. Congress; and a significant increase in mass shootings. We must also consider that there are two generations of children who have been raised in prison communities in the Country Called Prison, since the 1980s, who are now between 18 and 30 years of age. While not all of these young adults commit violent crimes, there is a strong likelihood that the number of violent crimes will increase as more children in the Country Called Prison become adults.

The nonviolent crime category in Table 4.6 shows a 55% decrease in property crime since 2011. As noted earlier, in the past decade there

has been an increase in the use of specialty courts, diversion programs, restorative justice programs for adolescents, and community
programs in crime prevention through community policing activities.
There appears to be a larger focus by the criminal justice system on
reducing the rate incarceration (which has become known as *ware-
housing*) and creating habilitation programs in the community that
can increase prosocial, working community members. Within the
nonviolent crime category, property crimes decreased by 55% and
drug crimes decreased by 57%; these two crime categories account for
the significant reduction in nonviolent crimes. However, the increase
in violent crimes tends to overshadow the significance of this. In the
last 10 years, we have seen more effort by criminal justice professionals
and community leaders to address the needs of people who live in prisons and prison communities. Many leaders have begun to realize that
you cannot just punish people for the culture they grew up in. Failure
to change has to do with socialization. Most offenders behave as they
have been socialized to behave in *their* culture. Their behavior in prosocial cultures, however, is not appropriate. In England, driving on the
left side of the road is appropriate, but it is not in America. Since the
root of the problem for many is a debilitated childhood development
process, we must address this issue in the solution if we hope to prevent future crimes. Extending punishment to people who are used to
being punished does little. If we hope to transform the current culture
of the Country Called Prison to a more prosocial one, we will need a
plan that focuses on socializing offenders to American culture.

Although children learn culture through conditioning, Albert
Bandura's research in social learning suggests that adults learn new
cultural behaviors through observation and instruction, retention of
new information and skills, reproduction and reinforcement, and self-
motivation to continue or internalization (Bandura, 1963). Increasing
inmates' self-esteem is key since self-esteem is foundational to healthy
adult functioning.

Branden (1994), a leading expert on self-esteem, believed that
adequate self-esteem is essential to our success in life because "it is a
motivator. It inspires behavior" (p. 4). Another leading expert in self-
esteem, Christopher Mruk (2006), suggests that self-efficacy—the
belief that we can learn new things and accomplish tasks—goes hand

Table 4.7. ALPHA BEHAVIORS OF SELF-EFFICACY

Trait	Self-Efficacy Behavior
Awareness	Can identify own thoughts, emotions, and behaviors
Acceptance	Can identify own strengths and flaws
	Can engage in an affirming manner with others by accepting their attributes
Accountability	Responsible for own emotions, actions, and achievements
Assertive	Able to overcome obstacles to achieve goals
Admirable	Able to transform dreams and thoughts into productive tasks and relationships
Altruism	Adheres to universal values of goodness
	Contributes to the wellness of society

Source: Looman (2012).

in hand with self-esteem. In other words, the internal traits of healthy adult functioning are found in self-esteem, and the outward signs are found in self-efficacy. By blending the research of Branden and Mruk, six measurable traits emerge that demonstrate healthy adult functioning. These alpha behaviors of self-efficacy are listed in Table 4.7 (Looman, 2012). With measurable goals, we have outcomes that can drive the transformation process necessary to take down the incarceration mountain. Obviously, the mountain was not built overnight, and simple changes will not remove it. Transformation will require long-term solutions that will significantly change society's social structures. However, some immediate, smaller changes can begin our journey toward a socially justice system.

In this chapter, as well as the next two, we propose some simple, inexpensive changes that we hope will start a chain reaction in shifting the culture of the Country Called Prison to include qualities that create full inclusion, rather than marginalization, within American culture. Our proposals focus on nonviolent offenders, who are the majority population in the Country Called Prison.

PROPOSAL 4.1: INCREASE EXECUTIVE FUNCTIONING SKILLS

As identified earlier, one of the most important outcomes of childhood development is executive functioning, which is a prerequisite for learning prosocial behavior. Therefore, improving executive functioning (planning, organization, time management, problem-solving, and emotional reasoning) is foundational in transforming the prison culture. A search on Amazon for "executive functioning workbook for high school students" will provide several practical choices. Many nonviolent, noncombative computer games are currently available that teach executive functioning and emotional reasoning skills. By succeeding in the game, the gamers improves their skills in time management, strategizing (setting goals and steps to achieve goals), organizing resources, managing emotions, and prosocial problem-solving. EdTechReview and The Pathway 2 Success are suitable internet sources for finding electronic games that teach emotional reasoning and executive functioning skills. These materials could be used in prison training and community diversion programs.

Some in the prison industry believe that allowing incarcerated offenders computer access is dangerous. They fear prisoners will use the internet to hack into websites, buy contraband, circulate hard-core porn, and so on. However, with a little ingenuity, these types of games could be made available to nonviolent prisoners without creating a security risk, such as scheduled game time on resident units.

Prisons could create training rooms in lieu of weight rooms. Instead of muscling up (which also is a security risk), inmates could learn executive functioning skills. Games designed specifically for offenders could create new business opportunities for Silicon Valley. If a reward structure was tied to successful completion of game levels, prison residents might be motivated to play in their free time. These games could also be used in halfway houses and diversion programs to accomplish the same goals.

When people have adequate executive functioning skills, they can curb reckless and dangerous behaviors such as using illegal substances, obtaining contraband materials, or being disrespectful to staff. They can establish long-term goals and identify behaviors and activities that will help them achieve those goals. They can manage work assignments and life obligations (laundry, room cleanliness, hygiene, and so on) effectively and overcome challenges without undue stress. They can make good use of leisure time and engage in self-fulfilling, growth-oriented activities. They can develop humane attitudes toward others and identify ways to be altruistic. In other words, if offenders improved their executive functioning skills, prisons would experience fewer security issues and lowered medical costs for injuries resulting from violence. For community diversion programs and probation/parole officers, there would be less need for supervision and monitoring and more time could be spent on assisting their clients in reassimilating to American culture.

PROPOSAL 4.2: INCREASE LITERACY AND GENERAL KNOWLEDGE AND FOSTER VALUES TO BUILD CHARACTER, IMPROVE PARENTING SKILLS, AND PARTICIPATE IN CIVIC RESPONSIBILITIES

Increase Literacy Through Education and Book Clubs

To change a society's culture, one must consider changing the language, values, and norms of that culture. These cannot be easily changed because they have evolved over time. However, research has shown that education is one of the most powerful and easily implemented processes to shift a culture toward democracy and cooperative, prosocial behavior (Harrison, 2006). Although the importance of education has been recognized by leaders in the criminal justice system for many years, implementation has not been easy due to security issues and funding for educational staff, especially in prisons.

Again, we suggest the use of technology as a low-cost alternative. Today we have computer programs that can teach literacy and prepare students for GED tests, college entrance exams, and licensed certification exams. Other programs teach technical skills and assist in learning vocational trades. Through the internet and television, one teacher can present to several classrooms in different locations at once as well as interact with students.

Imagine if every prison resident obtained a GED, learned vocational skills, and/or even attended college prior to discharge. Again, security remains a concern. However, if China can restrict internet access to its citizens, why can't prisons? Online education is more available than ever. Inmates with access to a computer lab could even use this technology to plan for their lives after release, such as finding employment and housing. With proper monitoring, we believe this plan is viable.

In November 2007, the One Laptop Per Child nonprofit organization began shipping their hand-crank laptops to children in third-world countries where little access to electricity is available, to educate and connect these cultures with the 21st century. Surely we can bring this same technology to nonviolent inmates safely and with little cost.

Research by Kong and Fitch (2002) has shown that students who participate in book clubs and current events discussion groups benefit greatly. They better their scores on standardized tests, improve their speaking and listening skills, increase their prosocial behavior, expand their problem-solving skills, and build their general knowledge base. These clubs also promote a sense of community and fellowship, which opens minds to alternative perceptions and improves the ability to empathize with others.

One of the best resources for implementing a quality book club program is the Great Books Foundation (http://www.greatbooks.org), a nonprofit organization that was founded in 1947. The original purpose of the organization was to promote the reading and discussion of great literature within the general population. In 1962, it expanded its mission to include children with the introduction of Junior Great Books. Over the years, the foundation has helped hundreds of thousands of people throughout the United States start their own discussion groups in schools, libraries, and community centers. One of the reasons for the great success of book clubs developed with assistance from Great Books is the foundation's use of the *shared inquiry* discussion method. Participants learn to read more keenly, ask introspective questions, listen open-mindedly, and respond to others effectively. Participants also practice leading discussions and reflect on the discussion process.

Implementing these clubs in prison would allow offenders to reflect on their lives and to think about the larger world. Of course, a reward system would need to be instituted to encourage offenders to join. In one prison in which John worked, prisoners earned a gold card for good behavior. The gold card allowed them to go first in the dinner line and provided an earlier shopping time at the canteen. No-cost rewards could be put in place to help the incarcerated learn to make choices that benefit them.

Having knowledge and understanding of the world is a good thing. So too is connecting to others in the community. Prison life is a community. Currently the only connections available to many offenders in prison are gangs. While church services and Alcoholics Anonymous (AA) meetings are provided in many prisons, we believe that expanding residents' social interactions can only help. Busy residents are easier to manage, and if residents work on a degree or a GED or just learn to read, they may see a future for their lives. In short, all these ideas could help prisoners develop executive functioning skills, which would be good for both prison safety and American society to which inmates will return.

Of all the proposals outlined in this chapter, implementing book clubs in prisons is perhaps the easiest and least expensive. It also has the highest probability of success and will quickly lead to positive change (https://libromaniacs.com/). The first step would be to contact a local librarian, either at the local high school or community public library. In addition, many community organizations—churches, civic groups, book clubs—want to help those in need. These organizations might want to volunteer to facilitate discussion groups, help purchase books, or train residents to become club facilitators.

The next step toward implementation would be to assign a champion, an employee who works at the prison who is excited about the idea and understands the value of such a program. The champion would focus on implementing the program. Then identify residents who could be the first facilitators; they will need to have training in facilitator skills. The last step would be to identify a prison to start a book club, perhaps a small minimum security facility or a few units in a medium security prison that have mature offenders willing to start something new. Obviously, policies and procedures will need to be written so the program could be implemented in all prisons. Different rules for different types of facilities would likely need to be written, but everyone should be able to participate in some fashion.

Foster Values to Build Character, Improve Parenting Skills, and Participate in Civic Responsibilities

Beyond increasing literacy and general knowledge, offenders and their families need training and education in three specific areas: character, parenting, and civics. *Character education* is essential to the dignity and development of society (Lickona, 1992). Character includes respecting the norms of society, self-discipline, honor, loyalty, consideration of others, and a desire to be your best while accepting failure. Curricula and resources for initiating character education programs and discussion groups can be found at http://www.charactercounts.org.

Although *parenting education* has been around for many years, typical curricula focus on skills and behaviors. Because lifelong patterning is developed within the first 7 years of life through parent–child interactions, mothers and fathers are the primary source to help children develop prosocial values and attitudes. Since many who live in the Country Called Prison did not experience effective parenting, they first must learn to self-parent. Every child protective services office in the United States recommends a set of parenting classes to families. These programs teach proper discipline, boundaries, and rules for healthy families. These parenting classes could be taught to offenders to better understand their own childhoods while at the same time preparing to parent their own children. Self-help groups are often effective in this regard, and, with proper training, long-term prison residents could lead the groups for little or no cost.

Civic education involves imparting the knowledge, skills, attitudes, and experiences that allow someone to be an active participant in American life. The United States needs informed, active, and thoughtful citizens to remain democratic. Civic education encourages personal responsibility for community endeavors, growth, and safety. An excellent guideline for developing curriculum for civic education programs and discussion groups is *Making Civics Count: Citizenship Education for a New Generation* (D. Campbell et al., 2012).

PROPOSAL 4.3: MODIFY PRISON ENVIRONMENTS TO INTRINSICALLY HABILITATE DELAYED PSYCHOSOCIAL SKILLS

In most correctional systems, residents are just thrown together without much thought to their age and rehabilitation needs. This practice is one of the root causes of the predatory culture of prisons. Prisoners with psychopathic personalities are usually the minority in most prisons. However, they often cause the most problems for nonviolent residents, who, with a little help, could be transformed into taxpayers. This situation must change if we are going to stop the growth of the Country Called Prison.

Separate Predators From Prey

First, we need to separate the predators from the prey. Zoos with natural habitats don't let lions roam loose in the same area as antelopes. Yet prison administrators irrationally do the same thing with offenders. Predators can be identified by using one or two psychological clinical assessments, such as the Hare Psychopathy Checklist–Revised (Hare, 2004) and the Millon Clinical Multiaxial Inventory–III (Millon et al., 2009). These assessments, which are specifically designed to determine psychopathy and predatory behavior, are inexpensive and easy to administer to groups and to score and analyze. In public health, identifying and isolating the virus is the first step in stopping an epidemic. These same practices could make prisons safer.

The assessments can also identify mental health symptoms and socialization issues for all offenders, not just the predators. In our experience, we find that many residents have undiagnosed mental disorders and frequently have dual diagnosis issues related to mental health and addiction. Couple this with the trauma from childhood abuse, and one can see the reasons for the poor interpersonal relationship and problem-solving skills. Residents with serious mental disorders (such as schizophrenia and bipolar disorder), intellectual disability, and serious medical disorders could then be housed in specialty units that offered standard mental health and medical services. These inmates require expert services and specialized discharge planning.

Smaller Is Better

Criminology theories of social control propose that when a society's moral codes are internalized and individuals have a stake in their wider community, they will voluntarily limit their propensity to commit deviant acts. Recall our earlier discussion of social bonding theory developed by Travis Hirschi (1969). He suggests that strong internal controls, which are influenced by social bonds, prevent criminality. While individuals with prosocial characteristics developed these strong internal controls by bonding with prosocial adults in their families and schools, most offenders did not because they likely grew up in families where prosocial values were not practiced. To correct this, prison environments need to support the four key bonds that influence internal control. First is affiliation with those who follow the rules. Separating prisoners from prey would go a long way to supporting this bond. Second, commitment to or investment in conventional action is vital, and it will increase when prisoners obtain adequate educational and vocational programs. Third, involvement in prosocial activities improves our social bonds. Activities such as participating in book clubs, playing educational computer games, and learning new skills will be supportive as well. Finally, belief in or agreement with society's value system would increase through participation in civic engagement and self-help groups.

All these bonds would be easier to strengthen if prisons were smaller. Research on school size suggests 20 students per teacher have more student commitment and involvement and, therefore, fewer delinquency problems (Kennedy, 2014). The military divides up companies into smaller units or platoons because it realizes that soldiers fight best when they bond to a group. Smaller is better for general learning as well. How we learn and grow is often a reciprocal process, where we observe and learn from each other during day-to-day interactions. Research suggests that reciprocity takes place more frequently in groups with fewer than 10 members (Nowak & Sigmund, 1998). Smaller living units can be created by fencing off larger prison facilities into smaller sections or dividing large units into smaller units via wall partitions.

Use Discernment in Placement Considerations

Prison residents need to be assigned to housing units based on demographic factors. Age, for example, is an important characteristic to consider. Separating inmates by age aligns them with natural growth and development processes. School systems rarely place high school students in the same building as first graders. Humans naturally associate with people who are going through the same life processes, since we learn and grow by sharing concerns and experiences. If prisons are to become places for correcting behavior, we should use the natural socialization process of age to assist.

Length of sentence is another consideration for housing placement. Residents should be housed according to how long they are going to be in prison because the needs are very different. *Fast-track units* designated for residents serving sentences that are fewer than 5 calendar years should be created. Optimally, these units would be divided by age and offense, as well as number of offenses. It is important to not house first-time, nonviolent offenders with repeat offenders.

Developmentally, all young adults are figuring out their self-identity and their own moral principles. They are discovering their purpose in life, choosing a career, and forming close relationships with friends with whom they will stay connected throughout their lives. These developmental challenges for young adults in prison could be better addressed if they were housed in units with residents of similar age characteristics.

Prison residents in their midyears (ages 30 to 50) have often been employed and have families and aging parents. Developmentally, they are realizing that life is not just about them, that others depend on them. For this group, guilt and shame for their addictions and criminal behaviors often trouble them deeply and make their poor decision-making worse because of fatalism and depression.

If age groups need to be mixed, we propose housing the over-50 group with the midyear group and not the young. An "older and wiser" resident serving a life sentence might positively influence younger inmates, like housing a college senior on the freshmen dormitory floor. The older student likely has gained some understanding and wisdom, which can help the younger student. In short, a deliberate effort should be made to house people in groups that are most likely to help them restart their development process and learn healthy prosocial skills.

We envision that these units will have rehabilitative milieus focusing on the psychosocial needs of the age group. Prison residents could be given planners and workbooks, appropriate for the different age groups, to guide them in their recovery. In college, we often create *plans of study* for students so that they know their roadmap to graduation. In prison, residents could create *life roadmaps* to be used during their time in confinement and after their release.

Again, reward systems need to be in place to help motivate residents to develop self-discipline and improve their executive functioning and interpersonal skills. Of course, all units will have case managers and security personnel; however, in most rehabilitative programs, the goal is to have each group govern itself, just as families and neighborhoods do in the United States.

There also needs to be special *reintegration units* for offenders who have been in prison for longer than 5 years and who are about to receive parole. Residents who have been in prison for this amount of time tend to be institutionalized. Some long-term prisoners develop PTSD due to the warlike conditions of some prisons and will need to be treated before they are released with follow-up care in the community. Since reintegration is a major and complex process for residents leaving prison, we will discuss it at length in a later chapter.

Prison residents who are likely to spend their lives (or most of their lives) in prison might do better if they are allowed to create pseudo-family units where they form lifelong friendships and a support system (again, separating the predators from the prey). Reformed "lifers" can serve as unit program and club facilitators or as teacher's aides after completing training courses. Such responsibilities could provide lifers with a valuable way to contribute to their community and allow them the human dignity of atonement. Program facilitators can lead various club meetings, AA sessions, and educational groups (such as life skills, GED preparation, parenting skills, or employment skills) and assist with online classroom programs.

For over 100 years, social scientists have recognized and identified that human development is based on peer group processes and patterning that intertwine cognitive, emotional, psychosocial, sexual, and moral internal systems. To disrupt this natural process assures functional impairment. By grouping prison residents in natural developmental peer groups, they can fill in the gaps left by their incomplete childhood development. As residents resume normal developmental growth patterns, they will be better able to appropriately care for their own needs. If offenders are to leave the Country Called Prison, they will need to be independent, be able to maintain healthy relationships with others, and possess the skills to manage their responses to challenges in appropriate ways. While they have been taught that they must accept responsibility for their actions, they must also learn to self-correct their behavior.

The citizens of the Country Called Prison are diverse. In many ways, they are a lot like all of us, merely trying to get through life. However, for most of them, their socialization has been sorely lacking, leading them to make choices that land them in prison. The question for the taxpayer is this: Since most prison residents will eventually leave prison, what do we want them to be like when they get out?

Currently, we tend to release residents from prison in the same or a worse condition than when they came in. The educational, social, and even spiritual resources that were lacking in the community are not provided in the prison system either. Thus, the boundaries of the Country Called Prison extend far beyond the walls of a correctional facility to prison communities across America.

SUMMARY

If we want to decrease the number of people in prison and prison communities, we need to integrate them into American society. To transform prisons so that they habilitate offenders does not require a lot of money or a lot of staff. Transformation requires a belief that it can be done and that the citizens of a Country Called Prison are worth assimilating into American society.

CHAPTER 5

Living in a Country Called Prison

The vilest deeds like poison weeds bloom well in prison air: It's only what is
good in Man that wastes and withers there.

Oscar Wilde

When people live in the same place long enough, the day-to-day
process of living together eventually becomes a way of life, a
way of life that is distinct from other groups of people who have lived
together long enough in another place. It is a way of life that continues long after the first people living together in that space die or leave.
Culture is the word that social scientists use to describe the symbolic
system that represents a specific people's way of life.

To change a culture, one must first understand it. Anthropologists
study cultures in several ways. Most people are familiar with archaeol-
ogy, physical anthropology (the study of bones), and linguistics (the
study of language). Fewer people are aware of *social-cultural anthropology*, a subfield of archeology that focuses on the social and psychological behavior of a group of people who live together. Two basic schools
of thought exist as to how one should study this behavior. One group
of researchers assumes that social institutions create the cultural
domains of a society, while the other assumes that culture drives the
development of social institutions (Delaney & Kaspin, 2011). In this
chapter, we are going to discuss both perspectives.

When anthropologists conduct research, they immerse themselves
into the culture they are studying by living with the group; this is

A Country Called Prison, Second Edition. John D. Carl and Mary D. Looman, Oxford University Press.
© Oxford University Press 2024. DOI: 10.1093/oso/9780197768310.003.0005

called *fieldwork*. They take extensive notes on their experiences and observations (research clues) to understand the reasons a particular group of people does what it does, what motivates the group, and how the group's way of life constrains or develops the group. Their findings are usually published as an ethnography.

In the years we have worked in prisons and ancillary community social service agencies, we have asked why prisons are the way they are. We have looked through research by others to find answers to our questions. While the research has been valuable, it has mostly come from "outside" the culture. There have been very few anthropological studies of prison culture.

James Waldram has conducted such studies for over 20 years. He notes that "few are willing to venture into the 'belly of the beast' for three basic reasons: 1) prison inmates are not embraceable research participants in a discipline strongly focused on the innocent, disempowered, and disenfranchised; 2) researchers assume that inmates will be uncooperative and too difficult to work with; and 3) prisons are highly regulated environments that constrain more than they enable research" (Waldram, 2009, p. 4). These are the reasons we include our experiences in this book. Although our stories have not been generated from the rigorous notes of fieldwork, we have tried our best to make our anecdotes accurate.

Why is culture important to understand when it comes to the mass incarceration epidemic? It is important because culture is the way each of us thinks, feels, speaks, and behaves. We all believe that the way we see and experience the world is the same for everyone else. In fact, our minds interpret our life as we experience it based on cultural patterning from our childhood. As we grow up, we learn behavior patterns, values, and beliefs that are considered normal within the family, community, and country in which we live. As we learn these patterns, the mind stores this information as concepts and schemes—the framework for understanding relationships when cultural information is different. By the time we are young adults, these patterns have developed into our own unique sense of reality—the way we each interpret and experience *normal*. This is why, when two people witness the same accident, they often tell the police officer a different story. This is also the reason we sometimes have difficulty communicating with each other and have conflicts over the simplest things, such as the way laundry should be done.

Research by Wakefield and Wildeman (2014) illustrates why we need to study and understand the culture of the Country Called Prison. Their work suggests that children who are raised in households where a parent, particularly a father, goes to prison suffer throughout their lives. The act of incarcerating a parent sets a child up for a host of problems, including long-term economic inequality, increased like-lihood of incarceration, higher rates of mental health and behavioral problems, higher rates of infant mortality, and a host of other com-plicating factors. Their findings clearly support our thesis that prison affects not only those who live in it but also the future generations who are raised in prison communities.

Within a culture, we learn our roles and how to play them. The experience of life within a culture is dependent on the role a per-son plays in it. In 1971, Philip Zimbardo, a professor at Stanford University, designed a 2-week experiment to study the way systemic power differences in prison corrupt people (http://www.prisonexp. org). Zimbardo divided students into two groups: One group was prison guards and the other was prisoners. He guessed that these roles would affect outcomes, but no one could have predicted what occurred. He theorized that four factors would contribute to the corruption of the student guards: (a) anonymity of place and per-son, which creates states of de-individuation; (b) dehumanization of victims; (c) permission to control others; and (d) an environment that sanctions malevolence through significant differences in control and power (Zimbardo, 2004). Zimbardo assessed the physical and mental health of the research participants prior to the experiment and found them all to be healthy. By the sixth day of the experiment, student guards began mistreating student prisoners. As student pris-oners grew more and more resentful, Zimbardo feared that violence was about to erupt and stopped the experiment. Over the years, we have witnessed Zimbardo's corruption factors play out time and again in the Country Called Prison with similar results—only no one stops the real-life scenario. Box 5.1 summarizes Zimbardo's find-ings related to who is most likely to abuse their authority if given the opportunity.

Mary's career in criminal justice began about the same time as Zimbardo's experiment, and the study greatly influenced her perceptions and attitudes toward the behaviors and relationships of and between criminals and criminal justice professionals. To this day, she sees great differences in the roles of people who live or work in the Country Called Prison. The imbalance of power often leads some who work in the prison system to act in a callous and uncaring way. At the same time, residents abuse and rape one another to maintain their own power. In prison, power is key. Everyone wants it, but few have it.

Before we continue, however, we emphasize that, for the most part, the people we have met working in the criminal justice system are compassionate and want to help offenders turn their lives around. Most understand, at least on some level, that offenders have had difficult childhoods and are not inherently bad people. In other words, the criminal justice system is not an industry where budding despots come to work for the sole purpose of being mean to other people.

We believe that the abuse of power, the inhumane care of prisoners, and the callousness sometimes exhibited by employees stems from the overall objective of the system, which is to *contain* criminals, not correct their behavior. Therefore, we have observed that as soon as a person is charged with a crime and given a number-name that person becomes an object, no different than a piece of furniture that needs to be moved from here to there or stored in a warehouse. To work with this number-name object and ignore its humanity, criminal justice personnel must shut down, or at least turn down, their emotional reasoning center. When humans detach from this center, they become insensitive and potentially cruel.

Why haven't prison operations changed much since Zimbardo's enlightening research? Beyond isolating those we are afraid of, do prisons serve a psychological or sociological purpose? Philosopher Kenneth Burke (1954) coined the term *scapegoat mechanism*, which Rene Girard (1986) developed more broadly as a cultural phenomenon that occurs when a person is singled out to be expelled from society, or sacrificed, to psychologically reduce tension created by the human desire to have what someone else has. Although the initial conflict over an object likely started a long time ago, the antagonism between the two groups or individuals builds to the point that the desired object is forgotten and only the antagonism remains. Since growing antagonism ultimately threatens human survival, the antagonistic feelings are projected onto a designated scapegoat who can then be destroyed, thus restoring peace between the individuals or groups.

Although he was not speaking directly about criminals, Carl Jung, a Swiss psychiatrist, described the role scapegoats play in society when he stated, "There must be some people who behave in the wrong way; they act as scapegoats and objects of interest for the normal ones" (Jung & Campbell, 1976, p. 108). The killing of Native Americans in America's early history and the killing of Jewish people during World War II are examples of large-scale scapegoat events.

About the same time Girard and Jung were developing the scapegoat theory, American social scientist Lee Ross (1977) proposed a slightly different idea. His fundamental attribution of error theory postulates that humans tend to explain a person's behavior as a choice rather than a result of situational context. For example, if I have no money and I steal medication to take care of my child, Ross's research suggests that people would judge me as a bad person because I stole something and ignore the extenuating circumstances of my poverty and my sick child.

In our experience, we believe that many people judge offenders the same way. Over the years, we have heard many people say, "Well, she's a criminal; she gets what she deserves"; "What did he expect? He should have thought about that before he stole the car"; or "All of them lie; don't believe a word they say." Yet, as we identified in previous chapters, statistics demonstrate year after year that most people in prison are poor, are inadequately educated, and have poor problem-solving skills. Add to these characteristics the fact that most are in prison for nonviolent offenses and the picture becomes cloudier. Most people from the Country Called Prison are not inherently *bad*, yet we treat them as if they are.

We wonder if society has made prisons, and the millions of non-violent offenders that fill them, the scapegoat for society's frustrated desires. What is society projecting on the millions of nonviolent offenders who have been expelled from American culture over the past 50 years and expression of its frustration with modernity? Is our growing diversity of race, gender, and ideology? Is it the growing inequality between the wealthy and the poor? These remain open questions.

Obviously, mass incarceration has not made our society any better or safer from crime. We contend that it is making things worse. So when solutions don't solve the problem, oftentimes it is because researchers have asked the wrong questions. Instead of asking, "What should we do with people we think are bad?", we might want to ask, "How can we help humans make cooperative choices rather than antagonistic ones?" or "How can we change the environment so that antagonistic choices don't have to be made?"

The concept of culture is complex and entails many dimensions and attributes. A major dimension of culture is the way a group of people view the concept of "self" (Storti & Bennhold-Samaan, 1997). In *individualistic cultures*, members identify primarily with themselves; independence and self-reliance are valued (Figure 5.1). Although members may join groups or clubs and attend family gatherings, they tend to distance themselves psychologically and emotionally from each other. In other words, a person's sense of identity and success is not tied to what others think but to their sense of accomplishment. The United States, Great Britain, Australia, and Canada are examples of individualistic cultures.

Within this typology, two divisions identify the way individuals relate to one another. In *horizontal individualism*, each person views themselves as autonomous and relatively equal with others. In *vertical individualism*, each person views themselves as autonomous but unequal with each other; thus, competition is valued. This describes America's culture.

In a *collectivist culture*, one's sense of identity stems from one's membership and role in a group; the harmony of the group and the

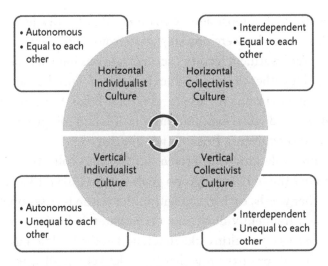

Figure 5.1. Individualist and Collectivist Culture Typology.
Source: Storti and Bennhold-Samaan (1997).

interdependence of group members are valued. Group members are relatively close emotionally and psychologically but distant toward members of other groups. Japan, Pakistan, and India are examples of collectivist cultures.

Within this typology are two divisions that specify the way group members interact with each other. *Horizontal collectivism* encourages collective decision-making among equal individuals and is based on decentralization and egalitarianism. *Vertical collectivism* stresses hierarchical structures of power and conformity; it is based on centralization and hierarchy. Vertical collectivism generally describes the four major groups we have observed interacting with each other in jails and prisons: prison residents, security personnel, administrative staff, and licensed professionals.

We believe each of these four major groups experiences life in prison differently and has developed a subculture within the larger prison culture. Inside prison is the only place Mary has worked where the different employee groups do not seem to have a common purpose regarding prisoner care. For example, Mary worked at an inpatient treatment facility for teenagers where everyone focused on treatment objectives. At the facility, even the housekeepers, security officers, and kitchen personnel were trained to interact with each patient in a therapeutic and compassionate manner. This facility housed very difficult patients who were one step away from being sent to juvenile prison. Yet the treatment facility's success rate was high because everyone worked together to create an environment focused on a common goal. In this environment, where everyone holds the same values, belief system, and social expectations, the different role groups did not develop into subcultures. Prison is not like this.

Over time, role groups in prison develop into collectivist subcultures because the individual group goals are not linked to a common goal. In other words, each group within the prison focuses on its own goals, which frequently don't support inmates' behavior correction. Prison then sets up a culture like that found in the Middle East, where different subcultures exist together in a relatively small space but are often at odds with each other. Since each subculture has its own goals, peace is hard to achieve. So it is with prisons.

Figure 5.2 provides a visual image of the four groups—security, administration, licensed professionals, and prisoners—found within prison walls. Each has different goals to which their efforts are usually directed. For instance, the goal of the mental and physical health professionals who work in prisons is different from that of the "break-even, fill-the-beds" mentality of administration. However, security always holds the trump card in a prison.

Figure 5.2. Goals of Four Main Role Groups in the Prison System.

Later we will discuss the characteristics of the different subcultures. First, we relate one of Mary's prison experiences that led her to the insight that the four subcultures within prison work against each other.

"Doc, it's Sgt. Lane on Unit 6. Jane's acting up again; I think she's probably going to start cutting herself again." "Can you send her up to my office?" "No, the yard's locked down and everyone has to stay put." "Is there an officer that can escort her?" "No, our roving officer had to make a medical run; someone got hurt in the kitchen." Mary knew better than to ask if she could come and get her. She had tried to escort an offender several months earlier and had received a scolding from the chief of security, who adamantly reviewed the security regulations with her. In another 30 days Jane would be out in the community without a police escort. Why couldn't security use some common sense? Resigned to the situation, Mary told the officer she'd be there soon.

Mary hung up the phone feeling frustrated. Jane had some very serious mental health problems and should never have been sent to prison in the first place. Mary had been expecting this acting-out behavior, this cry for help, for the last few days. Now that Jane was going to be discharged soon, she didn't want to leave because no one in her family wanted her. Mary wasn't sure what good she could do visiting her in the corner of the dayroom surrounded by the other residents.

Mary first spoke to Jane's case manager to see how her discharge plan was coming along. The case manager explained, "Well, I've called a couple of shelters to see if they've got any beds open. To tell you the truth, though, I've had six discharges this week, and I really haven't had time to work on her plan. There's very little out there for anyone with her issues. I don't know what can be done. She's probably not going to make it anyway." Although Mary knew he was probably right, she was a little perturbed by his pessimism. She wondered if he was really trying to find her a good placement or just going through the motions.

As Mary walked into Jane's unit, about a third of the residents were in the dayroom. There weren't enough jobs for all the prisoners, so many residents spent the day trying to figure out ways to occupy their time without getting into trouble. Some of them were styling each other's hair, while others ironed or drew on art paper. They all smiled at Mary when she entered, obviously glad that help had arrived for Jane.

They knew not to say anything though; the officer on duty was fussy about residents talking to staff without permission. This officer had once said, "Doc, you got to set better boundaries with them. They're going to take advantage of you. You got to make sure they know their place."

Jane was sitting on a bench by a window off to one side of the day-room. Two residents were doing their best to befriend her, although one of them had just about as many issues as Jane. The friends stood up to leave when Mary arrived, but Mary asked them to stay. Without divulging anything her friends didn't already know, Jane said she was distressed about her imminent discharge. However, she also made some statements that suggested that the real issue concerned a known gang member pressuring her to do things before her discharge. Mary validated her concerns and educated her friends on ways they could help her cope with the stress. After talking with her for about 30 minutes, Mary invited her to her office as soon as lockdown cleared so the two of them could talk more privately.

Mary feared that helping Jane would get her into more trouble, but she wanted to try. If you tell on someone in prison, you're setting yourself up for a savage beating if not death; but if you don't, your life can become wretched. As a licensed professional, Mary was supposed to be caring and helpful, but as a Department of Corrections employee she is supposed to follow policy, which states that Jane should request separation from the gang member who is threatening her. Each day is a catch-22.

Mary then went to speak with the duty officer. Upon entering the control room, she surprised a couple of officers excitedly discussing the fight that had broken out in the kitchen that initiated the need for the medical run. A resident who owed money for drugs had been stabbed by the woman who sold her the drugs. The officers' language was coarse and filled with expletives. Mary told them of her plan and assured them that Jane was not suicidal. They complained, but only because they feared Jane would create more problems for them if her mental health continued to deteriorate. Mary walked back to her office feeling tired and irritable, recognizing the absurdity of prison life. No one worked toward the same goals for Jane or anyone else. How could Jane ever hope to recover in such a setting?

As this story demonstrates, the subcultural group in prison that is viewed as essential is security and it therefore has the most intrinsic power. After all, there are dangerous people in prison, and it is the officers' job to keep them in prison. In addition to supervising prisoners and ensuring their safety, security is also responsible for keeping all staff safe as well. The security subculture tends to be based on a military-style system that includes a hierarchical structure of decision-making. It tends to have exact rules of conduct and defined roles, ranks, and statuses. Members tend to have a strong sense of tradition and adherence to values that often remain even if someone leaves the group. There is consistency across units and organizations; for instance, if you are a captain at one place, you know you will be a captain at another place. There is a clearly defined career path with expected promotions based on the passage of time as well as abilities. Bill's story illustrates the general beliefs and attitudes of this subculture.

Bill was convicted of possessing a relatively large amount of methamphetamine. It was his first time in prison. As he got off the transport bus and began walking toward the prison entrance, a security officer told him to get in line and walk straight. Bill had difficulty walking straight because of a limp. The officer, a kind-hearted family man outside of prison, pulled him from the line and berated him, screaming, "Hey Gimpy, walk where you are told!" Bill cowered in terror and tried to comply. Later this officer joked with the staff, saying, "It's good to find one and make him an example; it keeps the others in line." Everyone laughed and agreed. John knew this man well and knew he would never laugh or yell at a person limping at the mall or in his church. Yet in prison, he submitted to the dominant value of the security subculture, which is to maintain power over the residents. No one cared if Bill's feelings were hurt. That was not the point. After all, he was just an inmate.

Employees in the administrative subculture are responsible for the business end of criminal justice organizations. They are concerned with such activities as processing prisoners, filling beds, overseeing facility maintenance, providing for personnel supplies and needs, and managing the finances of the organization. This subculture tends to have a collaborative, matrix structure, with rules of conduct that are generally implied rather than specifically identified. The roles and statuses of members are more flexible and ambiguous, with both formal and informal decision-making practices. Considerable variation across units exists within this subculture, with leadership usually establishing the distinctiveness. Career paths are open and usually based on individual abilities and personal interest. The following story highlights the values of this subculture.

The prison at which Mary worked for several years experienced an unusual flood of new residents. Over the course of 3 weeks, the prison received more residents than it would normally receive in 6 months. Clothing ran short, food at the intake unit grew scarce, and hygiene products, such as toilet paper, disappeared. When security brought the situation to the administration's attention, the secretary in charge of ordering supplies stated in front of her manager, "What's the hurry? They're not going anywhere. If they're a bit dirty, it's no big deal. Eventually they'll get what they're supposed to get." The secretary was a grandmother who loved to tell stories about how she spoiled her grandchildren. Kindness in one environment, disdain in another.

Although the subculture of licensed professionals (mental and physical health care professionals and religious ministry) is like administration, there are some unique differences that are important to understand. Of all the subcultural groups, this group tends to be the most educated, and members are professionally licensed or certified, which can put them at odds with the criminal justice professionals because their allegiances are to an external professional code of ethics, not just the prison. This may be the reason that this group is sometimes seen by security or administration as "soft" on residents.

At a prison in which John worked, Dion, a 20-something resident incarcerated for drug offenses, received news that his mother, with whom he was close, was dying. He went through the proper channels to obtain permission to contact her, but because he had previously had some conduct issues, his requests were denied. As a social worker, John knew that his code of ethics required him to advocate for the client. In this case, Dion was his client, not the prison. He began with security and worked his way up to the warden, asking, "Can Dion have a private phone call to speak with his terminally ill mother before she dies?" The reaction from the other two subcultures was telling. He was accused of "babying" the resident. The most fascinating part of this story was that most of the people who refused to allow a phone call were the same ones who gladly gave him permission to attend her funeral.

The fourth subculture is made up of the prison residents. Within the Country Called Prison, they are the largest subculture, but they have the least amount of inherent power. Of course, this is with good reason; after all, they are convicted felons. Interestingly, residents outnumber security and staff in every prison. Yet most willingly submit to the authority of smaller subcultures. It certainly seems possible that at any given moment prison residents could easily overtake a prison, but prison riots are rare. Why?

As mentioned in an earlier chapter, Donald Clemmer (1940) believed that prisoners become institutionalized by the submissive position they assume in prison to avoid harsh consequences. Years later, Martin Seligman (1975) published his theory on learned helplessness, which supports Clemmer's research. Learned helplessness occurs when someone endures adversity or a painful situation for a long time. Later, when the person has the chance to leave the situation, they don't leave, because they believe they have no control. This can occur over time as residents must repeatedly play a submissive role.

Recent research by Terence Gorski (2014), a leading expert on the long-term effects of incarceration, suggests the learned helplessness occurring in prison should more aptly be called *institutionalized personality*. The institutionalized personality results from people living "in an oppressive environment that demands passive compliance to the demands of authority figures, passive acceptance of severely restricted acts of daily living, the repression of personal lifestyle preferences, the elimination of critical thinking and individual decision making, and internalized acceptance of severe restrictions on the honest self-expression of thoughts and feelings" (Gorski, 2014, p. 1). Gorski's research demonstrates that prison residents can develop marked hopelessness, intense immobilizing fear, free-floating anger, and impulsive violence with minimal provocation, which can lead to a host of problems, particularly the use of addictive substances to self-medicate after discharge. Gorski believes, as we do, that learned helplessness from living in prison significantly increases the chance of failure after discharge.

We have personally seen this happen. Monique was given a 3-year sentence for possession of methamphetamine. Upon admission, she was defiant and angry. It was her first round of incarceration, and she made it known to everyone. She frequently raised her voice with staff and complained about living conditions. Mary spent nearly twice the normal amount of time with her intake assessment in the hope that Monique would better understand the culture of prison. Mary introduced ways that would help Monique assimilate before she ended up in solitary confinement with a longer sentence. A year passed before Mary saw her again, walking alone across the prison yard, head bowed, eyes on the ground. Mary greeted her with a "Good morning," which Monique ignored. Mary asked what her plans were for her imminent discharge. She mumbled, "I don't know; I'll have to see where they send me." Her spirit was gone. She was an ideal inmate because she'd learned to be obedient and to depend on authority to make decisions for her. Most important, she was getting out on time because she hadn't caused any trouble. Unfortunately for society, she had not learned anything that would help her stay out of prison.

Although at first glance prison residents appear to be a homogenous group with their similar nondescript attire, they are not. Residents make up the most complex subculture in prison, for there are several factions within it. Prison gangs are powerful groups that directly influence the overall milieu of jails and prisons. Although residents are adults, as we pointed out in an earlier chapter, most are developmentally and psychosocially delayed in their early teen years. Additionally, while prison is home to residents, they are not in charge of their home; they are supervised much like teenagers are by their parents. Is it surprising that these *mental teens* would form gangs?

From our observations, prison residents have many of the cultural characteristics of an American middle school (CA-EDU, 1989). Residents display a wide range of individual intellectual development, as some are still in the concrete stages of adolescent reasoning while others have progressed into the abstract thinking of early adulthood. They tend to learn through active experiences and often argue with each other and staff merely to demonstrate being independent.

Prisoners' behaviors are inconsistent, at times conforming and cooperative, at other times anxious and needy or aggressive and devious. Typical of teenage behavior, residents tend to challenge authority, testing the limits of acceptable behavior; yet at the same time they want frequent reassurance that they are accepted and cared about. They experience intense conflict regarding loyalty to their subculture in prison, while at the same time they want to get out of prison and stay out.

From our experience, much of the conflict in prison between staff and residents, as well as among residents themselves, stems from the fact that most residents are egocentric. They are easily offended and believe their personal problems, experiences, and feelings are unique. Residents are also idealistic and demand fairness from their own perspective. Conversely, they often lack the capacity to understand the unfairness they caused their families and victims through their wrongdoing, as the following story illustrates.

Jim was always a large kid and the anchor of his high school football defensive line. Throughout school he'd had issues related to fighting and learning. Although school never came easy for him, he was good enough to have a shot at playing college football. One night, after a big game, Jim, who had just turned 18, got drunk with some friends by the local river. He then tried to drive home. On the way, his car slammed into an elderly couple who were returning home after a movie, killing the wife. In a panic, Jim fled the scene but was quickly tracked down thanks to numerous eyewitness reports. The judge convicted him of manslaughter, and he was sent to prison. In John's intake interview with him, John asked Jim if he was sorry for his crime. He said, "Of course! I'm here, aren't I?" He did not mention the grandchildren who will never see their grandmother again or the lost football scholarship or the shame brought to his family. The consequences of his actions were assessed only by how they affected him. Jim was a good fit for prison. Everything was all about him.

We want to emphasize something that we believe directly affects how good people working in prison can be cruel. As we noted earlier, American culture is vertical individualist, where competition is valued; however, the three employee subculture groups—security, administration, and licensed professionals—are part of the vertical collectivist category. So employees of the criminal justice system pass between two very different cultural worlds every day.

Both American culture and prison culture have their own beliefs, expected behaviors, communication styles, and reward systems. They are fundamentally incongruous to each other, one individualist and the other collectivist. When people experience significant cultural differences for extended periods of time, they develop something known as "cultural stress" (Koteskey, 2014). They become anxious and disoriented as they lose all familiar cues, which leads to frustration, verbally (and sometimes physically) aggressive behavior, an irrational need for familiar and comforting things, and disproportionate anger at trivial restrictions and delays (Delaney & Kaspin, 2011).

It has been only recently that we have begun to understand this kind of behavior as cultural stress. We have noticed that employees get irritated if the security gate does not open quickly and they usually make a disparaging remark about the officer operating it. When Mary observes this behavior at work, she now humorously reminds the irritated person, "Just think. We get paid the same whether we are standing at the gate or not."

This kind of humorous statement helps people relax because it reminds them that they are employees (a familiar cue) who can therefore go home at the end of the day (safety). We believe cultural stress accounts for many episodes of cruelty toward prisoners by otherwise socially just employees. We also wonder if cultural stress is the reason for the unexpected extreme violence that erupted during the Stanford study.

Stanley Milgram's (1965) famous obedience experiment also shows the powerful external control that prison environments have on good people. Recall that Milgram tested a subject's ability to reject the orders of a perceived superior. In the experiment, subjects are told that they are going to be a part of a study to test the effects of punishment on learning. The person being studied is called the *teacher*, and it is their job to give an electric shock to the *learner* when that person fails to answer the given question correctly. The teacher cannot see the learner, and the learner is not really getting shocked, but the teacher doesn't know this. With each error, the *supervisor* instructed the *teacher* to increase the voltage of the shock. Eventually the *learners* pretend to cry in pain; the *supervisor* instructs the *teacher* to continue.

Milgram found that 65% of the teachers administered up to 450 volts, even when the learner stopped responding and the dial on the machine for this voltage read "danger." Some people quit the experiment before their session ended, but most continued to administer what they thought was a strong electric shock even after the learner had supposedly passed out. After observing thousands of participants, Milgram (1965) wrote, "With numbing regularity good people were seen to knuckle under the demands of authority and perform actions that were callous and severe. Men who are in everyday life responsible and decent were seduced by the trappings of authority, by the control of their perceptions, and by the uncritical acceptance of the experimenter's definition of the situation, into performing harsh acts" (p. 74).

The same seems true for prison employees. Frequently they seem callous and uncaring. But how can employees hope to correct a resident's behavior when many of their interactions are adversarial? Certainly, strong boundaries are needed with the hardened criminals who occupy today's prisons. However, in the Country Called Prison, most are nonviolent drug offenders. Could the use of abrasive and demeaning authoritarian techniques be partly the reason for high recidivism rates? Why don't criminal justice professionals see this?

Groupthink is a term coined by social psychologist Irving Janis (1972). It is used to describe decisions that are made without objective reasoning. When in groupthink mode, people conform to what they believe is the consensus of their peers, which can lead them to make decisions they would not normally make. Groupthink frequently results in bad decisions that people later agree were a mistake. The prison environment is prone to groupthink for the following reasons:

- **Cohesiveness:** Groups that are highly integrated are more likely to engage in groupthink. Prisons have subcultures, and workers see themselves as the status they occupy. Thus, security doesn't care if the toilet paper runs out—that's administration's job. Add to this the hundreds of policies and procedures that specifically govern nearly every action needed to operate a prison. These statuses and roles become thoroughly entrenched in the culture of a prison. This provides predictability in an environment where at any moment things can get out of hand and become dangerous.

- **Threats:** When groups encounter an external threat, solidarity increases because common enemies unify groups. In prison, all staff realize that they are outnumbered by the residents and their control of the institution hangs on a thin margin.
- **Strong leadership:** Since administrative and security personnel follow an almost military-like authority structure, directives from wardens and their assistants are rarely questioned.

Here is an example of the way groupthink plays out in prison. When a prison resident reported a rape, he was immediately placed in protective custody, which means he was locked in a cell for 23 hours a day with 1 hour of private time in a fenced exercise area about 15 feet square. When the time came for the resident to testify to the investigator, policy required the resident to be handcuffed and escorted through the facility to the interview office. Now, we have a victim of a prison rape with the courage to report the crime being paraded through the prison facility in handcuffs. Imagine if we did this to a rape victim in a hospital emergency room setting.

When Mary asked if the interview could be conducted more privately, the shift captain said, "Sorry, Doc. It's policy. You'll have to talk to the warden." When Mary asked the warden, the warden seemed quite irritated that she asked and referred her to the state deputy director over prison operations. The director mindlessly told Mary that this was current policy. However, in a feeble attempt to be helpful, he said, "Well, the policy is up for review next year, and you should write a letter then and make your suggestions to the review committee." No one knew why rape investigations were handled this way and no one questioned it. Groupthink at its best!

The various subcultures of prison are all likely to be wrapped in groupthink. They each have different goals for their jobs, but they tend to have one thing in common: They carry out their roles without much thought. This is true for both the employees, who forget that their job includes inmate rehabilitation, and the offenders, who forget that they're supposed to learn from this punishment.

Now that we have a better idea of the factions and ideologies that make up prison culture, let's try to understand the life residents lead within the boundaries of prison. We could write a lengthy book if we described everything we knew about life behind the razor-wire fences. So we are only going to discuss the characteristics that we believe contribute to an unhealthy prison culture and that our proposals hope to change.

Daily life in prison is strange, to say the least. No babies are born, but people grow old and die. The people who live there just wait for the sentencing clock to run out so they can leave. While many count the minutes until they are released, feeling their life slipping away, others work at meaningless jobs to earn enough money to buy something special, like a chocolate bar, at the overpriced prison commissary. In prison, the natural human sex drive is often reduced to animal barbarianism, and materialism and status rest on a few pictures on a cell wall and a bag of goodies purchased at the commissary. Rules define what relationships can form, how they form, and for what purpose. Rules and security are the most important things, and human dignity is always the least.

For prison residents, cultural stress is more problematic than it is for employees. While residents tend to be poorly socialized, they did grow up in a culture where autonomy and competition are valued, just like most employees in the criminal justice system. Offenders are incarcerated into a dual society where authority figures no longer view them as people but as objects with a number-name. Prison residents must also form allegiances with the collectivist subculture groups formed by the residents with whom they live while at the same time striving to be individualistic and autonomous to change and not return to prison. Since continuous stress is not healthy and can cause many physical and psychological problems, prison residents must let go of their familiar American cues and adapt to prison life.

Two processes can help people adapt to a different culture. One is assimilation, in which a person's language and culture come to resemble those of the other culture. While the process is usually gradual, full assimilation occurs when the new member of the society is indistinguishable from current members of the culture. In prison, these residents are often referred to as "convicts" because they have become prisonized. Second is acculturation. Acculturation is the process by which the new person keeps some of their customs, which the other culture embraces. In prison, many of the trustees starch and iron the clothes they wear to their jobs, which can be likened to people wearing suits rather than casual clothes to work.

Rather than being a positive change agent, prison life often duplicates residents' lives they had outside prison communities. Many grew up without caring, loving parents. In prison, many staff would like to be more caring toward residents, but policy prohibits this behavior. Other staff treat residents as if they are a bother, just as their parents did when they were children. Rules and discipline in prison are as arbitrary as they were in their childhood depending on the officer on duty.

Education was not often valued by parents of prison residents. Prisons don't seem to value education either, since many residents leave prison without a GED even though they had time to earn one. Much like on the outside, many residents in prison do not have work assignments. If they do have a work assignment, the work is usually meaningless. Many residents did not have jobs prior to their arrest, and those who did worked at jobs that just covered their basic human needs. Most did not have a career, and they likely will not receive training on the inside to begin one when they leave prison.

Another way living outside of prison is like a prison community, will have to do with relationships. Prior to being incarcerated, many prisoners did not have their own place to live and drifted from one friend's couch to another. In prison, some people are difficult to get along with, and officers move them from one cell to another. Friends come and go, as individual security levels change and residents are transferred to other prisons or other units. Just like on the outside, nothing is permanent, and relationships are unpredictable. Relationships have very little continuity. How can you develop trust and respect for others when you aren't given enough time to bond? How can you develop social allegiance if the members of society continually shift and change?

The threat of danger is with all of us all the time. We never know if a car accident will take our lives or if someone will attack us. Most of us, however, have coping skills that put these fears to rest when we get home, locking ourselves into the safety of our nest. But if you are a prison resident who has been placed in a cell with an inmate who wants to regularly dominate you, you have trouble. Tell staff, and you will be isolated, moved, and singled out as a snitch. Ignore it, and you're a punk, a sex toy for a domineering and violent resident. Certainly not everyone is tormented in prison, but residents never know if their new cellmate might be that kind of person. Few people in the outside community have this worry.

Of course, for many prison residents, life might not be as absurd as we imagine. After all, most come from fractured backgrounds, so perhaps their lives are not much different from when they lived in the outside community. If they were homeless and poor, perhaps prison would improve their lives. At least once a week, an offender tells Mary that prison saved their life. Usually, the resident notes that if they had remained in the community, they would have probably died from violence or drugs within the year. Nonetheless, even in these circumstances, prison culture makes little sense compared to the American way of life.

It is important to understand the dynamics that create a specific culture, especially if that culture needs to change. The main dynamics we will explore in this chapter are language, customs/etiquette, clothing, spatial relations, economics, and social relationships.

Just like other nations, the Country Called Prison has its own language and style of communication. Communication is not just words; it also includes body language, voice tone, eye contact, and the use of silence. All communication, sent and received, must pass through cultural filters. Therefore, one of the first things we learn as children is language. Language is important to the Country Called Prison as well.

A major dimension of communication is *context*—the amount of innate understanding a person can be expected to bring to a particular communication setting (Storti & Bennhold-Samaan, 1997). Language in the Country Called Prison varies a great deal depending on the subculture to which you belong. Security, administration, and licensed professional staff all use similar terms. For example, the number-name that is given to offenders and the process of stripping them of their birth name turn them into an object, a nonperson. Since they are now deemed *objects*, other words reinforce that perception.

An offender is *booked* at the police station when the district attorney decides the person will be charged with a crime and placed in jail. The judge tells the *defendant* to rise prior to the verdict being announced, instead of saying, "Mr. Smith, please rise." When a convicted felon is transferred from jail to prison, this is referred to as *pulling chain*, which originated as a term in the 1800s when prisoners were chained together in a line and an officer pulled on the chain to lead them.

In prison, offenders are called *inmates*, implying that all criminals are the same, that they are all mates. Residents live in *cells* on *units* or *quads* with a *cellmate*. When young adults go off to college, we say they live in student dorms. They are referred to as dorm residents, and they are assigned a room with a roommate. Offenders are often referred to by the crime they committed: thief, chomo (child molester), murderer, druggie—again, not their name.

Why are prisoners objectified? Recall that the fundamental attribution of error theory, developed by Lee Ross (1977), suggests that humans tend to explain a person's behavior as a choice rather than a result of situational context. Carmon has been housed in a medium security prison for 2 years and has earned the privilege to be transferred to a minimum security facility. The minimum security prison she will be sent to has cottage-like living quarters with two sets of bunk beds and a private bath area; everyone eats in the central cafeteria area. The prison has no fence, but residents can easily tell where the boundaries are because of the tree line. No one leaves the prison because being caught trying to escape would land them back into medium security, along with an extended 3-year, day-for-day sentence. Almost everyone at the minimum security prison is within 2 years of discharge. Carmon needs to complete only 9 more months of her sentence and she will go home to her mother, who is caring for her 3-year-old son.

Here's the power of objectification and the fundamental attribution error. Before Carmon can get on the bus to be transported to the minimum security prison where she will be free to walk off any time, she must be strip-searched, then handcuffed to a belly chain with her ankles shackled. Although she has earned the right to be trusted at a prison without a fence, on the bus her ankle chains will be locked into the floor. From security's point of view, Carmon is an object that is being shipped. How does Carmon feel about herself as she is riding in the bus? Is there a difference between being shackled and unshackled? It seems that if she were unshackled, she might see that she's being rewarded for her good behavior instead of feeling shamed.

In prison, communication involves more than just words. Customs and etiquette are the observable signs of the cultural beliefs of a nation. These dynamics of culture dictate the way we greet people (a handshake in the United States or a bow in Japan), appropriately eat a meal (belching at the end of a meal is expected in some countries), enter someone's house (in Japan, shoes are removed first), or respect someone's privacy (the tendency not to talk in an elevator full of strangers). The Country Called Prison has customs and etiquette as well. But in America, if someone does not follow a custom or display proper etiquette, that person will be looked at with disdain or merely laughed at. In prison, not following customs and etiquette rules can get you killed.

In talking to and observing residents, we have learned that *respect* is the number one aspect of most of the customs in the Country Called Prison. Conflicts in prison usually involve the dayroom, which often has a television, a telephone area, and a chow hall. These are common areas where behavior toward an inmate can show respect or disdain. There is a pecking order for residents that determines who gets which seat, how close you stand to someone while they're on the phone, and who gets to be first in line for meals. These are just some of the unwritten rules that substantiate residents as a collectivist culture. Remember that in nations in which people have limited space and know each other well, customs and etiquette develop to create psychological space and privacy for everyone.

Since prison residents spend a great deal of time in their units, it is important to quickly learn the proper way to act in the dayroom. Rules dictate the use of dayroom property, such as the television, microwave, coffeepot, and laundry equipment. Residents usually develop an unwritten schedule for use of dayroom property, which residents are expected to know. Telephones are usually tightly spaced on a wall in the dayroom. Residents expect each other to act as if they are in a telephone booth, being sure not to touch each other and to talk quietly so as not to disturb the person next to them.

Since food in prison is limited and the chow hall crowded, offenders are expected to stay in the space created by their chairs and to share any leftover food on their tray. However, the leftover food rule gets a little tricky, as sharing food with someone might be a lure to later use the recipient for something inappropriate, such as sex or a *mule* carrying drugs from one unit to another.

The most important etiquette rules to quickly grasp are those governing toilet use. Obviously, when the toilet is in the bedroom, which is shared with other people, residents must use the toilet in a way that reduces the smell. The rule is to flush quickly and often while using the toilet. Cellmates turn their backs when others use the toilet or step outside the cell if the door is unlocked. How might this daily prison etiquette affect a resident when released from prison? Generally, these roles and rules don't translate very well to American culture.

Interestingly, cleanliness and good health are important in prison, no doubt because of cramped quarters. Obese people are perceived as weak and are preyed upon. Sickly people are also perceived as weak but also as a threat because of possible contagion. Residents are expected to practice good hygiene such as washing their hands after using the toilet and brushing their teeth. It is a sign of respect; it shows that a resident cares about their peers' health.

There are also very specific customs and etiquette rules regarding interactions between residents and employees. Residents must never whisper with staff or be seen talking with an employee alone as they might be suspected of snitching. Many prisons require residents to refrain from talking to employees unless employees talk to them first. Residents are mindful of their closeness to staff and maintain an adequate distance; this applies even to trustees and others who work in the offices with employees. When a security gate opens, all employees go first and then residents.

Culturally, clothing has meaning in terms of status, age, gender, occupation, and degree of formality (Delaney & Kaspin, 2011). Cultures identify the type of clothing one should wear to celebrations, to work, and for leisure activities. One would never consider wearing athletic wear to a formal wedding. Clothing for prison residents is as bland as their lives. They have no choice in their clothing because all residents are the same. Choice of dress isn't really needed because not many activities require different styles of dress. Residents are also told how to wear their clothes, much like parents instruct their young children. As might be assumed, clothing for residents is designed to identify them as inmates; residents' shirts usually have "inmate" or "corrections" printed on the back.

Clothing provided by prisons is designed to be worn by many different sizes of people and is made with easy-to-launder material. Clothing usually consists of a T-shirt, a long-sleeved shirt with buttons, and elastic-waist pull-on long pants. For men, the T-shirt and pants are not much different than T-shirts and sweatpants that they wore on the outside. For women, prison clothing is often demeaning because the clothing looks unfeminine. Many state systems just make one style of clothing and do not differentiate between male and female styles. Thus, women frequently wear unisex clothing, another subtle form of punishment. Is this because having one style of clothing is cheaper? Or is this a fundamental attribution error? Is genderless clothing provided because no one wants to acknowledge the increasing numbers of women in prison?

While space (geographic location, structures, landscapes, physical distance) is a universal concept, the meaning it holds is different for each culture. Mary worked in and visited many different prisons in several states. Prisons are like little towns and are often reminiscent of castles. They have razor-wire fences that serve as moats separating those inside the castle from those on the outside. Once inside, it is difficult to get outside.

Most prisons have two rows of 20-foot-high fencing with razor wire in rolls along the top and bottom; the rows are about 15 feet apart. Why are there two rows of fencing? Per foot, prison fence wire is very expensive. The probability of someone making it over the top of one razor-wire fence is very small. It could be a security precaution to prevent an outside person from throwing something over the fence and into the prison. Many of the prisons that we have been inside or have seen on state Department of Corrections websites look structurally like small college campuses from the outside. Yet once inside the buildings, the solid cement walls and clanging steel doors that echo throughout the building remind us of a cave. The echoing sound in units and hallways makes it difficult to hear staff requests, so sometimes residents don't respond when they should. Staff also cannot hear inmates' responses. The diminished ability to hear each other often leads to conflicts between staff and residents.

If the staff already think residents are "just a bunch of lazy criminals" and residents think staff are "mean and deliberately unfair," it's difficult to mediate disputes. For residents, this dynamic may be reminiscent of their childhood. They would come home from school, walk in the door, and get yelled at. They would ask for something to eat and get yelled at. Mom would tell them to do something, only she'd be drunk and not make much sense, so they would ask mom to repeat the instructions and get yelled at.

Most prisons are a contradiction in spatial elements. While the landscape is large, the space for residents is very small. While the entrance is often beautifully landscaped, the living conditions for residents are deplorable. Although there is plenty of space for residents to do various things (e.g., classrooms, craft shops, vocational training areas, leisure activity areas), residents sit in their units for long hours and many are confined to their tiny cells, with nothing to do except read or draw, usually in the name of security.

One of the annual training courses Mary attends focuses on *games offenders play*. Its goal is to educate staff about ways prison residents attempt to manipulate them. According to the training, residents are experts at getting staff to give them things they are not supposed to have. Year after year, instructors tell employees that "residents don't have anything to do all day long except watch staff and think about ways to use staff weaknesses to their advantage." If prison leadership knows this to be true, then why haven't they done something to keep residents active in a productive manner? Groupthink?

Providing productive opportunities for residents would improve their lives and make the prison community safer and more egalitarian. If residents learn and grow, then they will likely be successful in society when they are released. Recidivism would decrease because corrections departments would have corrected residents' criminal behaviors. And taxpayers might not be so angry about the billion-dollar corrections budget.

Prisons are supposedly designed to control the movement of residents. We use the word *supposedly* because, in our experience, the reason that we have stayed safe when we worked in prisons has nothing to do with security. We are safe because the residents decided not to hurt us because they will likely receive a life sentence. We have seen security gates left open, officers asleep in control rooms because they were working a double shift, too few officers managing too many offenders outside of their cells, and easily weaponizable items left accessible to prison residents. So if prison residents choose to *do no harm*, then why all the security and its resulting costs?

Obviously, some prisons house violent offenders, and security is very important. At these prisons though, residents are usually confined to their cells most of the day and only one to two residents are allowed out at any given time. But this is not the norm. Remember that we are talking about nonviolent offenders who are going to be in prison for only a few years. They just want to get back home. Shaming them with overzealous control mechanisms only makes them more prisonized, more helpless, and angrier. If you treat adults like children, you are going to get childish behavior.

Mary was in a unit with an officer who was controlling and mean. This officer had let about 20 residents out of their cells to get their lunch. The lunches lately had been of poor quality and small. So the men were already grouchy. One of the residents did not have a slice of bread on his tray, and so he politely asked the officer, who had let him out of his cell, for a slice of bread. The officer snapped back, "Be quiet and go to your cell." Not a good call on the officer's part. The resident, of course, got angry and began arguing with the officer using profanity. The other residents became alarmed, with some backing away and others moving closer to fortify his stand. Mary could tell that the situation was going to escalate quickly, so she intervened and was able to calm everyone. Although the officer and resident were still angry, they stopped yelling. Although most of the time residents will have their say and eventually back down and return to their cells, there are moments when an episode like this one could go the wrong way quickly. However, most nonviolent residents don't want to be tagged with a misconduct charge, which could result in more time being added to their sentences. The threat of a longer sentence keeps most nonviolent offenders in check.

All nations have their own economy and legitimate and illegitimate ways to obtain items to satisfy needs. So do prisons. The money that residents have is referred to as "money on my books." If they have a job in prison, they receive a small salary (usually less than $20 a month). Family and friends can also send money to be placed in residents' accounts. Residents are not supposed to flaunt their money by buying large amounts of commissary items or having lots of items in their cells to demonstrate wealth, but some do.

Residents can also earn money through *self-employment*. Some residents with artistic talent create greeting cards in exchange for something another resident can do for them. Some residents make money illegally the same way they did on the outside, selling drugs, sex, and cell phones. These kinds of trades are where most of the trouble between residents begins. If you owe a debt, you pay or you die; there are no bankruptcy laws in prison.

One of the most important dimensions of a culture is kinship. Social relationships are significant because humans need to be with others; we do not do well in isolation, as Abraham Maslow's research (1954) on human needs identified. Relationships are important because they affect who we are and who we will become; they connect us to a family. Prison residents, for the most part, do not get to choose with whom they have a relationship in prison. They are assigned to a specific group of people day and night. They eat together, sleep together, play together, shower together, and get in trouble together (even if an individual in the group doesn't do anything wrong). Residents are forced to form familiar relationships with people they do not call a friend. Imagine going to a public restroom where there are no stalls. In prison, two people who may hate each other share a small room with bunk beds, a sink, and a toilet.

As in all cultures, hierarchies and politics are closely related in prison. All prison yards have their hierarchies, with one or two residents serving as the informal leaders—and they are usually gang leaders. Officers work with resident leaders to keep the prison manageable since residents outnumber security officers. Some inmates who are not gang leaders have a lot of influence in the prison, usually in terms of mediation and common sense. In some ways, all prisons have a dual leadership that mirrors a traditional family, with the father figure (gang leader) as the protector and controller alongside the mother figure (non–gang leader) who focuses on relationship and harmony.

Knowing the gangs, and the hierarchy within the gangs, is crucial to survival in prison. Gangs are often ethnically oriented, but residents can choose to stay out of gangs. Staying out of gangs is harder for younger residents, since gangs are eager to increase their numbers.

Gang members threaten new residents by promising retribution if they don't join. Residents must be politically savvy to avoid a problem. Young residents often join out of fear, believing that ties to gangs will make prison easier for them. Later, if a person wants out of the gang, the resident sadly finds out that membership is not easily dropped.

As social scientists, we believe that human relationships are paramount to healthy living. After all, everything we have done, and will do, generally occurs within the framework of a relationship. In the world outside of prison, relationships might persist, or they may come and go. Think of your best friend at work at your first job. Odds are that you were very close and now you have no idea where that person lives. In prison, relationships are no different. For some who can establish a relationship with a mentor, prison gives them an opportunity to develop their self-identity, complete their GED, learn a vocational trade, and develop the socialization skills needed to successfully emigrate from the Country Called Prison. Others connect to gangs and dominant residents who might make them even worse off, sealing their fate to live their entire life in the Country Called Prison.

In America, people form friendships based on race, ethnic heritage, age, gender, and religious beliefs. Prison residents also bond in the same way, although there are some differences. Some prison residents form relationships with each other based on interests or skills. However, other relationships are chosen for survival purposes. Men tend to be competitive and hierarchical; therefore, where a man stands within the pecking order is important. Smaller men or men who are not accustomed to fighting might form relationships with larger men or men who know ways to fight. These relationships are often mutually beneficial. The protector might need help in learning a skill, such as reading or writing; the protected benefits from the protection he receives.

In American culture, women form friendships based on their family status. Women with children tend to make friends with other women with children, and so forth. In prison we've seen similar affiliations. In prison, women tend to form more family-like relationships. An older woman might have "children" (younger offenders) whom she looks after. A middle-aged female resident might care for an elderly resident, much like she would care for her mother outside of prison.

Just like male relationships, female relationships are seen by security as troublesome. Our experiences show that women in prison tend to place very high value on their relationships with others in the institution. This surrogate family is important to women and yet frequently discouraged by security. In prison, when a female breaks off a relationship with a friend, serious consequences can result. The first day Mary worked at a female prison, she had to counsel a resident whose ex-friend threw boiling syrup on her face because of their break-up; they had been close friends for only 3 months.

Dating and marriage are universal concepts in all cultures, even in prison. Just because prisons house a single gender does not mean that sex doesn't take place. Sex in prison, much like in the outside world, takes place under three circumstances—consensual, prostitution, and rape. Some residents abstain from all forms of sexual activity while in prison. Other residents willingly prostitute themselves as payment for protection, drugs, and other needs. And then there is rape, which is not about sex at all; it is about power and control.

Prison rape is perhaps the ultimate abuse of power and most symbolizes the corruptive nature of prison. In 2013, the Bureau of Justice Statistics collected data on the incidence of prison rape in the United States in all forms of secure confinement (Beck et al., 2013a, 2013b). When John addresses the issue of prison rape in his university criminology course, students usually snicker. Some suggest prison rape is just part of the cost of committing a crime. In short, our perception is that few people understand the data on prison rape, and most don't care. However, the research is clear; there has been a steady increase in prison rapes over time. While not all reported rapes are substantiated, of those reported in 2011, only slightly more than half involved non-consensual acts between residents. The rest involved staff-on-resident sexual violations. Resident-on-resident rape generally includes the use of force or threat of force. Most staff-on-resident rapes were reported as consensual; however, no state allows staff to have sexual relations with residents. Although sexual activity between staff and residents appears to be consensual, true consent can never be obtained due to the power differential. So these acts are classified as rape. The research indicated that female staff most often engaged in illegal sexual activity with prison residents, accounting for almost 60% of the crimes.

Resident-on-resident sexual violence is most common in the victim's room, while staff victimization tends to occur in program service areas. For a complete look at this topic, one should consider Michael Singer's book, *Prison Rape: An American Institution* (2013).

Every weekend and on most holidays, families and friends visit residents in prison. Visiting a prisoner is not like visiting your son or daughter at college. Visitors must have passed a background check and can only bring with them an ID and some coins for the vending machine. Visitors must pass through a security checkpoint, much like at an airport. Visitation is public, with all the residents and visitors in one large room. Little to no touching is allowed, but that does not mean it doesn't happen. We have seen residents create disturbances to cover a conjugal visit of a friend right in the visiting room. Conversations are limited since everyone can hear everyone else. Some residents don't want their families to visit because the heartache after they leave is worse than not seeing them at all. Many just choose to keep in touch by phone.

There is another aspect of a Country Called Prison that has not received the significant attention of researchers that we think it deserves. These are the prison communities that most incarcerated persons have been born into and will likely return when they discharge.

In the 1980s, Todd Clear, a penologist, noticed that for 15 years prison populations were rapidly increasing along with a 15-year rapid increase in crime growth. Along with other penologists and sociologists, he began his lifelong study of the negative influence that mass incarceration policies were having on the American way of life. In 2007, Clear published his eye-opening book, *Imprisoning Communities: How Mass Incarceration Makes Disadvantaged Neighborhoods Worse.* His research clearly identified four main factors that contributed to increased poverty, increased crime, and increased prison populations in disadvantaged neighborhoods (Clear, 2007, pp. 5–6):

1. The significant growth of U.S. prisons, sustained over 30 years, has had small impact on crime reduction.
2. The concentration of prison growth comes from poor, minority males who live in communities with high poverty rates.

3. Concentrated incarceration of Black men from poor communities has broken families, weakened social-control capacity of parents, eroded economic strength, soured attitudes toward society, distorted politics, and increased rather than decreased crime rates.
4. Attempts to overcome high rates of crime will need to encompass sentencing reforms and philosophical realignment.

Clear's succinct explanation of the factors that create prison communities provide the criteria for evidence-based research for rebuilding communities:

> When impoverished communities lose a large percentage of their young working men to the criminal justice system, three legitimate systems of neighborhood order are negatively influenced which increases poverty and crime. The family system is a community's source of private social controls. With a high percentage of arrests, there are high rates of family disruption, single-parent families, and teenage pregnancies. Concentrated incarceration and reentry cycles reduce labor market opportunities for men that already experience difficulties finding work. The obvious discrimination that members of impoverished communities experience diminishes the willingness of community members to participate in local politics; thus, deserting the socially acceptable way to make improvements. (Clear, 2007, pp. 87–88)

About 10 years after Clear published his insights about the influence of mass incarceration on prison communities, Sara Wakefield and Christopher Wildeman (2014) published their book, *Children of the Prison Boom: Mass Incarceration and the Future of American Inequality*. Their research focused on the way mass incarceration has influenced three outcomes of childhood: (a) mental health and behavioral problems, (b) infant mortality, and (c) homelessness.

Childhood mental health and behavior have been found to be prescriptive for adult criminal behavior, especially for violent crimes. Wakefield and Wildeman's research suggests that the risk of paternal imprisonment in adulthood has become unequally distributed between Black and White people and represents a significant harm to Black children in prison communities. Total behavioral problems in schools have risen by at least 7% for Black–White inequality. Infant mortality is important to research because it portrays the way childhood disadvantages influence a community's ability to provide health services to poor families. Wakefield and Wildeman's research data suggest that mass incarceration had increased infant mortality in prison communities by about 40% by 2014. The focus on childhood homelessness is important because the data often follows children into adulthood and show that homelessness contributes to increases in nonviolent crime rates. "Homeless children experience high rates of victimization, exposure to infectious disease, limited access to health care and compromises health in adulthood" (Wakefield & Wildeman, p. 10). Their research indicates that mass incarceration has increased childhood homelessness by 65% in Prison communities. "In an era in which it is hoped that blacks and whites have increasingly open channels to a quality life, these findings are all the more disheartening since they portend the creation of a new underclass" (Wakefield & Wildeman, 2014, p. 148). According to our research, we believe that the new underclass already exists in the Country Called Prison.

Life in the Country Called Prison is different than life in America. We may have told you more about it than you really wanted to know. Many Americans believe that people in prison are locked away in dingy, dark cells or building roads on some chain gang. What most people don't realize is that prison is a place where criminals live out their lives in a town rather like any town in America. The biggest difference is that this prison town only teaches those who live there to become more disenfranchised from American society, to become more mentally ill, to become filled with more anger and hate, and to become more criminal.

So how can prisons change? Nowak and Highfield (2011), experts on evolution and game theory, have recently demonstrated that cooperation is as fundamental as DNA in terms of human progress. Their research indicates that altruism and cooperation are not just nice things we do but are essential in our struggle to survive. "Our ability to cooperate is one of the main reasons we have managed to survive in every ecosystem on Earth, from scorched, sunbaked deserts to frozen wastelands of Antarctica to the dark, crushing ocean depths" (Nowak & Highfield, 2011, p. xvi). In terms of genetic selection, far too many people are involved in the mass incarceration epidemic to ignore its effect on all of us.

Cooperation, as a survival mechanism, is not about being nice to one another. It is about competitors voluntarily helping an enemy. Every November we celebrate Thanksgiving, which reminds us that without the help of Native Americans we would not be the country we are today. Nowak (Nowak & Highfield, 2011) points out that when individuals are forced into the same area, working together helps everyone do better. In his research he noticed that when you take out the concept of forgiveness, you create a vendetta rather than the ability to move toward a better condition.

Nowak identified five mechanisms that lead toward evolutionary social change:

- Direct reciprocity: *I will if you will.*
- Indirect reciprocity: *I will help you because you are my sister's friend.*
- Spatial selection: *We live in the same unit. Let's work together.*
- Multilevel selection: *We all work for the same company. Let's help each other.*
- Kinship selection: *You're my cousin. Come live with me till you find your own place.*

In terms of helping offenders emigrate from the Country Called Prison, the most important part of Nowak's cooperation instinct theory is that cooperation does not require an institution to direct altruistic behavior. Cooperation is an instinct, an innate part of who we are. Correctional departments merely need to let it flourish (Nowak & Highfield, 2011).

Just as the great glaciers of Earth's Ice Age melted so that land could be formed and humans could eventually populate Earth, the mass incarceration mountain needs to melt away. We need to migrate away from a belief system that causes us to see enemies where there are none. We need to create prison environments that encourage cooperation and altruistic behavior, that help people self-actualize, to become what they are innately capable of. A human is a terrible thing to waste.

We recognize that prison culture has evolved over many years and will be difficult to change. However, if we want people to leave prison and never return, then we must try. Changing a culture requires not only new rules and regulations but also new psychological and social acuities, which are hardest to acquire. Therefore, the proposals that follow are intended to only get the ball rolling. Our hope is that as small changes take place and life within prison becomes more psychologically healthy for everyone, people will be motivated to try more healthy ideas until we have a society that more closely resembles the egalitarian culture we all want to live in. Once again, our proposals are focused on the nonviolent offender population.

PROPOSAL 5.1: MODIFY PRISON ENVIRONMENTS TO PROMOTE COOPERATIVE BEHAVIOR AND PROSOCIAL AMERICAN VALUES

Promote Prosocial Behaviors, Cooperation, and Compassion

Procedures should be put in place whereby residents and staff are rewarded for being charitable to each other. In the outside world, people are often rewarded for compassion. In prison, compassion happens rarely; when it does it should be encouraged.

Perhaps some simple reward structure could be instituted so that when a resident does something nice for someone else, a note is placed in their file, which will be reviewed when that inmate comes up for parole. So too with staff. Currently, a staff member who lends a book to a resident or goes out of their way to assist a felon in contacting their children is often deemed to have "bad boundaries." While it is certainly true that residents try to "con" staff for favors, this is not universally true. Prison officers and staff should be able to reward prison workers for going above and beyond their jobs. Much in the same way schools vote on "teacher of the year," perhaps prisons could have "staff of the month" awards based on who showed the most compassion. Policies and procedures, as well as reward systems, should be created to encourage both prison residents and employees to follow the five mechanisms of cooperation: direct reciprocity, indirect reciprocity, spatial selection, multilevel selection, and kinship selection.

Promote Personal Pride and Self-Respect in Prison Residents

In sociology, the symbolic interactionist paradigm suggests that how we talk about things creates the social world. We believe such a paradigm should be applied to prisons. It would cost almost nothing and could create significant change in the prison atmosphere.

We should remove objectifying language from policy and procedure by using words to describe tasks that are affirming of human dignity. Instead of "shipping" a resident to a new prison, we should talk about "transferring" people. Prisons could easily improve civility by insisting that all people use niceties (please, thank you, excuse me) and greetings that are respectful (such as Mr. Smith, Ms. Jones, rather than someone's last name only).

Only changing prison language will not change everything, any more than eliminating racial slurs has eliminated racism. However, no one questions that reducing racial slurs has been a good thing for race relations in the United States. If we were to eliminate terms that do not translate to life outside prison walls, perhaps life would improve within them.

Imagine if instead of "inmates," we had "residents." What if the "cell" was called a "room"? What might occur if we used the same language we use in the public arenas to describe prison functions? Instead of going to "chow," prisoners would go to "dinner." If residents could purchase a candy bar from the "store" instead of the "canteen," the prison experience could be more normalized, thereby helping prepare residents for life outside the walls and reducing the effects of institutionalization.

Reduce Learned Helplessness and Institutionalization

We should promote opportunities for residents to make choices that reduce learned helplessness and increase their sense of competence. Research by McRaney (2013) shows that when people in prison were given responsibilities and choices, such as choosing their roommate or the movie to watch for group movie night, they were more cooperative, less argumentative, and less demanding. Making good choices is central to maturity and the development of proper executive functioning. While security must remain a primary concern, residents can make many choices, such as electing a resident leadership group to help make decisions on matters like meal menus, store hours, and even paint colors for common areas.

The point is that the more power people have over their own lives, the more cooperative they become. Prison exists to protect the public and to eliminate harmful behaviors from society. If we hope for that to happen, we need to teach proper social skills that will translate to the community.

Establish Multidisciplinary Unit Teams

Multidisciplinary health care teams have been in existence for over 20 years, and research has shown that they are highly effective (Fay et al., 2006) with complex cases. When unit teams consist of members from security, case management, and social work (health care and discharge planning), they can focus on individual cases. Much like individual departments in corporations, multidisciplinary unit teams should have the power to establish unit rules and procedures that provide structure and social development based on the unique needs of the unit as well as complement the larger organization. The team should teach and model civic responsibility through unit meetings and democratic processes with residents.

Increase Employees' Knowledge and Understanding of Social Science Principles

We need to encourage all employees to obtain at least a bachelor's degree in one of the social sciences (psychology, sociology, social work, and criminal justice) and encourage management personnel to have a master's degree. By expanding employee training programs to include information on childhood development, social psychology, mental illness, addictions, diplomacy, mentoring and coaching skills, and egalitarian principles, we could radically change prisons. Research in progressive cultural change shows that education is crucial to successful transformation, along with structural changes in the environment and clearly identified behavioral outcomes (Harrison, 2006). Training curricula should cover a broad range of social science topics as well as pragmatic how-to skills for learning new behaviors. If processes were implemented within the context of a multidisciplinary team, prison could be transformed into an environment where all subcultures in prison—administration, security, professional staff, and prisoners—work together. If we reward staff and residents both intrinsically and extrinsically for practicing these new skills, life within prison walls could change. We transform the coercive culture that currently exists within prison toward one that is more cooperative and altruistic.

PRISON COMMUNITIES

Initiate discussions with informal and formal community leaders to develop community policing programs, reentry programs (like Homeboy Industries), court diversion programs, and community problem-solving task forces. Empower citizens to find solutions that will transform their culture into cooperative and affirming processes.

SUMMARY

When Mary was a child, she often visited her grandparents' farm in western Kansas. Their home did not have a bathroom; it had an outhouse about 50 feet from the house. Even though her father volunteered repeatedly to pay for and build a bathroom in their house, they did not see a need for it. They did not see how it would improve their lives.

We think people cannot envision a prison ever being a place where people will be nice to each other voluntarily. Yet, kindness and cooperation are the foundation of American culture, as evidenced by our celebration of Thanksgiving. We have seen the same kind of kindness and cooperation that we celebrate occur every day in prison.

Although these acts of kindness and cooperation only last a few minutes, random acts of kindness do happen, which means they can happen again. Once or twice a week, a resident will tell Mary that his cellmate is having a rough time and ask if she can help. An elderly resident was having trouble walking, and another resident broke the rules to assist him. The weather outside was extremely hot one day, making the cells feel like ovens. An officer went against policy and unlocked all the tray holes in the cell doors so air could circulate. In many prisons we have worked in, we have seen staff office walls covered with beautiful pictures drawn by residents. A gentler, kinder prison environment will allow both employees and residents a greater opportunity to grow and is fiscally prudent as well.

CHAPTER 6

Visiting America From a Country Called Prison

Compassion, in which all ethics must take root, can only attain its full breadth
and depth if it embraces all living creatures.

Albert Schweitzer

In 2008, for the first time, the U.S. Bureau of Justice Statistics began a 10-year study (2008 to 2018) of prisoners released from incarceration in hopes of learning more about the causes of ex-prisoners' relapses into criminal behavior after release from incarceration, commonly referred to as *recidivism* (Antenangeli & Durose, 2021). The bureau's researchers randomly selected 73,600 men and women from a total population of 409,300 in 24 states. Overall, 6% of prisoners in the study were arrested within 3 years, with 82% arrested at least once during the 10-year study. Nevertheless, arrests of prisoners in the study declined over time: year 1, 43%; year 5, 29%; and year 10, 22%. Nearly 50% of released prisoners across 18 states (six states were unable to provide data) returned to prison within the first 3 years of release for probation/parole violations or a new crime. At the end of the study, 62% of offenders from the 18 states had returned to prison. Considering the 62% recidivism rate for prisoners across these 18 states, the total number of released prisoners returning to prison was approximately 249,673 in 2018—these prisoners failed to learn how to be successful within American culture. That is a lot of people placing

A Country Called Prison, Second Edition. John D. Carl and Mary D. Looman, Oxford University Press.
© Oxford University Press 2024. DOI: 10.1093/oso/9780197768310.003.0006

a burden on the economy. Imagine what might happen to the national debt if these people paid taxes instead of using them.

Why do so many ex-prisoners return to prison? After living in the dreadful conditions of prison, why would anyone ever do anything to risk going back? Some think prison must be too easy and that it should be more brutal. However, with all the violence and isolation of prison that you read about previously, we can't imagine that prison could be any harder.

As we've shown, for some prisoners, conditions are quite like the environment in which they were raised. For others, return to prison might occur because they've become prisonized, a tragic end to a wasted life. For others it may not be a clear decision, but the result of years of flawed thinking. One thing is certain: For most people adequate support is unavailable to them to help them change, so when they leave prison, they often repeat the same mistakes.

What do we not understand? All over the world, people successfully transition from one country to another, from one culture to another. How does this happen? Can we duplicate this successful immigration with prison residents returning to their communities? What can we do differently that will make their homecoming permanent and beneficial?

Over the years, Mary helped three people during their first year out of prison to reassimilate to American culture. Her experiences with these three people were part of the reason we wrote this book. The focus of this chapter is Avalon's story, which is a good representation of Mary's experience with the people she helped. We have also met many former prisoners who shared their experiences with us and have read books by former prisoners that relate their experiences, such as *The Dedicated Ex-Prisoner's Guide to Life and Success on the Outside* (Bovan, 2018), *The End of Recidivism* (LaBeet, 2021), and *Life After Prison* (Loshi, 2021). While the anecdote about Avalon is a compilation of several experiences, it is an accurate portrayal of the challenges and difficulties newly discharged prisoners face.

Mary met Avalon while working as a psychologist at a women's prison. Avalon related that she was going to leave prison in a couple of years and wanted to "get better and not come back." She met with Mary for psychotherapy twice a week for several months until Mary left the facility for another job. Mary learned through these sessions that Avalon's childhood was filled with psychological trauma from severe abuse and neglect at home that was offset by nurturance from caring teachers and a female neighbor she thought of as her aunt. Avalon became pregnant at age 15, left school, and began living with her boyfriend. By their mid-20s, they both had been convicted of drug crimes and child neglect, and Avalon had also been convicted of prostitution. A year after their arrest, they lost their parental rights, and their two children were placed in an adoptive home. Avalon and her boyfriend both ended up in prison.

In 1996, the late Stanley Greenspan, then clinical professor of psychiatry and pediatrics at George Washington University Medical School and chair of the Interdisciplinary Council on Developmental and Learning Disorders, invited leading researchers and clinicians on childhood development to form a study group to determine the universal needs of children. Although he thought the group would need several weeks to create the list, they finished within a few days. The list can be found in Box 6.1.

Without stability and nurturing guardianship, children develop learned helplessness and exhibit many of the symptoms of Terrence Gorski's (2014) institutionalized personality: passive acceptance of deprivation, impaired critical thinking and emotional reasoning abilities, and a deep-seated rage that is often drowned out by drug and alcohol use. By the time Avalon became a teenage mother and a drug addict, she had already been socialized as a member of the Country

---

Box 6.1. UNIVERSAL NEEDS OF CHILDREN

- Safe and secure environment
- At least one stable, nurturing, and protective adult
- Consistent, nurturing relationship with same caregivers
- Rich, ongoing interactions with caregivers
- Child allowed to progress in own style and timeline
- Opportunities to experiment, take risks, and find solutions
- Structure and clear boundaries
- Stable neighborhood and community

Source: Greenspan (1997).

Called Prison. In many ways, she was destined to become a felon, as children who grow up with abuse and neglect are significantly more likely to develop addictions and commit nonviolent crimes (Dube et al., 2003; Wakefield & Wildeman, 2014).

About 2 years after Mary left the prison where Avalon lived, her case manager asked Mary if she was still interested in helping her. Their journey together began about a month later. On the day Mary met Avalon on the "prison border," she was wearing the clothes Mary had mailed her 2 weeks earlier and was carrying a small bag containing 2 weeks' worth of medication she took for a psychological disorder, a form confirming that she had been released from the facility, and a piece of paper on which was written her parole officer's name and address. As the metal gate clanged behind her, Avalon said with a slight smile and a bit of a quivery voice, "Hi. I didn't know if you were really going to come."

Mary's maternal instincts kicked in, but she resisted the desire to hug her. Instead, with the most nonchalant voice she could muster, she said, "Of course I came. I said I would." Avalon stared at Mary, her eyes betraying no hint of her emotions. They walked to Mary's car without a word. Avalon got in, and they drove toward America.

Mary assumed Avalon would need time to adjust to her new freedom, so she waited for her to initiate a conversation. When she did, she asked about Mary's job and other trivial things. Mary responded with brief answers but let her know that she didn't have to talk. Mary told her, "I know you must be having all kinds of emotions and thoughts running through your head. Take care of yourself. If you want to talk, we can, or if you want to be quiet, that is good too." Avalon responded, her voice uncertain, "I don't know what to do. I don't even know what to think. It's been so long since I've even let myself have feelings that I don't know what I am feeling. In the facility, kindness is used for no good and to hurt people. Even though I know your kindness is a good thing, I don't know what to do or what to say to you." Mary gently responded, "Avalon, I cannot imagine what you are going through right now. . . . Whatever you need to help yourself adjust to your new surroundings, just tell me."

As they rode on in silence, the music from the car radio offering some relief from their uncomfortable feelings, Mary thought about Avalon's comment about kindness and her disbelief that she would really honor her commitment to her. Even though Mary had heard the statement "kindness is weakness" many times in prisons, she thought of it colloquially, much like Americans saying, "How's your day going?" yet not expecting an honest response.

As Mary reflected on the hundreds of residents of the Country Called Prison she had met over the years, both inside and outside prison facilities, she had an *aha!* moment. Their stories followed similar themes—abuse, neglect (either physical or emotional), and poverty. She realized these themes were the observable patterns, not the foundational issue. The real issue was that children who grew up the way Avalon did were not usually socialized for human attachment.

Attachment is the emotional bond that forms between an infant and a primary caregiver. Attachment is crucial to the social and emotional development of an infant, and it needs to form within the first 8 months of life. Table 6.1 identifies four types of parenting styles and the resultant outcome regarding child development (Ainsworth & Bell, 1970; Bowlby, 1960). During this time, the child must master two-way, intentional communication, which can only be achieved by routine interactions with a nurturing caregiver. Without this skill, further cognitive, psychological, emotional, and social patterns develop in an idiosyncratic, piecemeal, and disorganized manner (Greenspan, 1997). Attachment creates the trusses that allow the brain to interconnect cognitive and emotional reasoning centers so the mind can operate with intentionality and purpose, grasping ever more complex concepts, meaning, and empathy that make relationships possible.

Table 6.1. HUMAN ATTACHMENT: PARENTAL
INVOLVEMENT AND OUTCOME

Secure	Predicable caregiving
	Child secure
Ambivalent	Unpredictable caregiving
	Child passive and very independent
Avoidant	Abusive caregiving
	Child insecure and anxious
Disorganized	Inconsistent caregiving
	Child very impaired

Sources: Ainsworth and Bell (1970); Bowlby (1960).

Poor attachment in children is highly correlated with having a caregiver who consistently avoids the infant's needs or who is coldly rejecting, indifferent, inconsistent, or abusive.

Poor attachment results in long-term problems with emotional control, interpersonal relationships, learning, organizational and planning skills, self-identity and self-esteem, task completion, and perseverance. For many offenders like Avalon, the early years are filled with violence and deprivation, which means that they are not able to organize their experiences and information into a logical order from which they can develop solutions and consider consequences. Their emotions are not able to corroborate their experiences so that their needs can be satisfied through relationships with others. Therefore, they are often overwhelmed by situations, and their reactions to events can be irrational and at times counterproductive.

Mary and Avalon had driven about 30 minutes when they arrived in town. Mary asked, "Avalon, did the discharge clerk give you a cashier's check before you left?" When Avalon replied "yes," Mary suggested that they go to a bank to cash the check and Avalon agreed. When they arrived at the bank, Mary, as a matter of habit, started thinking through the checklist of items needed for banking. Suddenly she realized that Avalon would not have a driver's license or a state ID card; she had no way to prove her identity.

Even though for the last 4 years Avalon had to always have her prison ID card with her, she left prison without an ID card of any kind. The moment the gate closed behind Avalon she became a *legal alien*—an American without any legal status. In disbelief, Mary wondered if this was some kind of cruel joke that correctional employees played on the prisoners. Was this the last "gotcha," the last little reminder that felons, even those who have completed their punishment, are not wanted in America? Surely this was just an oversight. Many Americans do not realize that a state ID card or a driver's license signifies American citizenship. Although an oversight by correctional personnel, for Avalon it was a huge stumbling block toward successful reassimilation into American culture. Not only was she unable to cash her check but also she would not be able to get a job, rent an apartment, or go to a doctor's appointment.

While an ex-felon may automatically lose some rights that go along with citizenship, the right to have a driver's license is not one of those rights (Stefanski, 2023). However, due to the length of sentence, a felon's license may expire before the felon leaves prison. All states have laws on ways a person may reactivate an expired license. Unfortunately, the process is expensive, often exceeding $200, and most ex-felons do not have a job because they don't have a driver's license to prove citizenship. It's a catch-22 situation. If convicted for a violent crime or drug crime, each state has laws on the process for renewing a license; often a felon must wait 3 years after release. An ex-felon also needs a copy of their Social Security card to prove citizenship when seeking employment. Although there is no expense to obtain a Social Security card because the application process is online through the Social Security Administration, most ex-felons do not have access to or knowledge of online application processes.

As soon as the shock of not having an ID card passed, Mary came up with a plan. Avalon would sign the check over to Mary, who could deposit it, then withdraw the cash and give it to Avalon. When Mary returned from the bank, she could tell Avalon had been crying. Mary laid the cash on her lap and confidently said, "Well, we solved that problem. No doubt we will have more ahead of us. I'm frustrated, but I'm not going to give up and you aren't either." Looking out the window, Avalon tearfully mumbled, "Thanks." It was at this point that Mary realized that helping Avalon would require a lot of patience.

When they arrived at Avalon's father's house about 2 hours later, the welcome that was not given said everything. Her father did not come outside. When the two women walked in the door, he grumbled, "Hello." No hug, no smile, no thanks for bringing his daughter home. One didn't need to be a forensic expert to understand the body language of father and daughter—neither of them wanted to be with the other. "You can have your old room," her father grumbled again.

Successful reentry to America requires being able to meet basic needs such as housing, food, clothing, employment, comprehensive health care, and, for some, child care, beginning day 1 (Burnside, 2022). The inability to meet these critical human needs for released prisoners is often the cause behind continued high recidivism rates each year. Although Avalon might not like living with her dad, at least her survival needs would be met until she could get a job and financially care for herself. This is not true for most released offenders.

At the height of the War on Drugs, President Clinton signed into law the Personal Responsibility and Work Opportunity Reconciliation Act (1996). For drug offenders, the act imposed a lifetime ban on several social support programs, such as public housing, food stamps, and Temporary Assistance to Needy Families. Fortunately, states could choose to disregard the bans. As states began to realize that these bans were ineffective in reducing crime, reducing recidivism, and increasing homelessness, they stopped using them (Burnside, 2022). During this time, the U.S. Department of Housing and Urban Development (HUD) began to allow most people with felony convictions to receive housing choice vouchers (HUD Exchange, 2022). Today, HUD denies public housing to applicants in only three instances: (a) individuals convicted of manufacturing/producing methamphetamine on the premises of federally assisted housing, (b) sex offenders subject to a lifetime registration requirement under a state sex offender registration program, and (c) persons who abuse or show a pattern of abuse of alcohol.

Let's get back to Avalon's story. After greeting her dad, Avalon carried the bags of clothing and personal hygiene products that Mary had bought her to her room. Even after spending nearly $400, Mary realized that the summer clothes she'd purchased would only be suitable for another couple of months, as winter was coming. There was no way Avalon would have her own income by then. Since the signs of poverty were everywhere in the house, it was clear that her father would not be able to provide much for her. Mary made a mental note to locate a church in town that offered clothes for destitute people.

Mary had wanted Avalon to return home to a deserved celebration. Trying to salvage the moment, Mary suggested that Avalon might enjoy going through her new clothes. Although her heart wasn't in it, Avalon began pulling the outfits from the bags and making favorable comments about them before hanging them in her closet. Although she seemed happy with her new clothes, her body language portrayed only rejection, shame, and unworthiness. How could Avalon's father have been so insensitive and impassive? Mary grew up in prosocial, middle-class America. Maybe there was something about Avalon's culture that she did not understand.

Most people view family as necessary for obtaining food, clothing, shelter, and, most important, nurturance. According to Collier et al.

(1982), "Nurturance is a certain kind of relationship that entails affection and love, that is based on cooperation as opposed to competition, that is enduring rather than temporary, that is non-contingent rather than contingent upon performance, and that is governed by feeling and morality instead of law and contract" (p. 77). However, this idealized concept of family prevented Mary from understanding Avalon's choice to live with her father, someone who had beat her as a child and terrified her with his rage when he was drunk. However, to Avalon, this was normal. This was her family.

As we grow and experience life, we form attitudes—positive or negative viewpoints about ideas, relationships, people, objects, or situations. Attitudes about life develop from our experiences, either through direct behaviors or through observation. Social roles and norms, especially in childhood, have a strong effect on attitude development. Attitudes involve our thoughts about something and our emotions, the way something makes us feel. We can be consciously (explicit) or unconsciously (implicit) aware of our attitudes. Nonetheless, our attitudes influence our beliefs and behaviors.

Not only do we form attitudes about other people, situations, places, and so on, but also we form them about ourselves. Our attitudes about ourselves are referred to as *ego-identity*. Although grounded in childhood development processes, ego-identity is constantly in flux and influenced by one's experiences all through life, especially the way people react to your decisions and behaviors.

The attitudes that children growing up in abusive and neglectful homes form are the ingredients for intergenerational criminality and learned helplessness. These children believe that they cannot have what others have. They believe that they are incapable of doing things correctly. They believe that they are worthless and a burden. Drugs, alcohol, and sex temporarily numb their despair and sense of hopelessness.

From Avalon's point of view, she had basically three choices of where to live when she left prison—with her father, with her mother, or at a homeless shelter. Although some offenders choose homeless shelters, for Avalon, the homeless shelter was not a good choice; it would bring back too many horrible memories that would likely return her to a life of drugs and prostitution. Avalon did not want to live with her mother because she felt betrayed by her for not protecting her from her father's abuse. Avalon rationalized that her father beat her occasionally, but only when he had been drinking. And now he was sober. As a child, when he was not drinking, her father would often take her places and was nurturing and fun. He worked, so the family had food and clothing. She believed that she would be safe with him and that he would provide for her needs.

Unfortunately, Avalon was blinded by a false image of her father's ability to provide the love and nurturance she needed because of her idealized concept of family. She viewed her father's house as a place where she would be accepted, supported, and encouraged. However, according to Ruby Payne's research (2005), living in poverty can lead to expectations on men to be lovers and fighters and women to be martyrs and rescuers. In such a setting, frequently the mother is all-powerful if she is viewed as nurturing and attentive, while men are seen as largely irrelevant to the family structure. Avalon did not view her mother as such. After all, her mother turned a blind eye to the abuse she had suffered as a child.

Avalon's childhood memories of her father caring for and loving her occurred when he fulfilled his nurturing ("lover") role as a father toward his little girl. But she was no longer a little girl, and he obviously was unable to nurture her in that way. Therefore, he no longer had a culturally prescribed relationship with her; Avalon was now merely someone living in his house.

Later Mary discovered that Avalon also chose to live with her father to provide care for him as he was ill. She had unconsciously assumed the "rescuer" role and would later take on the role of "martyr," as she gave up her needs to care for him, ignoring her need to get a job. These gender roles may have worked out well for both father and daughter if her father had had the financial resources to provide for her and they had lived in a community where she would have access to resources to meet her social and psychological needs.

Because Mary didn't share Avalon's idealized concept of family, she was unable to understand Avalon's choice to live with her formerly abusive and absent father. However, to Avalon, her father was her family. Avalon had related during sessions in prison that she was going to live with her father because he had worked and provided for the family when she was a child. She rationalized that his abuse and ambivalence only happened when he was drinking, and he no longer drank. She believed that since she was now an adult, she would be safe with him and that he would provide for her needs.

When you grow up in one culture or value system and change to another, a distressful mental state called *cognitive dissonance* can occur. In this mental state, you experience myriad emotions, such as frustration, anxiety, guilt, dread, embarrassment, and anger, as you attempt to shift from one value system to another. For this reason, humans resist change. They want their expectations to meet reality and to avoid situations or information sources that may cause them to feel uneasy. When we encounter the uneasiness or dissonance caused by change, we attempt to reduce our tension in one of three ways:

1. Lowering the importance of one of the factors that makes us uneasy: "I know cigarettes are supposedly bad for me, but no one in my family ever got cancer."
2. Adding elements that help us feel better: "I know cigarettes are supposedly bad for me, but I don't have the smoker's cough so I should be okay."
3. Changing one of the factors that make us uneasy: "I know cigarettes are supposedly bad for me, but I eat healthy and exercise a few times a week. So I think I'll be all right."

People who are unaware of the unconscious influence cognitive dissonance has on decision-making have difficulty managing their frustration and tend to make quick decisions without fully evaluating consequences. While Avalon was in prison, she did not want to think about not having a home to go to when she discharged. She did not want to face the reality that she had been abandoned by her parents, not only as a child, but also as an adult. Therefore, she rationalized the fact that her father was abusive by saying that he only was abusive when he was drunk. She also changed one of the factors by believing that since she was an adult, he would not abuse her anymore. Therefore, she could justify her decision to live with her father after discharge.

After Mary witnessed Avalon's father's behavior, she realized that she had been naive about the length of time and amount of nurturance and support Avalon would need to be successful. She told Avalon,

"I have just realized that the plans we made for getting you back on your feet again are going to need a little adjusting. I can see that your father is not going to help you and you are very uncomfortable being here." Avalon stared at Mary with sad eyes while she made fists with her hands, driving her nails into her palms, hoping that the pain would stop her from crying. Mary had seen this behavior in prison when residents did not want to show their fear, anger, or sadness, which is a sign of weakness in prison.

Mary declared, "Avalon, I will come back in the morning, and we will go into town and see what we can get accomplished. Do you think your father will hurt you?" Avalon stoically stated, "No, he'll just ignore me and watch TV. I'll be okay. Don't worry about me. I've been living in a cell the size of this room for 4 years with a cellmate. At least tonight I can be by myself." Avalon's mind was already busy figuring out ways to survive, to make do, to escape if she had to. Although Mary wasn't experienced in this kind of problem-solving, clearly Avalon had had a whole childhood of training.

Mary already knew from her therapy sessions with Avalon that she was an intelligent young woman. But why was she not able to solve problems effectively? Why was she not able to think about her options, make plans, or come up with different solutions? Why did she choose to live with her father, who lived in the country? How could she not realize that she would have fewer resources available to her and she would need transportation? Why was she setting herself up to fail?

In prosocial cultures, young children learn fundamental ways of processing information from their parents and other caring adults. These people guide them through problems by identifying the situation, telling them the meaning or importance of it, and helping them solve the problem. As an example, Aaron bites Lilly because Lilly took a toy from Aaron. The adult stops the action. The adult asks the children to explain the situation and helps them identify the details. Then the adult explains the prosocial way to handle the situation, by teaching rules about sharing or providing ways to appropriately manage anger. Over time, children develop cognitive and emotional neurological pathways for processing complex information, which is critical for problem-solving, interpersonal relationships, and developing prosocial attitudes and behaviors (Feuerstein, 1980).

Many children in the Country Called Prison do not have these kinds of adult–child interactions. They generally must figure things out on their own, which might work for some but not for others. The problems in childhood are relatively minor, so the methods children develop on their own are rarely effective in adulthood. Many people in prison continue to use problem-solving methods from childhood. If someone disrespects them, they try to get even. If someone has something they want, they take it. If they get in trouble, they complain that it's not their fault. As a child, when they complained, their parents either scolded them harshly or rescued them. A whipping or a candy bar was the natural outcome of complaints. These outcomes can be duplicated in prison, where complaints rarely are rewarded but might result in a transfer (punishment) to another unit or prison.

The next morning Mary picked up Avalon from her father's house. Mary had realized that the first thing Avalon needed was a copy of her birth certificate—the one document that would prove she was an American citizen. Avalon did not know the process for obtaining a copy of her birth certificate or replacing her Social Security card. How would Avalon have been able to get these critical citizenship documents if Mary had not assisted her?

By mid-afternoon, the task had been completed, but it was more difficult than expected. Avalon and Mary had to stand in line for nearly an hour, with crying babies and mothers scolding misbehaving children. The crowded room was making Avalon anxious. The clerk asked Avalon for her driver's license, which she did not have. All she had was the paper showing that she had been discharged from prison. As the clerk read the paper, his body language slowly began to display aversion instead of boredom. His eyes were filled with disgust and in a terse voice he said, "I'll have to check with my supervisor." Avalon's eyes began to fill with tears. Finally, the clerk returned and processed the paperwork necessary for Avalon to get her birth certificate.

After they got in the car, Avalon reminded Mary that she had to see her parole officer the next day. After Mary told her that she would drive her to the meeting, Avalon began to sob. Mary felt powerless and inept. The government agency they had spent the day dealing with was just like the fence that surrounded the prison Avalon had come from. She was still in prison, only now in a prison community. She had finally acquired a passport but still knew little about America's culture, norms, and hidden social rules. Culturally, Mary realized that Avalon had always been a *legal alien* because she grew up in poverty, not just because she committed a crime. Mary also came to realize that many illegal immigrants understand American culture better than Avalon.

More than 11 million undocumented immigrants are in America on any given day, and about 8 million work to support their families (http://www.numbersusa.org). While they might be breaking immigration laws, illegal immigrants are generally prosocial and abide by and appreciate the customs and laws in the United States. Unlike legal aliens like Avalon, who have poor coping strategies and planning skills, the undocumented immigrants had to plan and save money for several years to cross the border in search of a better life. Most of these immigrants had support from employers, family members, and churches. Not so for the Avalons of the world.

Legal aliens rarely have a support structure, either emotionally or physically. If they do, it is usually ineffective in meeting the numerous needs formerly incarcerated people have. For the most part, children who grow up in the Country Called Prison do not learn prosocial coping strategies as children. They do not develop goal-directed attitudes. No one teaches them the self-talk that helps us persevere through difficult times. Rarely are lessons taught about positive, nonviolent ways to solve conflicts that promote satisfying interpersonal relationships. While some may believe that illegal immigrants are a financial threat to the United States, we suggest that legal aliens like Avalon create a greater burden on taxpayers, and will likely continue to do so for decades to come if America does not repeal the rules that created the mass incarceration epidemic.

When Avalon visited her parole officer the next day, she was told that she had to pay a monthly parole fee as well as $1,750 for court fees that were incurred prior to her imprisonment. Mary was stunned when she told her this news. Carceral debt is the amount of money a person convicted of a felony owes the court for expenses incurred while waiting for the settlement of the legal case. According to Alexes Harris in her book *A Pound of Flesh* (2016), after prisoners complete their prison sentence, they often are tied to the criminal justice system for the rest of their lives. This is complicated by the court imposed fines and fees that often accompany them. Court fees are often assigned to people who were in poverty before they came to prison and, like Avalon, will have difficulty obtaining a job to repay the debt and care for themselves. This carceral debt also prevents people with felonies from voting until their debt is paid, and they can be taken back to prison if they miss a payment. Sounds like a new kind of indentured servitude.

How was Avalon supposed to pay for these expenses? Her prison sentence was her punishment and that was over now. How was she going to find a job with her felony record so she could pay these fees? After all, nearly every employment application asks if you have been convicted of a crime. And if Mary hadn't assisted, she would not have been able to get a job anyway since she left prison without two forms of legal identification. It is no wonder so many former prisoners turn to drugs and crime. Carceral debt creates a lifetime sentence for most people convicted of a felony.

In a longitudinal study conducted from 2001 to 2006, sponsored by the Urban Institute (Visher et al., 2011), 740 ethically/racially diverse male offenders, who had been in prison at least 1 year, were monitored for their postrelease income and employment sources. Table 6.2 identifies some of the key findings. After 8 months, nearly half of the men did not have employment. Although 65% of the men had employment training in prison, it did not seem to help many obtain a job in the community. The Urban Institute study showed that nearly half of the men had been financially supported by their family and friends both before and after prison. Former prisoners must overcome prejudice and the stigma of incarceration regardless of their job skills. Sadly, nearly half of the men did not know where to get help in the community for learning or improving their job skills. Why were they not given this information prior to their release?

As we have discussed throughout this book, once someone has been sent to prison, their lives are forever changed and reentry to America is hard. Note in Table 6.2 that 61% of the men had been working prior to prison, yet 8 months after release, only 41% were working at a traditional job. Although an additional 47% were working at informal jobs, these jobs usually do not produce adequate or steady income. While the study indicated that illegal income dropped significantly from before to after prison, we are not sure that percentage would hold

Table 6.2. EMPLOYMENT AND INCOME FOR FORMER PRISONERS

Key Findings

Percent employed in prison	53%
Percent received employment training in prison	65%
Percent employed 8 months past release	45%
Percent who had no knowledge of how to obtain training	48%

		Time Past Release	
Sources of Income	Before Prison	2 Months	8 Months
Family/friends	43%	66%	48%
Formal employment	61%	30%	41%
Informal employment	—	28%	47%
Government program	10%	25%	24%
Illegal	35%	02%	06%

Source: Visher et al. (2011).

the longer the person was out of work. Although research by Petersilia (2011) has shown time and again that employment for former prisoners is crucial in reducing recidivism, parole officers often are unable to provide much assistance. The barriers to employment are huge. Without a job, how can you live?

Although the aforementioned Urban Institute research is 12 years old, unfortunately, it is still relevant. However, the last decade seems to show a light at the end of the tunnel that will likely improve an ex-offender's ability to gain employment. As of 2018, most states have adopted *ban the box* laws whereby an applicant's qualifications must be considered first in employment decisions (Ban the Box, 2018). Applicants go through their application process without having to answer any questions about previous criminal arrests and/or convictions. In a majority of the ban the box jurisdictions, a conditional job offer must be made to a candidate before inquiring about previous criminal records. But even if application barriers to employment are removed, it is difficult to obtain employment without money. It's a catch-22 situation. You need money for transportation and for fuel or bus fare. Money is needed for a haircut and for clothes so you look presentable for interviews. You need a cell phone so that employers can call you to schedule an interview. But you need a job to get the money.

Since Avalon's father clearly was not going to drive her to work, she was going to need a driver's license. As for a car, maybe her father would at least let her borrow his truck. Much like getting a copy of her birth certificate, obtaining a driver's license took much longer than expected. At the driver's license agency, Avalon was told that she had to pay an extra $150 because the court had fined her for an old traffic violation that she did not even remember. Although Mary offered to pay, Avalon became so upset that she was not able to take her written test.

Avalon had acted like this every time she interacted with a clerk at a government office or a volunteer at a social service agency, such as the church that provided her winter clothes. She became extremely anxious and frustrated, and Mary had to translate most of the communication from the workers at these places. In response, Avalon talked about trivial information or related stories about other government workers she had encountered in the past, which had nothing to do with the present day. Mary sometimes wondered if she had an auditory learning disability. She needed a significant amount of encouragement to stay with the processes that had to be gone through to obtain documents, appointments, and possessions. Mary found that on the days she worked with Avalon she would end up mentally exhausted, with little energy for her own chores.

Mary's struggles with Avalon reminded her of the foreign exchange student she befriended in high school. While the student could speak and understand English, Mary often had to help translate, especially when formal processes were involved. Avalon grew up speaking English. Why did Mary have to translate for her?

Language in any culture is spoken in five registers (Joos, 1967). Differing situations determine which register is appropriate depending on the audience (who), the topic (what), the purpose (why), and the location (where). These are summarized in Box 6.2. Static Frozen register is rarely used; prayer and the Pledge of Allegiance are examples. Formal register is usually one-way and used to give instructions or make announcements. Consultative register is commonly used and is a two-way dialogue based on social dialogue etiquette. Casual register is informative and used by peers and friends in a group setting. Intimate register is used for private conversations and generally contains endearments.

For those growing up in the Country Called Prison, frozen and casual register are most often used, whereas school, work, and professional settings use formal and consultative register. During conversation, formal register information is organized, and the goal is to get to the point quickly and precisely, conveying information, meaning, and importance; there is little body language. In casual register, "the pattern is to go around and around and finally get to the point" (Payne, 2005, p. 28). This accounts for the frustration Mary felt when Avalon produced meandering responses when Mary tried to explain things to her. Research by Montano-Harmon (1991) identified that to function in a prosocial culture, one must be able to move back and forth from formal to casual register, much like someone who is bilingual and can move easily between English and French.

For Avalon to acquire the skill of easily changing language registers, she would need to immerse herself in the formal language register through a relationship with someone who speaks formal and consultative register regularly, just as one might live in a foreign country to learn a language. In short, she would need to be taught this register, much as students are taught a foreign language in school. Unfortunately, in prison, personnel are not supposed to have consultative conversations with residents; they are only supposed to talk with them when they ask them to complete tasks or paperwork, which requires frozen register. Therefore, while residents live day after day immersed in an environment where they could learn important skills for success in America, they cannot because of the us-versus-them mentality of prison.

The more Mary worked with Avalon, the more she reminded her of her daughters when they were teenagers. Although teenagers can often make good decisions, they can also make some big mistakes. Since Mary was Avalon's teacher and mentor, and not her mother, she had to be careful in the way she talked with Avalon about these issues.

As we discussed in Chapter 4, most people from the Country Called Prison are psychosocially delayed. They generally stopped developing in their early teens, which is usually when they also began using drugs. To help Avalon, Mary needed to review the psychosocial goals for adolescent development. Adolescence is the most complex of all the developmental stages. It involves five areas: physical, cognitive, emotional, social, and behavioral.

Table 6.3 identifies the major psychosocial goals that need to be met during adolescence. First, teens must achieve a new level of closeness with and trust in their peers. Mary needed to help Avalon try out more adult ways to interact with others. Mary would need to model the behavior as well as give Avalon feedback regarding her attempts. Second, teens must gain independence from parents and develop a new status within their family. Rather than just telling Avalon the rules for their relationship while mentoring her, Mary would need to involve her in the decision-making process. Third, and most important, teens must develop a sense of their own personal identity that distinguishes their abilities, skills, and unique personality. Mary would need to engage Avalon in discussions about her preferences and her thoughts about different ethical and moral problems and give her feedback regarding her decisions. Fourth, teens must move toward autonomy. Mary would need to help Avalon take on more responsibility without overwhelming her with too much, too soon. Finally, Mary would also need to help her become involved in work, social activities, and planning future goals, such as an education.

Table 6.3. ADOLESCENT DEVELOPMENT GOALS

Goal	Task
Achieve new level of trust with peers	Practice different ways to interact
Gain independence from parents	Collaborative rule-setting with guardians
Develop new status with family	Evaluate and consider different options
Develop own sense of identity	Increase responsibility
Become more autonomous	Increase activities in the community

Source: Pruitt (1999).

During the months that Mary worked with Avalon, she would get frustrated and impatient with her. She kept expecting her to act like an adult but then would remind herself that, developmentally, she was working with a teenager. A few times Mary needed to be stern with her as she made a few serious mistakes that could have led her back to prison. But just like a typical teenager, Avalon was testing limits. Slowly, though, she began to move along the developmental pathway, assuming the qualities of a young adult, although she was already in her 30s. With luck, she would continue to grow and catch up with her peer group.

Three weeks after Avalon's release, she applied for food stamps and Medicaid. Although she was able to get food stamps right away, she was unable to get Medicaid immediately. She was able to go to a community mental health clinic without medical insurance, but she had no money to pay for medications. Although her father was not abusive, he remained emotionally distant and resistant to offering financial support. Avalon grew more and more discouraged and depressed. Since the COVID epidemic, obtaining Medicaid health insurance is now easier and faster.

Nearly 6 weeks passed before Avalon was emotionally ready to look for a job. Before she went to prison, she had worked at a fast-food restaurant and at a daycare. Because of her posttraumatic stress disorder acquired while she was in prison because of the violence she experienced and witnessed nearly every day, she did not believe she could handle being around a lot of people, so she did not want to work in either of those jobs again. After some discussion, she agreed to apply at a temporary employment service agency.

Thanks to a local church, Avalon was able to find a couple of outfits that were suitable to wear when applying for work. Without telling Avalon, Mary had already checked with her parole office and discovered that the agency worked with former prisoners and knew several companies willing to employ them. Avalon was able to get through the application process calmly, and within a few days she was offered a job by a small company that needed someone to mail brochures. Although the job was only going to last a month, Avalon was happy and proud to have it. Mary kept in touch with her over the next month. Although she needed a lot of coaching on employment skills and relationship situations, she steadily improved.

Mary's biggest worry was that she would fall in with a bad crowd and get back into drugs. Mary discussed Avalon's situation with a friend who sponsored adults in Alcoholics Anonymous and learned some valuable mentoring skills. Even in the absence of addiction problems, former prison residents would probably do better if they had a sponsor as well as a support group to help them stay on the right path.

Avalon had been out of prison for about 5 months when she called Mary wheezing and coughing. After seeing her in person, Mary realized she was very ill and took her to the nearest emergency room. Her breathing was labored, and the beds of her nails were blue, indicating that she was getting little oxygen. Diagnosed with severe pneumonia, Avalon was admitted to the hospital, where she stayed for about 2 weeks. The nurse told Mary that she would have died within a week had she not gotten medical attention. This is one category of statistics we have not seen in research but that should be studied.

Mary visited Avalon in the hospital the day after she was admitted. Avalon told her that she'd been sick for days but had thought her father would recognize she was sick and get her help. By the time she figured out that he was not going to help, she was gravely ill. She told Mary, "I thought I was dying. I knew if I died that you'd be mad about all you did for me and that I let myself die. So I called you." While her logic was a little off, Mary noted her learned helplessness. She was still struggling with being a victim. But one positive result was that she finally realized that Mary was trying to help her because she genuinely cared about her.

A few weeks earlier, Avalon had told Mary that she did not think she was "going to make it." She thought she should just go back to prison. She said, "If I don't see my parole officer next week and I don't pay my fines, then the officer will just revoke my parole, and I can go back to prison. At least I'd have a place to live, and I have friends still there." Remembering that conversation, Mary wondered if Avalon's reason for not calling her sooner about her illness had been a form of suicidal thinking. Mary remembered the character in *The Shawshank Redemption* (Darabont, 1994) who hung himself a few weeks after being released from prison.

Individuals raised in the Country Called Prison tend to think in black-and-white terms, much like children. They tend to have little self-awareness and make decisions to neutralize their internal anxiety as quickly as possible. If the decision turns out to have bad consequences, then they quickly rationalize their situation by explaining it away, blaming others, or convincing themselves that there is no problem. They often use anger to intimidate others so that they can feel in control of the difficult situation they created by their impulsive decision. They have developed numerous thinking errors that help them defend against their fear of change. The severe anxiety that comes with change is extremely difficult for many former prisoners as they shift from the culture of prison to the culture of prosocial America. We believe this is why so many unconsciously return to the familiar rules and expectations of prison life.

As Avalon began to recover from her illness, Mary approached her with the idea of finding another place to live. Mary offered one idea after another that Avalon always found a reason to dismiss, even though she acknowledged that living at her father's house was not working out. She again would talk about "just going back to prison," which caused Mary's frustration to grow. What was causing this impasse?

As children grow up in a structured and nurturing home, they progress through three levels of prosocial maturity, as shown in Table 6.4. In his book *7 Habits of Highly Effective People*, Covey (1989) points out that, at first, children need a great deal of help from their parents but gradually learn to do more and more things on their own. Parents often view teenagers as difficult to parent because one minute the teen functions independently, sometimes too independently, and then suddenly they become clingy and needy again. By age 25 or so most young adults realize that achieving goals requires working with others.

Most children growing up in the Country Called Prison do not encounter situations or form parental relationships that help them move through these levels. Although humans have an innate drive to

Table 6.4. LEVELS OF MATURITY

Dependence	"You take care of me."
Independence	"I take care of myself."
Interdependence	"We can cooperate and do things together better."

Source: Covey (1989).

seek positive reinforcement and avoid punishment, the chaotic environment of most homes in the Country Called Prison prevents children from learning patterns by which to predict outcomes. Therefore, they do not develop self-efficacy—the confidence in one's ability to succeed at a task. Self-efficacy is critical in developing independence. Without a sense that one can control the outcome through choices and relevant behavior, one falls into the pattern of learned helplessness, depression, and criminal behavior to meet needs (Peterson, 1995).

For adults in the Country Called Prison, antisocial dependent maturity is demonstrated in a pattern of manipulation, anger, threats, and violence as the person expects to be cared for and the mentality of "when you don't come through for me, I will blame you for the results" arises. This is one of the main reasons for the predatory milieu in prisons and the hundreds of grievances filed by residents against prison employees. Prison residents demonstrate antisocial independent maturity also by seeking to get their way through criminal behavior, such as lying, stealing, breaking rules, and so on.

Although prison is an environment that could provide prisoners with positive role modeling and reciprocal interactions through which they could learn appropriate expectancy patterns, corrections personnel often believe that prisoners will manipulate them to obtain illegal items or special privileges. Therefore, personnel limit their interactions with prisoners as much as possible. Once again, the us-versus-them mentality prevents residents from interacting with role models and mentors who could help them develop the skills necessary for success in America.

Once Mary realized the reason that Avalon was being so resistant to change, she tried a new approach—talking with her about her mother. Avalon proudly said that her mother had divorced her father after Avalon left home, then went on to earn a medical office management certificate at the local technology school and had been steadily working at a medical clinic ever since. After hearing Avalon talk about her mother, Mary realized that Avalon's mother was in a better position to care for her than her father.

After leaving the hospital, Mary took Avalon to her mother's house. Although her mother also offered no hugs of welcome, she was polite and appeared to care. In addition, Avalon's mother lived in the city where Avalon grew up and Avalon hoped to reunite with some of her school friends who could offer her emotional support as well as drive her to job interviews. Avalon also had more access to social services and would be able to continue her counseling.

Once Avalon moved in with her mother, her life began to slowly improve, although Mary still periodically received a frantic phone call and a request for help. Mary spoke with Avalon for the last time a little over a year after Avalon was released from prison. She was still living in her mother's home but was on the waiting list for housing through HUD. She had found a job at a florist's shop and was being encouraged by two friends to attend the community college where they had gotten associate degrees. She was seeing a therapist and was taking her mental health medication.

In their last call, Avalon told Mary, "I'm never doing drugs again or hanging out with anyone who does. I'm never doing anything that will get me sent back to prison." Avalon had learned to love herself enough to keep the gift of freedom. She had fallen off the human development pathway when she got pregnant and dropped out of school as a teenager. Now she was back on track, developing her authentic adult self.

Eighteen months later, Mary called Avalon's parole officer and discovered that Avalon was doing well. The parole officer told Mary that when Avalon graduates with an associate degree in about 6 months, she would release Avalon from parole. She will be completely free at last.

While Mary had the training, knowledge, and maturity to manage the frustrations they experienced and the problem-solving skills to overcome challenges and barriers, Avalon certainly did not. In trying to help her help herself and not treating her like a child, Mary had to develop new ways of thinking about solving typical life challenges and a whole new level of patience and compassion.

What did Mary learn from her experiences helping former prisoners emigrate from the Country Called Prison? First, while paying for a host of social services (housing, employment training, food stamps, transportation, medical insurance, etc.) for former prisoners may seem expensive, it is cheaper for taxpayers than incarceration. If we're going to make a choice based on fiscal responsibility, then dollars spent for community support and programs will beat dollars spent on incarceration hands down.

Secondly, often released prison residents were socialized into a prison culture and that culture frequently doesn't translate well into the typical societal expressions of American culture. They unconsciously see the world as rejecting them and themselves as unworthy. Psychologically, they are immature, helpless, and chronically fearful of people. Cognitively, they have poor problem-solving and social communication skills. They have little understanding of the internet, word processing systems, or other technology that could help them find and keep a job. They have impaired adaptive skills and little understanding of ways to achieve their goals and are frightened of authority figures or people "in the government." To help released prisoners succeed, it will take a team of people and organizations with the vision to inspire social justice processes within their communities for all members.

The former prisoners Mary helped entered the criminal justice system with poor social skills, few problem-solving abilities, and no idea about how to improve their lives. While at the prison, nothing about this framework changed. The offenders were merely contained like toddlers in time-out. While in time-out, they learned more about isolation and abuse. They were degraded as human beings and viewed by the prison system as a package to be shipped to the next prison. They witnessed peers being stabbed and raped. They had to be strip-searched every time they had a visitor. They did not receive occupational training so they could support themselves when they returned to America. When they were released from prison, they left without proof of citizenship. How were people with few problem-solving skills and no self-esteem or self-confidence supposed to crawl out of that deep hole?

The hierarchy of needs, the humanistic psychology theory developed by Abraham Maslow (1954), provides a foundation for ways to help Avalon and those like her (Figure 6.1). The theory suggests that human motivation is based on a series of needs that must be met for human development to occur. The first two needs are physiological and safety. You might think of these as survival needs that include food, clothing, shelter, and a safe environment. Next come needs related to love and belonging. In other words, we need social relationships. The

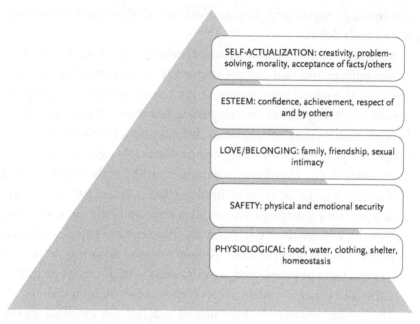

Figure 6.1. Abraham Maslow's Hierarchy of Needs Model.

Source: Maslow (1954).

fourth need—self-esteem—comes after meeting physiological, safety, and belonging needs. One way to build self-esteem is to succeed cognitively in areas we thought were weaknesses. Finally, we cannot feel comfortable in our own skin and reach self-actualization, where creativity and resourcefulness develop, until all these lower-level needs are met.

Since Maslow's theory was published, hundreds of social science and business research endeavors have used it as a basis for their studies. Maslow's theory is taught in high schools, colleges, and universities all over the world, not only in social sciences degrees but also in degrees in business, marketing, management, leadership, and law. Why? His model provides structure and intuitive clarity from which to create effective strategies for transformation involving human growth and development. To ensure that prisoners will leave prison and never come back, we must help them satisfy these needs through prosocial cultural norms and standards. Remember, these are innate human needs, and they will be satisfied in one way or another.

PROPOSAL 6.1: PROVIDE PRISON RESIDENTS WHO ARE DISCHARGING WITH THE IMMEDIATE AND ESSENTIAL NEEDS TO REENTER SOCIETY SUCCESSFULLY AND WITH DIGNITY

Most case managers who supervise prison residents have a list of things to do prior to a resident's release date. But the focus is on discharge needs—getting them out the door—rather than helping them flourish when they leave so they don't come back. In doing research for this book, we found a workbook designed by the Peace Corps (Storti & Bennhold-Samaan, 1997) that helps to prepare people for life in a foreign country. Containing more than 250 pages, it includes information and self-directed study assignments. It covers all the important things one would need to know about assimilating and adapting to another country's culture.

We also searched the internet for the topics "checklist for going to college" and "checklist for going on a trip." We found numerous websites with comprehensive lists of things to do before going somewhere for an extended period. Given these examples and the success of the Peace Corps and colleges in transitioning people from one home to another (if only temporarily), we think that prisons could learn from these organizations. If prisons could create a checklist for assimilating to life outside of prison, former prison residents would have a better chance of successfully transitioning.

Since Maslow's hierarchy of needs model has been recognized as the foundational checklist for humans in transition, let's look at a basic checklist for residents leaving prison. While this list may seem excessive and more costly than current discharge checklists, prevention is always cheaper.

Survival Needs

- Legal documents, including a driver's license or state ID card, Social Security card, and birth certificate. To get a job, the driver's license and Social Security card are critical. Departments of Corrections could collaborate with state and federal agencies to obtain these documents via the internet. Prison residents should be able to renew their driver's license while at the prison or halfway house. All fines should be removed that impede a resident from getting their license.

- Clothes, hygiene products, and first aid supplies to last at least 3 months, including casual and work clothes, socks and shoes, undergarments, sleepwear, and outerwear—basically everything a person would pack if they were going on a 3-month trip. A suitcase would also be needed. Prison staff could collaborate with local churches or agencies, such as the Salvation Army, in providing a "clothes closet" where residents could shop. Residents leaving prison should be given a list of churches and agencies from which they can find additional clothing and supplies in the town where they are going to live. Additionally, to reduce any potential feelings of shame, these support agencies could include a flyer in the resident's planner that assures the resident that they are welcome.
- Food vouchers or food stamps to last at least 6 months to a year, depending on the resident's situation.
- Safe and affordable housing, where the resident can stay for 6 months to a year. Housing might be with a relative or friend or in a program or the resident can use housing vouchers. The emphasis is on a safe environment and affordability. Many residents, especially women, can only choose places where they were once victims or where they are more likely to return to substance abuse, because many people in the home or the neighborhood are addicts.
- Health care needs, including Medicaid (or some other type of insurance) for at least 1 year, prescription medication for at least 90 days, over-the-counter medications, and health supplies (bandages, diabetic test strips, and so on) or equipment (eyeglasses, cane, knee braces, and so on) that the resident had been receiving in prison. Many prison doctors give the resident a prescription to have filled at a community pharmacy, but without money or insurance the resident is unable to have it filled. For residents with chronic medical and mental health needs, follow-up appointments and transportation to those appointments should be arranged prior to discharge.
- Residents should leave prison with some type of short-term, prepaid debit card (like Social Security disability income) that provides them with funds to meet basic needs, such as transportation to job interviews, for 3 to 6 months depending on individual

circumstances. They should be required to attend a 6-hour training course on budgeting and money management.

- Employment or approved Social Security disability income. Prisons should provide ways for residents to seek employment before they leave. We will address this proposal in the next chapter. Residents who are unable to work due to medical or mental health issues should be able to apply for Social Security disability income using an online application system.

Belonging (Social) Needs

- Residents should have opportunities to talk with—either in person or via phone—family, friends, or sponsors who will assist them after they are released to discuss the release plan. Contact should be outside of normal visiting hours and should be used to thoroughly plan the reintegration process to increase the likelihood of success. Discussion topics should include the residents' needs, possible obstacles to success, and the individuals on the reintegration support team who will help with the various needs.
- If the resident has children with whom they will have contact after release, arrangements should be made for family counseling in the community to assist the family in the reunification process. The military provides a similar service for military personnel who have been away from their families on lengthy deployments.
- For residents who attend religious services, they should have the opportunity to talk with—either by phone or in person—the priest, minister, rabbi, or imam of the house of worship they plan to attend. This would ensure residents will be welcomed and transportation can be arranged, if necessary.

Self-Esteem Needs

- For some residents, contact with universities or vocational schools should be made prior to their release and appointments made with the enrollment coordinator. Funding, transportation, and other obstacles to success should also be addressed prior to discharge.

- Prisoner residents should be involved in reintegration group therapy prior to discharge, with group therapy continuing at community agencies or parole offices for at least 1 year after release. Group therapy should focus on increasing self-efficacy, confidence, problem-solving skills, interpersonal relationship skills, and moral reasoning.

Self-Fulfillment Needs

- A discharge planner that not only lists preparation steps, items to obtain, people to contact, and decisions to make but also provides instructions on the importance of maintaining and organizing personal documents and life plans. The planner should include pages noting planned accomplishments in prison and during the first year out of prison. We will discuss this further in the next chapter.
- A plastic storage bin (about 12×18 inches) with a sealable lid where prison residents can keep personal papers and items.
- A binder with pocket pages and tabs for important documents.

SUMMARY

To solve the U.S. incarceration problem, we must focus on ways to improve success and win the game—a whole America with everyone included and flourishing. We need to count ways to score, not penalties. College football teams develop elaborate strategies and practice long hours to win the national championship. They don't practice ways to get penalty flags during the game. Surely, we can do the same for offenders who have served their time in prison and want a fresh start when they are released.

CHAPTER 7

Decarceration

Emigrating From a Country Called Prison

The ultimate measure of a man is not where he stands in moments of comfort
and convenience, but where he stands at times of challenge and controversy.

Martin Luther King, Jr.

Just like alcoholics who believe they can cure a hangover by drinking
more, the current solution of incarcerating more to cure crime in
America seems more likely to create more problems than it will solve.
It has, as we have already noted, created a legion of former citizens who
are essentially disenfranchised in their own land at the cost of billions
of taxpayer dollars and even more in lost productivity. Of course, these
efforts have almost nothing to do with crime control. Most solutions
focus on punishment, not on education and socialization.

A difference exists between our best efforts to punish and our efforts
to prevent crime from occurring in the first place. If we understood
better ways to stop criminal behavior before it happens, then we could
significantly decrease the prison population, as well as improve the
millions of lives and communities that exist within prisons and prison
communities. However, stopping any human action before it has
occurred is virtually impossible. If we could accurately predict people's behavior, most of the problems we have in society would stop. So
our solution cannot be the complete elimination of miscreant behavior, but how we respond to it. Are our responses making this better or

A Country Called Prison, Second Edition. John D. Carl and Mary D. Looman, Oxford University Press.
© Oxford University Press 2024. DOI: 10.1093/oso/9780197768310.003.0007

worse? In this chapter, we investigate ways to change the criminal justice system. These changes can be applied at national, state, and local levels. In our proposals to reinvent the local criminal justice system, we use theories and models from sociology, public health, social work, and psychology to orchestrate legitimate changes. Our assumptions in this discussion rest on our belief that change is essential because the current system of mass incarceration:

1. is economically unsustainable;
2. is in opposition to the dominant values of the United States, namely that all people should have equal opportunity regardless of their race, creed, or social class;
3. has created more problems than it has solved; and
4. has created a new nation within the United States, the Country Called Prison, that is populated by millions of marginalized U.S. citizens who are tax users rather than taxpayers and social contributors.

All social structures have manifest (intended) and latent (unintended) consequences. The manifest consequence of incarceration is to protect us from those we fear. The latent consequence created a dysfunctional and expensive Country Called Prison. Since social systems are designed by people, they can be changed by people. The status quo has evolved over time, and it can change again over time. So how can the system change so that everyone wins?

Social conflict theory teaches us that in every social situation there are winners and losers. To paraphrase what a wise old professor once told John, "If something is functioning in a society, it must be functional for someone." The key question is, functional for whom?

Many of the winners of the current system are not bad people. They are merely smart enough to figure out ways to make a buck under the rules of our current society. Politicians win when they run for office on the "tough on crime" mantra. Entrepreneurs win when they build private, for-profit prisons by claiming that they can house dangerous people more cheaply and effectively, all the while turning a profit. Prison staff win when they cash paychecks and pay their bills. Each of these groups will resist change because it is in their vested interest to maintain the status quo. If change is to occur, these winners must be safeguarded in some way and encouraged to see that their short-term win is really a long-term loss for them and everyone else.

At the same time, those who lose are not always eager for change either. Many people who live in dangerous neighborhoods prefer dangerous people to be locked up to rid them from the neighborhood so it can be safe. They know that drug dealers cause problems, so they support locking them up too. In many poor neighborhoods, so many people are in prison that it often may seem more like a rite of passage for young adults than a punishment.

John once taught in a community college in a poor area. During class, when he asked if anyone knew someone who had been in prison, almost all the students raised their hands. Something is not quite right about that. People who are addicted and out of work may see crime as a means of survival and prison as merely the cost of doing business. It is certainly possible that the corner drug dealer may be a motivated guy because he is, at least, working and supporting himself financially. Taxpayers often protest change as well. Many believe that the only way to stay safe is to fill up prisons with everyone who is nonconforming. In short, many people believe that punishment works, and if crime persists it must be because the punishments are not harsh enough. We have shown throughout this book that harsh punishment does not, in and of itself, correct inappropriate behavior; it often makes criminal thinking and mental illness worse.

Of course, the total elimination of crime is only possible if we legalize everything, and few of us would want to live in that chaos. In all societies there are people who do very bad things, and societies must decide how to respond. Do we need to isolate them for everyone's protection? Is prison the best location to accomplish this goal?

Recently, in a conversation with a friend about this book, John mentioned that he was hopeful it could be used as a blueprint to decrease the prison population. The friend's first reply was, "Won't that hurt public safety?" He was shocked to learn that about half the prison residents in this country are incarcerated for illegal drugs and/or nonviolent offenses. This is an educated, well-read business owner who regularly votes, and yet he had no idea. We think many Americans are just like him.

We do not suggest that America should stop locking up dangerous people. A few years ago, John was leading a therapy group in prison when a serial rapist admitted to him that he "liked raping women" and that if he was ever released he'd "do it again." He is a criminal society should fear. No one questions the logic of locking him up for life.

However, as we have already shown, more than half of the people we incarcerate are nothing like this man. So are we locking up people out of fear or anger? Why do we incarcerate people who have mental health or addiction problems? And, most important, what are the consequences to the larger American society because we are doing this?

We have already discussed the economy of the prison system, including its hidden costs, in previous chapters. The way we calculate the cost of incarceration is flawed. Prison expenses far exceed prison bars and guards. Taxpayers never see the lost tax revenue when a worker is removed from society. We hide the increased welfare costs that arise when that person's children go into state welfare systems or the spouse and children need food stamps. It is nearly impossible to determine the actual price of a lifetime of lost income or costs of long-term unemployment for those incarcerated and their families. To thoroughly understand the futility of the current system, we need to look at the total costs.

In the current system, most of the financial incentives seem to fall on the side of incarceration, at least for police, district attorneys, and those who work in the criminal justice system. Full jails and prisons bring in state tax dollars, more jobs for the Departments of Correction, and increased funding for district attorneys' offices and other involved departments and agencies. What business doesn't want that? For local police chiefs, sheriffs, and district attorneys, reelection is perhaps an even more powerful force that drives high incarceration rates. District attorneys are elected because they are good at putting people in prison. They may not be good at justice at all. And the costs of their decisions do not come out of their local budgets. If America is going to significantly, and permanently, reduce the population of the Country Called Prison, this detached accountability much change.

DECARCERATION

In the last decade, several new philosophies have surfaced regarding ways to transform the criminal justice system from a punishment model to a restorative justice and redemption model. In their book *Smart Decarceration*, social workers Matthew Epperson and Carrie Pettus-Davis (2017a) suggest that as the era of mass incarceration ends, the era of decarceration will evolve. As it evolves, we need to decarcerate *smartly*. The smart way is to establish decarceration principles and not seek rapid patchwork quilt programs that do not relate to other projects or build a sustainable and collaborative transformation.

Decarceration is a relatively new philosophy in the criminal justice system. Originally, the word was hyphenated as *de-carceration*, implying that to end mass incarceration, the United States just needed to stop incarcerating drug users and people with mental illness. Once social science researchers began studying the idea, researchers and criminal justice leaders began to realize that to end the mass incarceration epidemic, a lot more ideas were needed because there were more people in the community needing help than inside prison walls.

Decarceration has grown into an empirically based philosophy that focuses on three broad goals: (a) reducing the incarcerated population, (b) addressing the social disparities among the incarcerated population, and (c) maintaining public safety (Epperson & Pettus-Davis, 2017). The guiding principles of smart decarceration reflect the following (Epperson & Pettus-Davis, 2017, pp. 4–5):

1. Change the narrative on incarceration and justice-involved people to positive and affirming as human beings.
2. Make criminal justice system–wide innovations using smart decarceration principles.
3. Implement multidisciplinary (collaborative) policy and practice interventions.
4. Employ evidence-driven strategies.

The challenges of working with the justice-involved population require more than a "one size fits all" framework. After all, individuals who are incarcerated frequently have a host of other issues, including mental health problems, suicide risk, integrating back into society after incarceration, children dealing with parents in prison, aging prisoners finding housing upon release, trauma from living in prison, and dealing with past trauma that occurred prior to incarceration. Incarcerated individuals also have the same issues that many in our society must deal with, particularly some that can be discriminatory, such as racism, sexism, homophobia, and a host of other issues (Ross & Richards, 2009).

Decarceration is more than decriminalizing drug offenses and letting people out of prisons and jails. Smart decarceration requires a broad social work strategy that entails safe housing, food, clothing, health insurance, temporary financial support, employment, psychological support, and mentoring. Most decarceration projects follow the public health model with three levels of care. The first level is for those needing few services because they have family and/or friends who can support them temporarily. Those needing moderate services will have family and/or friends who can help house them temporarily but will not be able to support them financially, so they will need help obtaining food stamps, a driver's license, a Social Security card, and a job. Some members of this group will likely need addiction and/or mental health services and a moderate level of parole supervision. The third level is for those who are diagnosed with serious mental illness and addiction (dual diagnosed). For the first 6 months at least, these clients will need daily contact and collaborative services from agencies in the community.

Many states are working to decarcerate (see Table 7.1). The Sentencing Project did a 10-year study of five states that were actively

Table 7.1. PERCENTAGE DECREASE OF PRISON POPULATION

State	Percent Decrease	Estimated Cost Savings
Connecticut	−25.2%	$398 million in 10 years
Michigan	−20.1%	$392 million in 10 years
Mississippi	−17.5%	$266 million in 10 years
Rhode Island	−23.3%	Unmeasured
South Carolina	−14.3%	$458 million in 10 years

Source: Schrantz et al., 2016.

working to decarcerate (Schrantz et al., 2016). From 2006 to 2016, these states decreased their prison populations by double digits and saved substantial tax money (Bocanegra, 2017).

You may ask, so what happened to crime? This is a logical question. In each state, index crimes decreased for both violent and nonviolent crimes. In other words, when the state used some other solution besides prison to deal with crime, tax money was saved, and crime actually decreased. As we have discussed, one way the prison system grew was due to recidivism rates, where high numbers of parolees return to prison. In each state, the recidivism rates also dropped, resulting in fewer people going back to prison. The strategies used to accomplish this varied somewhat by state, but in each case they used programs related to what we know about desistance from crime.

DESISTANCE

In 2021, the National Institute of Justice (NIJ) published an edited book, *Desistance From Crime* (Solomon & Scherer, 2021). The report highlights the concept of desistance as a key ingredient in transforming the criminal justice system and reducing criminal behavior. What is desistance? It refers to the developmental growth process of ceasing criminal activity after one has been involved in it. This field of study investigates criminal behavior over an individual's lifespan, much like the human development models we discussed in earlier chapters; it is a life-course perspective. In short, people tend to become less criminal as they age, but even younger people can experience events that may accelerate their criminality or lead them to desist from it. If decarceration is going to "work," the individuals being released must be encouraged to desist from criminal activity. Desistance theories generally follow the trilevel public health model: (a) crime prevention, (b) rehabilitation, and (c) incarceration.

Desistance is a process, not an event. Recognizing this will inform the types of interventions the criminal justice system delivers and the outcomes we expect to see from them. Practitioners can also incorporate practices informed by biosocial research, which will result in a better understanding of where the individual is coming from and how to build on their strengths. Continuing to build partnerships between practitioners and researchers is vital. (Solomon & Scherer, 2021, pp. 11–12)

For decades, recidivism research has dominated the criminal justice literature, emphasizing that nothing works to stop criminal thinking and behavior. However, with the help of technology that can analyze large databases, researchers are now identifying that about two-thirds of all people released from prison *do not return* (Solomon & Scherer, 2021). Notably, recidivism research does little to show us the pathways to success, whereas desistance research does because researchers are using empirical data grounded in social science theories and models regarding human behavior.

In *Desistance From Crime* (Solomon & Scherer, 2021), the authors provide a host of empirical evidence for successful desistance programs. It is important to remember, however, that desistence from any behavior is a process—anyone who has failed on a diet understands that our best intentions can quickly go awry. The same is true with criminality. While the individual's risk for antisocial conduct declines over the life course, generally after age 25, this does not mean it ever completely ends (Rocque, 2021).

Desistance follows the biopsychosocial perspective of transdisciplinary theories and models that examine the complex interconnection between the biological and the social (Boisvert, 2021). Researchers have found that long incarceration sentences not only negatively influence health but also potentially increase criminal thinking and behavior (Wildeman, 2021). This makes any smart decarceration challenging because as we've previously stated, the formerly incarcerated person does not lose their old habits, attitudes, and pains simply because they are released from an institution (Jannetta, 2015).

From a practitioner's point of view, research has identified that applying empirical-based treatment is difficult due to individual differences and life histories; researchers continue to explore different approaches and curriculums, including international perspectives (Bucklen, 2021). At this point, the work is not "done," but evidence does indicate what Travis Hirschi (1969) suggested long ago when he penned his social control theory. There seems to be a close connection between the relationship bonds criminals have with others and the likelihood of crime. If the criminal begins to make friends with pro-social behaviors, such as coworkers, romantic relationships, or social connections, the desistance from crime grows stronger (Farrall, 2021). Lila Kazemian (2021), professor of criminology at the John Jay College of Criminal Justice, summed up the key points of desistance principles (p. 154):

1. Programs should integrate the well-established fact that desistance from crime occurs gradually, and that setbacks are to be expected.
2. Programs should consider changes in individual and social outcomes in addition to behavioral measures.
3. Programs should offer a balanced assessment of both failure and success outcomes and invest resources in tracking progress before, during, and after any given intervention.
4. Programs should provide incentives for success.

CLINICAL ASSESSMENTS

Since 2015, the decarceration and desistance movement has grown, resulting in fewer members of a Country Called Prison. This new criminology movement has recently been recognized as a new era in the management of public safety and use of collaborative rehabilitation efforts to reduce the use of incarceration as the only form of correction services, rather than a service of last resort. This new era calls for programs, procedures, and policies that emphasize rigorous attention to evidence-based protocols, especially in the areas of (a) sentencing, (b) pretrial release and supervision, and (c) use of risk–needs and mental health assessments at all decision points and justice reinvestment (Taxman & Murphy, 2017, p. 193).

This attention to individual needs is critical, not only for justice-involved people, but also to determine interventions that improve the welfare of human conditions and reduce recidivism and the need to behave criminally to survive. Research has shown that when incarceration deferment programs and transition from jail/prison policies use decarceration and desistance protocols, criminal thinking and behavior decrease by 20% (Caudy et al., 2013). Following is a list of actuarial and clinical psychology assessments that Mary has used when evaluating the risk and needs of justice-involved people.

The Inventory of Risks, Needs, and Strengths (IORNS) was developed by Holly Miller (2006) to identify the justice-involved person's probability to reoffend, determine treatment needs, and predict the probability of successful habilitation through involvement in treatment programs. IORNS is published by http://www.parinc.com and takes about 30 minutes to administer and score. This assessment should be completed for most justice-involved individuals with violent crimes, addiction, psychopathic traits, and numerous incarcerations (Scott, 2010).

The Risk–Needs–Responsivity (RNR) assessment, originally developed by D. A. Andrews and J. Bonta in 2010, assists justice system professionals to evaluate the individual's risk factors for probable reoffense and the individual's needs that can increase the probability of successful rehabilitation and desistance from criminal behavior in the future (Berry et al., 2018, p. 293). After determining the risks and needs, the professional seeks community-based programs that match the individual's risks/needs.

While much attention has been focused on the RNR methodology, evidence-based psychological clinical assessments also provide important information for improving successful reentry and completion of specialty court deferment programs. Psychological clinical assessments are grounded in years of rigorous testing until the inventory instrument shows excellent validity and reliability.

The Millon Clinical Multiaxial Inventory (published by Pearson Education) provides diagnostic information on adult mental illness symptoms and adult personality traits (Millon et al., 2015). The inventory takes about 30 minutes to complete by the client and 20 minutes to hand-score by the mental health professional and is inexpensive. It can be given in a small group setting with supervision.

The Personality Assessment Inventory–Revised (PAI-R; published by http://www.parinc.com) was developed by Leslie C. Morey (2007) to assess adult personality and psychopathological symptoms. It provides information germane to clinical diagnosis and treatment planning. Administering and scoring the PAI takes about an hour; it can be administered in a group of 10 to 15 clients under supervision.

The Millon Index of Personality Styles–Revised, developed by Theodore Millon (1994), appraises personality traits of relatively healthy individuals. Personality styles are a combination of nature and nurture factors and are generally consistent after age 26. The assessment can be completed in about 30 minutes and hand-scored by the professional in about 20 minutes. The publisher is http://www.pearsonassessments.com.

The Psychopathic Personality Inventory–Revised is an objective, clinical assessment that evaluates traits of psychopathy in adults in less than an hour. Scott Lilienfeld and Brian Andrews developed the assessment to examine psychopathic traits in noncriminal and criminal populations (Lilienfeld & Andrews, 1996; Neumann et al., 2008). The publisher is http://www.parinc.com.

The Hare Psychopathy Checklist–Revised (PCL-R) is a subjective, psychological clinical assessment that evaluates psychopathic traits in individuals; Robert Hare developed the first assessment in the 1970s (Hare, 2004; Hare & Neumann, 2008). The PCL-R is a 20-item inventory of personality traits and behaviors, intended to be completed with the client in a semistructured interview, along with a review of the client's official records, such as case file notes. The scores predict the risk for criminal reoffense and probability of rehabilitation, especially for violent sexual offenders. This assessment takes about 3 hours to administer and score.

TRANSFORMATIONAL CHANGE

The conundrum with this era of decarceration and desistance is CHANGE—a really big change that influences many organizations' ways of getting their jobs done. The problem with change is that most of us don't like it, and with institutional changes, there will always be resistance from stakeholders who like the status quo (Loshi, 2021).

We need to change the U.S. criminal justice system because the system is broken in many ways and is leading us toward human rage—the human equivalent of global warming. Despite decreasing its incarceration rate, America still throws more people into incarceration warehouses than any other modern industrial democracy. Although

Chapter 1 identified about a 20% decrease in the number of incarcerated humans in the past 10 years, there are still over 1 million people in prisons and over 54 million people under some type of corrections supervision. There are not enough reentry programs to help these individuals regain their ability to contribute to American society. Once released, prisoners usually need to immediately care for themselves; however, they cannot usually get a job due to their criminal records. With no external support, is it any surprise that many return to criminal behaviors (Carson & Kluckow, 2023)?

Smart decarceration research identifies that transformative change need not be scary if we begin with interdisciplinary change task forces. Such groups seek to use the expertise of those in psychology, criminology, criminal justice, social work, health care, and social policy to work together to help with decarceration (Epperson & Pettus-Davis, 2017). In Chapter 1, we used a mountain analogy to visually simplify all the elements that were driving the mass incarceration epidemic. We would like to use another mountain figure (Figure 7.1) to talk about a rational process for organizing and implementing the many policies, procedures, new laws, and changed perspectives and attitudes related to decarceration.

Notice the center of the mountain (Figure 7.1). We call these the "core strategies." Transformational leadership envisions, directs, and manages the complexity of transformative change. The use of evidence-based practices (EBPs) in designing policies and procedures allows for clearly identified, and measurable outcomes. The Burj Khalifa Tower in Dubai, United Arab Emirates, is the world's tallest building, just over half a mile high and built in the harsh environment of the desert. It is a gorgeous building. Construction engineers had to invent several new construction methods to overcome the environmental demands, and all the different construction teams had to know the total processes at play on any given day. The building has an internal Y-shaped tripartite floor geometry design that optimizes the residential and hotel space around the central core of the building. The buttressed central core and wings support the height of the building. The core attaches to a new foundation designed to work in the desert sand (no solid ground available) and high winds. Engineers also invented a cladding system to withstand the extreme summer temperatures. This is an amazing

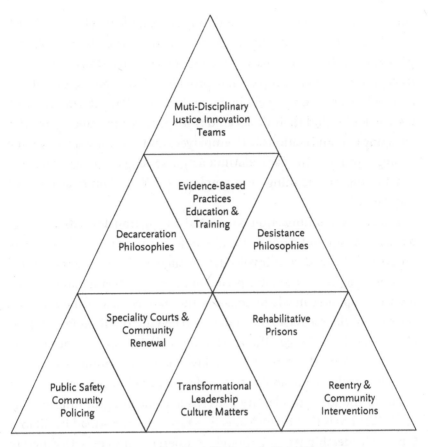

Figure 7.1. Components of a New Era of Social Justice in the United States.
Source: Created by M. Looman.

example of a transformational vision that exceeded everyone's imagination. We believe that Figure 7.1 represents the tower of the new era of social justice in the United States. Next, we will discuss each of the elements.

Transformational-style leadership and frequent and precise communication are crucial in any organization, especially when transformative changes are taking place (Figure 7.1). Leaders at all levels want to increase their organization's ability to move with environmental changes rather than resist. Effective leaders do this by using empirical-based principles and practices. The best way to do this is to create and develop a learning environment by encouraging multisector innovation teams that work together to find gaps between research and practice, improve quality, and simplify complexity. In today's fast-paced environment, effective leaders must create a flexible yet effective pathway that becomes a part of the organizational culture. Successful leaders know "their people" and provide opportunities, incentives, and tools to assist employees in doing their best. Transformative leaders are not behind their desks all day long; they are walking around, engaging in conversations with employees and planning activities and strategic actions. They are continuously assessing their organizations' functioning and making sure employees follow empirical research standards.

Effective communication is essential during transformative change because gossip and rumors are like new viruses that can shut down progress. Ideally, anyone involved in an ongoing project wants to know the outcomes in a reasonable period of time. Whoever is communicating these updates needs to consider the importance of the message, the tone of the message, the audience receiving the message, and the context of the message. There are several choices of communication technologies on the market that allow teams to communicate easily and effectively. Some applications offer ways to brainstorm and then organize the ideas to identify patterns and meaningful information. Table 7.2 shows that many leadership tasks are performed by all four types of leadership levels, although at different times or with different levels of intensity.

To begin a transformative change journey, leaders should identify the readiness of their organization to change. The criminal justice system is complex and made up of different types of institutions and agencies, all with different management styles, goals, and outcomes. Research regarding the success of new programs or projects identifies five cultural challenges that must be overcome to succeed (Hurley & Handley, 2010, p. 4):

1. A failure to engage in a strategic planning process for a new initiative
2. A failure to consider current organizational functioning
3. A failure to consider the organizational culture
4. A failure to monitor and adjust the implementation of the new practice as time passes
5. A failure to assess outcomes adequately

Table 7.2. CORE COMPETENCIES OF CORRECTIONAL LEADERSHIP

Executives	Senior Level	Managers	Supervisors
Self-awareness	Self-awareness	Ethics and values	Ethics and values
Ethics and values	Ethics and values	Interpersonal relationships	Interpersonal relationships
Vision and mission	Vision and mission	Motivating others	Oral and written communication
Strategic thinking	Strategic thinking	Developing direct reports	Motivating others
Managing the external environment	Managing the external environment	Managing conflict	Developing direct reports
Power and influence	Power and influence	Team building	Managing conflict
Collaboration	Strategic planning and performance	Collaboration	Team building
Team building	Team building	Problem-solving and decision-making	Collaboration
	Collaboration	Strategic thinking	Problem-solving and decision-making
		Managing change	Criminal justice system
		Program planning and performance monitoring	
		Criminal justice system	

Source: Originally from N. M. Campbell (2005, p. 3); from Hurley and Hanley (2010, p. 22).

These failures diminish if a transformative change baseline assessment takes place before any discussions about implementation occur. Throughout our book we have noted the importance of culture and its influence on a group's decision-making. Until his death in 2015, Lawrence Harrison (1932–2015) was one of the leading experts on culture's influence on decision-making. He is most famous for his 3-year research project, Culture Matters, in which he explored the cultural values of dozens of nations, examining ways each nation's culture propelled or retarded their political and economic progress. His book, *The Central Liberal Truth* (Harrison, 2006), addresses the findings from his research, which focuses on his belief that culture is the dominant factor influencing progress and development of groups and nations. His research and publications made *culture matters* a household phrase that rippled through all types of organizations and national discussions.

While conducting the Culture Matters research project, Harrison and Mariano Grondona, an Argentina scholar and journalist, developed a typology of progress-prone and progress-resistant cultures (Table 7.3). We think this typology could be an illuminating baseline assessment tool, using a Likert scale, to determine capability level. Since Grondona designed this typology to be used at the national level, some categories may not be needed at the organization or community level.

EBPs are essential during transformational changes. Most projects and habilitation programs that assist offenders in their transition from the criminal culture to a prosocial culture need pre- and post-evaluations designed to determine the baseline characteristics of participants and then their characteristics when finished. Program and project baselines evaluate the goals and outcomes desired. Participants take the evaluation prior to starting the program and then again after completing it. Depending on the length of the program, evaluations are completed to determine the offenders' progress toward achieving the desired outcomes. Periodic evaluations of long-term projects or practices are also necessary to identify barriers in the design that need corrective action. With transformative change, education is critical to success because the desired outcome is a total overhaul of an antiquated system, as well as a shift in culture characteristics. EBPs are essential in transformative change, and everyone should learn the importance of EBPs and ways to create and use these practices. EBPs integrate scientific research with goals, outcomes, and strategic plans (Hurley & Hanley, 2010). When implemented correctly, they often lead to improved organizational functioning and client functioning, which reduces recidivism. EBPs provide a common framework for discussing strategies and planning improvements.

All participants in the transformative change process need character and civic education. According to Thomas Lickona, a development psychologist, "Progressive culture change requires the widespread internalization of values such as democracy, social and economic justice, honesty, and individual initiative and responsibility. Such values must become virtues—habits of mind, heart, and conduct—in the character of large numbers of citizens" (Lickona, 1992, p. 71). Lickona's research shows that 10 virtues are affirmed by religious and cultural

Table 7.3. TYPOLOGY OF PROGRESS-PRONE AND PROGRESS-RESISTANT CULTURES (DUE TO SPACE LIMITATIONS SOME FACTORS HAVE BEEN JOINED TOGETHER)

Worldview	Progress-Prone Culture	Progress-Resistant Culture
Religion and destiny	Achievement and material pursuits I can influence my destiny	Irrationality; achievement inhibited Fatalism, resignation
Time orientation	Future focus promotes planning	Focus on present and past
Wealth and knowledge	Favor creativity to expand wealth Facts matter	Wealth is not expandable Theoretical, not verifiable
Values and Virtues		
Ethical code and lesser virtues	Realistic norms feed trust A job well done, courtesy, tidiness	Gap between norms and behavior = mistrust; does not care about lesser virtue
Education	Promotes autonomy and creativity	Promotes dependency; low priority
Economic Behavior		
Work/achievement	Work creates wealth; live to work	Work to live; work is for the poor
Frugality and prosperity	The mother of investment	Threat to equality
Entrepreneurship and innovation	Investment and creativity Rapid adaptation to innovation	Income comes from the government; suspicious; slow adaptation
Risk propensity	Moderate	Low
Competition and advancement	Leads to excellence Based on merit and connections	Sign of aggression; threat to equality Based on family/patron connections
Social Behavior		
Rule of law and corruption	Reasonably law abiding	Money and connections matter Corruption tolerated
Family	Concept expands to broader society	Family is fortress against society
The individual	Realistic emphasis on individual	Emphasis on the collective
Social capital and radius of identification and trust	Trust builds cooperation Strong identification with broader society	Mistrust breeds extreme individualism Identification with narrow group
Role of authority and elites	Dispersed; checks and balances Responsibility to society	Centralized Exploitive
Church–state relations	Wall between church and state	Religion has major role in civics
Gender relationship	Not inconsistent with value system	Women submissive to men
Fertility	Family's capacity to care for children	Economic asset; gift from God

Source: Adapted from Harrison (2006, pp. 36–37).

traditions: wisdom, justice, fortitude, self-mastery, love, positive attitude, hard work, integrity, gratitude, and humility (Lickona, 1992).

Education and literacy are major foundations underlying civic and political participation in a nation's (community's) governmental processes and growth. Civic education encourages people to participate in the political life of a democratic community. Community service is a good way for people to learn about their community's civil and democratic processes. Many offenders drop out of high school about the time they would be learning the importance of civic responsibilities and character virtues in terms of life success. This is one reason civic and character education is important for those who live in prison and those who participate in specialty court programs and reentry programs.

Multidisciplinary innovation teams push through the normal human resistance to change, especially the significant "turn my life upside down" kind of change. Transformational change for the criminal justice system is often referred to as a "paradigm shift" because it requires new ways of perceiving and responding to crime, as well as the policy and procedural infrastructure that will be needed to maintain order within the rumbling earthquake of massive change. This is where multidisciplinary innovation teams can save the day. Team members represent the variety of different sectors that will be affected by the change and recognize that a new way of doing things is needed. They begin with the development of foundational concepts and principles that will guide their new vision of a more just and efficient criminal justice system (Epperson & Pettus-Davis, 2017). Innovation teams are, in and of themselves, paradigm shifting.

We envision that decarceration and desistance elements are the forces that will drive transformative change within the U.S. criminal justice system (Figure 7.1). The focus of decarceration projects is to reconstruct the concept of crime and punishment within American culture. As we discussed earlier, punishment should reflect the seriousness of the crime and the context in which the behavior occurred. Punishment should not affect a citizen's fundamental rights, and the adjudication process should provide equal protection, opportunities, and resources. Desistance projects focus on the human development process with the understanding that growing up takes time and learning from mistakes. The philosophy and practices of desistance offer a balanced understanding of the outcomes of success and mistakes and provide interventions that teach and support positive changes leading to a pro-social lifestyle (Kazemian, 2021). Multidisciplinary innovation teams, using the philosophic power of decarceration and desistance, provide ongoing partnerships with community stakeholders, various agents of the criminal justice system (police, prosecution, community organizations, corrections), and economic resources within the community.

The bottom set of triangles in Figure 7.1 identifies the four main components of the U.S. justice system. This is where justice personnel put all the theories and innovations into practice. Following is a brief discussion of each component.

Public safety and community policing involves partnering with community members and organizations to improve community features and public safety. Officers often provide educational programs at public meetings and at schools regarding ways to be safe in various situations. By teaching community members about the crime triangle theory (Figure 7.2), officers can actively identify barriers to public safety quickly and work with community stakeholders to resolve problems using decarceration and desistance philosophies and strategies. The crime triangle shows the three ingredients of the criminogenic process. Only one side of the triangle needs to be stopped in order to stop criminal activity. As officers interact with community members, they learn about activities that make citizens feel unsafe. The officers work with innovation teams within the community to resolve concerns and prevent crime.

Specialty courts have five general characteristics. First, the court's strategies focus on smaller is better—in other words, keep as many

Figure 7.2. Crime Triangle Theory.
Source: Houston Police Department 2024; https://www.houstontx.gov/police/pdfs/brochures/english/Personal_Safety.pdf.

people out of prison as possible. Each offender placed under the court's supervision receives all the resources necessary for them to achieve success in overcoming a criminal lifestyle. Second, the court partners with agencies and resources in the community to provide clients with the means to succeed, such as a bus pass for traveling to work. Third, clients are encouraged to make a full disclosure about their past and the kind of help needed to overcome their past, such as mental health treatment or vocational training. Fourth, clients are rigorously supervised and held accountable for their behavior, usually for 1 to 2 years. Fifth, specialty courts offer results-focused programs.

The success rates for specialty courts are strong. Each specialty court works with one category of clients; substance addiction, domestic violence, mental health, veterans, and reentry are the most common. A latent benefit of specialty courts is the impact on community renewal and crime prevention. As clients (which often also include families) attend training classes and mental health treatment, they talk about their dilapidated neighborhoods and the challenges they face in avoiding criminal behavior (such as threats by gang members). This information is passed on to community police officers, who then organize innovation teams to reduce these challenges.

Rehabilitation prisons have been the topic of conversation and the focus of research for several decades. Criminology researchers have produced an increasing body of evidence showing that incarceration has a null effect on crime rates (Cullen et al., 2014). Furthermore, meta research projects suggest that too many low-risk offenders are needlessly incarcerated, and the money spent on incarceration would be better spent on treatment and rehabilitation in the community. Fortunately, there is a growing body of evidence that shows that prisons with small populations can provide treatment, training, and prosocial education that can help prisoners avoid a criminal lifestyle.

As we read research articles and books on innovative ideas, we often see several researchers discussing and testing similar ideas. Having smaller prisons, just like smaller classrooms, will allow prison administrators to take advantage of instructional technology, with educators being able to stay at one location while teaching satellite classrooms at several prisons at once. Smaller prisons will also allow prisoners to learn and practice trade skills and prosocial lifestyles. Most importantly, smaller prisons will allow staff to better prepare prisoners for reentry success, thus reducing recidivism.

Reentry and community support services have been the focus of much social science and criminology research. Obviously change cannot take place overnight, but the quicker the justice system can reduce admissions to prisons and develop successful, evidence-based reentry programs (reducing recidivism), the better. This will bring more healthy families and workers (thus taxpayers) back into their communities, which will increase public safety and urban renewal. Notably, these two categories of transformative change will significantly reduce justice system expenditures.

The Institute for Justice Research and Development (2023) at Florida State University has developed the five-key model for reentry. The model is based on a meta-review of over 100,000 studies, and the keys are as follows:

Key 1: healthy thinking patterns
Key 2: meaningful work trajectories
Key 3: effective coping strategies
Key 4: positive social engagement
Key 5: positive interpersonal relationships

The five-key model translates the key ingredients of successful reentry into a flexible approach that can be implemented at different levels of intensity, so resources are not wasted on a one-size-fits-all approach and they go beyond just getting a job after release. The five-key model can be implemented by a range of professionals working in a variety of settings and paired with evidence-driven engagement and retention strategies to help those leaving prison show up, participate, and succeed. The model encourages programs to pair clients with mentors and community resource services.

We believe that addiction, mental illness, and petty nonviolent crimes cannot be punished away. These are social issues, not criminal issues. We need to work on humanizing prisons so that both residents and employees can develop their potential and offenders can return to the community better off than they were when they entered prison. We need to provide incentives for people *not* to return to prison. We need to realize that without legitimate opportunities for success, petty criminals are unlikely to change their behavior.

We need to move forward with solutions that provide the public with accurate information as to consequences and costs associated with incarceration. We need to create programs in prisons that help prison residents change and prepare them for life outside the razor-wire boundaries. We need to help prison community residents learn ways to improve their lives and their communities. We need to provide a reason for felons to leave the criminal lifestyle and provide them with real opportunities for change and a real chance to be successful in America. The following is a little story to help the reader visualize a new cultural system that drives a socially fair and equitable justice system.

When Captain Tom (fictitious person) of the community policing department of the local police station finished reading a research article commonly referred to as "Broken Windows" by J. Q. Wilson and G. L. Kelling (1982), he thought about an abandoned parking lot with a 20×20-foot shed on it near Hamilton Park. Last year, someone had left an old car on the lot and large trash items began piling up, along with weeds and broken liquor bottles. Lately, Captain Tom had noticed that known drug dealers were hanging out more often near the shed, hiding in the shadows. The broken windows theory suggests that visible signs of crime and disorder, such as broken windows, vandalism, loitering, jaywalking, and graffiti, create an urban area that promotes crime and disorder. The criminal thinks, "If the people who live here don't care, then I should be able to do whatever I want."

Captain Tom asked the chief if he could start a transformative change project that would create a neighborhood garden on the lot. After getting the go-ahead, Captain Tom organized a task force of key stakeholders that included parishioners from two local churches, a member of the school board, the city's district attorney, and three business owners with businesses near the parking lot. Within a few months, Captain Tom and his task force had worked through all the legal items on their to-do list, and they were ready to let the local neighborhood know about the plan and the date and time of the first Neighborhood Garden Plots workday. About 15 people showed up and learned about the long-range plans; at the end of the day, all the trash was gone from the lot, even the old car that someone with a talent for fixing cars offered to buy. The money went towards buying supplies for the raised garden beds.

As things progressed, a large hardware store in the area agreed to buy and install solar-powered streetlights, which increased the safety of the area. Probation and parole officers joined in the efforts by creating a community service credit time for justice-involved people to contribute their expertise in carpentry, gardening, and mentoring. The high school counselor got involved by working with the superintendent to offer course credits for students who struggled with traditional math and science courses if they agreed to work at Neighborhood Garden Plots after school 3 days a week and one Saturday a month. The students would learn lessons a boring classroom would never be able to offer. There were many obstacles to overcome and some course corrections as the plan unfolded, but Captain Tom's task force and the first 15 people who showed up kept forging ahead. Giving up was never an option.

To bring down the mountain of incarceration, the United States needs a new paradigm of ways to solve problems. We cannot continue to view prisons and jails as the only solutions. We believe the basic solution is collaboration with all members of the community and organizations in solving problems with win–win solutions.

CHAPTER 8
Assimilating a Country Called Prison

The only thing necessary for evil to triumph is for good men to do nothing.
Edmund Burke

In this book, we have considered the mass incarceration epidemic in the United States and its latent consequences. Our intention in writing this book has been to provide readers with an opportunity to see the situation in a new light. The scope of the problem is significantly larger than most people realize, and while things are changing slowly, leading to a decrease in incarceration, it remains to be seen if this trend will continue, level off, or return to higher levels soon.

The expense of this experiment with mass incarceration has been monumental, and the public outcry over this spending is frequently absent from the conversation. In short, it seems that culturally, we would rather eliminate lawbreakers from society altogether, even if it is the least effective way to deal with later problems.

In the early chapters, we provided information that uncovered the deep underlying sources from which the incarceration mountain has steadily risen. In this final chapter, we propose a plan to eradicate the prison mountain and reintegrate those who are citizens of a Country Called Prison.

What we have attempted to do in this second edition of *A Country Called Prison* is to not only update the data but also add to our book some more clear-cut ideas about how we as a country might end mass incarceration. For the past 50 years the primary method used to deal

A Country Called Prison, Second Edition. John D. Carl and Mary D.Looman, Oxford University Press.
© Oxford University Press 2024. DOI: 10.1093/oso/9780197768310.003.0008

with those who commit crime is prison, even though we know that prison has not really been that effective. As John often tells his students, "We use prisons, not because they're good at changing behaviors, but because apparently we can't think of anything else to do with people who do things we don't want them to do."

While we identified in this second edition that criminal justice policies and practices are shifting toward restorative justice practices, we have a long way to go before we can reduce the latent effects of mass incarceration policies. Yet the data we have presented strongly suggest that prison is now as antiquated as the dunking stool. Statistics do not lie. The data clearly show that the policy decisions that have led to the mass incarceration of U.S. citizens, and the unintended creation of the Country Called Prison, must change. We must bring down the incarceration mountain now.

In this final chapter we attempt to start a conversation about plausible solutions to the problem of mass incarceration. The United States has a strong history of solving problems. Perhaps the most successful example involved the re-creating of nation-states and infrastructures following World War II. World War II ended September 2, 1945, when Japan surrendered to the United States. The war had damaged or destroyed most of the infrastructure of Germany and Japan, as well as large sections of France, Great Britain, and virtually every country in Europe.

Addressing the Harvard University graduating class of 1947, Secretary of State George C. Marshall advanced his idea of a comprehensive program to rebuild Europe (http://history.state.gov). Congress passed the Economic Cooperation Act of 1948, which later became known as the Marshall Plan. Over the next several years the approved funding rose to over $13 billion, and the Marshall Plan is credited for rebuilding war-torn regions, removing trade barriers, modernizing industry, and setting up Europe for a future of peace and prosperity. The Marshall Plan also stimulated the American economy by re-establishing markets for American goods in Europe, thus stabilizing the global economic market. In this way, the Marshall Plan was able to fix many of the massive problems left in the wake of a world war while at the same time creating a win–win solution. For his efforts, Marshall received the Nobel Peace Prize.

We make no claim to be as insightful as General Marshall, but after a combined effort of over 50 years of study, work, and educating others about crime and the criminal justice system, we present our own version of a Marshall plan, hoping that it can help our country emigrate from a Country Called Prison.

The criminal justice system has grown into a mountain, and taking this mountain down may seem impossible in large part due to its complexity. However, complexity brings a thousand different points at which interventions can be implemented to address the problem. If we are going to emigrate from our current mass incarceration nation, each component of the system will require some changes, and that will require an adjustment in the way we invest in crime control and punishment. Many of the changes we propose should, in the long run, decrease the cost of the system; however, in the short run there will be expenses that will need funding. It will not only require elected officials to review how money is spent on the criminal justice system but also require the public to have a collective willingness to support change. Perhaps, most importantly, it will require the current stakeholders of the status quo to review these changes with an open mind and see these proposals as an opportunity to expand their influence in the system.

POLICY IMPLICATION 1

To fix the massive problems of Europe, the Marshall Plan used some broad principles that led to practical policies. The same is true for our plan. Like Marshall, we start with funding. One of the first parts of the Marshall Plan was to make sure the United States provided enough food to Europe to rebuild it. After all, the farm fields were decimated by years of warfare. This follows Maslow's hierarchy of needs. In our plan as well, we suggest that funding needs to increase to pay for programs to address basic human needs. This must come first to successfully weaken the power of the prison industrial complex. Thus, public assistance funds for those released from prison need to be expanded. The availability of housing assistance, Medicaid, and food stamps needs to be normative for those released from prison. We cannot hope to convince people to stay out of prison without helping them at least in the short term when they leave prison. At the same time, employment placement should become a part of all discharge planning for inmates. If we hope to decrease the tax burden of caring for prisoners, we will need to make sure that upon release, they have their basic human needs met.

POLICY IMPLICATION 2

Criminal justice leaders need to conduct a national review of drug laws, punishments, and sentencing. The policies that were created to attempt to punish addiction need to be reconsidered, with alternative sentencing options expanded. Decreasing the rates of incarceration can be accomplished by increasing available drug treatments, thus allowing current stakeholders to transfer their efforts from prisons to treatment programs. While Congress could certainly control the federal drug criminal rate this way, each state would be left to their own devices, which would likely lead to 50 different plans. We suggest that Congress use the "grant" system much like it does for educational spending, welfare spending, and a host of other appropriations. States that fall within certain limits would qualify for increased federal dollars to pay for the increasing drug treatment programs. We suggest that for each percentage decrease in incarceration a state accomplishes, it receives increases in federal grant subsidies for increased drug treatment programs in that same percentage.

This would turn the United States into a system much more like our European allies, where addiction is treated as a medical problem, not a criminal one. At the same time, punishments for "dealers" and "traffickers" could remain, thus allowing the current system of asset forfeiture to apply to local police departments and causing them to target "big fish" dealers rather than "small fish" users.

We believe that such a plan would not only decrease the drug-to-prison connection but also have an overall positive effect on decreasing all crime. Data from the Bureau of Justice Statistics show that almost half of all perpetrators of crime are under the influence of drugs or alcohol at the time they commit the offense for which they are incarcerated. Thus, increasing drug treatment programs should have an inverse effect on all crime. This may be particularly valuable to decreasing the rates of violent crimes since intoxication is known to have a disinhibiting effect on human behavior, thus leading to the possibility of more violent crime (Bureau of Justice Statistics, 2021).

This first step would no doubt involve increased public spending, and so we strongly support full accountability of the costs of incarceration. The costs of incarceration are substantially different than merely looking at how many guards are needed per cell. As we have already shown, many costs are simply passed to other parts of the social safety network when in fact they are related to the cost of incarceration. In the current system incarceration is considered "free" to local communities because they have no idea of the direct costs of a district attorney's decision to prosecute a nonviolent offender. The costs of the system are divided across so many different facets of the criminal justice system that it becomes difficult to determine what it really does cost to send someone to prison.

We propose a system that directly accounts for the decision to incarcerate. We suggest that the costs of locking up nonviolent offenders be charged to the county from which they came. If a community wants to lock up every pot smoker in the county, that's fine; however, that community would need to pay for it. In this way, it is like public education, where property taxes from the local community pay for local public schools. Taxpayers are free to increase their own taxes to build new buildings or remodel old ones to help their community. If they want nice parks, they can tax themselves to build them. If a county believes that being tough on minor crimes is a good idea, then the county should pay for it.

We believe that the cost of incarcerating violent offenders should still be paid for by the state. This will avoid a geographic bias since violent crimes tend to occur more often in cities. We see incarceration of the violent as a public good, and so it should be paid for by everyone. Violent offenders are really everyone's problem, as murderers, rapists, and child molesters are unlikely to contain their illegal activities within one county.

An important component to this proposal is that the district attorney's office should oversee the budget for the county's use of prison bedspace for nonviolent offenders. This seems most logical, since the district attorney is the one responsible for charging, convicting, and sentencing offenders. While some might say it is the judges who are responsible, they should recall that over 90% of criminal cases in this country are settled through the plea-bargaining process (Devers, 2014). District attorney's offices decide the specifics of the plea deal. Therefore, the road to the Country Called Prison starts at the district attorney's office.

Where will the district attorney get the money to pay the bill? We believe that if we were to attach the county tax for incarceration to property taxes, we would most likely gain the attention of those who vote. Voters then would have some direct say in how their money is used for incarceration of nonviolent offenders. In this way, we could start the emigration from this Country Called Prison.

For this proposal to be successful, there must be a way for nonviolent offenders to be punished for their criminal behavior without going to prison. We believe that states should fund diversionary programs, based on decarceration and desistance principles, that will not only act as a judicial restraint but also provide socialization and treatment to help nonviolent offenders avoid going to the Country Called Prison. These community diversionary programs should also be covered by federal and state grants, thus spreading their cost across all taxpayers, making the county decision to use some alterative to prison a financially sound decision, which will likely appeal not only to voters but also to entrepreneurs and providers who create these diversionary programs. We stress, of course, that any new program must meet standards of transparency and accountability to assure the public that the programs are based on empirical evidence. Thus, we suggest the oversight of the criminal justice system should be treated like the oversight given to medical and social work interventions.

The most important part of this proposal is that it must be tax neutral. For every dollar that is passed to the county to pay the bills, the state should cut taxes by the same amount. States that contain exceptionally poor counties may wish to create some form of revenue sharing, much like the so-called Robin Hood laws related to school funding. A poor community should not be so worried about spending money on incarceration that the community becomes unsafe. This is another reason that we believe this proposal should only apply to nonviolent offenses. The primary point of this proposal is to hold the people who make the decision to incarcerate accountable for that choice.

Of course, those who are benefiting from the status quo will take some convincing. They would need some short-term financial incentives to expand their scope beyond the razor-wire boundaries of the Country Called Prison and into the untapped market of prison diversion. When diversion programs are expanded, job losses would occur in the prison system. However, these lost prison jobs should be easily replaceable with new jobs in the community diversion programs, thus creating a net-zero effect on employment.

As we see, much like the Marshall Plan, we need flexibility so that the specific implementation can be directed to the local level. The reality of the criminal justice system as it stands today is that frequently legislators who are far removed from a specific case create laws that tie the hands of judges and district attorneys. While the specific implementation can be variable based on the state, they should meet the criteria outlined here: financial accountability, empirical practice, and optimism for the possibility of human transformation.

The cynical nature of our current system may [mistakenly] indicate that people cannot change, despite the mountain of evidence that this is false. If we are going to eliminate the Country Called Prison, proven diversion programs, such as drug court, mental health court, restorative justice programs, drug treatment, group homes, halfway houses, vocational–technical/college programs, and electronic house arrest, will expand. As they expand, we expect a decrease in recidivism, crime, and the total criminal justice budget. More and more people will be able to emigrate from the Country Called Prison back to their country of birth. Tax users will be turned back into taxpayers, and eventually everyone will benefit.

POLICY IMPLICATION 3

As we have discussed, it is extremely difficult to determine the actual costs of incarceration. No state can provide a true accounting to the taxpayers of what it really costs to put someone in prison, because determining true costs is nearly impossible. However, we think other options worthy of consideration can help us get a clearer picture.

To account for the overall cost of the decision to incarcerate, we need to charge the prison system for all the actual and collateral costs we can. Currently, if we incarcerate a woman who is the sole custodian of her children and those children go into state custody, the bill for foster care is not paid by the criminal justice system. The same can be said for food stamps, Temporary Assistance for Needy Families, and housing assistance. This should change.

During the intake process at social service agencies, intake workers can easily assess whether someone is seeking services because of a family member being incarcerated. The intake worker could merely put in a code which would then tie that costs to incarceration, thus helping us keep track of how these issues are related.

We suggest this because we face an increasing issue with unhoused people, and as we have shown, a large share of these individuals are former inmates. The same idea could apply to a host of common ills that those released from prison face, such as disability costs, halfway house funding, and work-training costs. If all, or most, of the collateral expenditures were accounted for by the criminal justice system, we would have a clearer picture of the true costs of the criminal justice system to our society—and would likely be shocked by the number.

POLICY IMPLICATION 4

All criminologists understand that perpetration of crime decreases as people age. In short, the age–crime connection generally peaks at about 25 years of age and then starts to decline. Once a person is in their 40s, their risk to society rapidly declines. Once a person is over 60, the continued threat is almost nonexistent. However, this criminological fact is almost never considered in sentencing strategies. This same pattern follows drug and alcohol users as the number of users declines with age as well. Therefore, drug treatment tends to have greater efficacy in individuals who are past their 20s and is especially effective in individuals older than age 40 (Vasilenko et al., 2017).

When discussing this with his students, John usually finds someone in the room who had a relative sober up at about age 40. This interesting statistic has given criminologists a rule of thumb: "Nothing curbs criminality or drug use like a 40th birthday." This reality needs to be considered as we revisit the sentencing structure of crimes, particularly those that are nonviolent.

Laws like "three strikes you're out" and "truth in sentencing" need to be reviewed. Parole boards should be given the clinical assessments discussed in Chapter 7. Once reviewed, the boards should be empowered to make decisions that seem to best fit the specifics of an individual offender's situation. Expanding post release diversion spending should decrease recidivism and increase public safety.

We need to increase judicial discretion while reducing plea bargaining and determinate sentencing. Our roots in British common law emphasize the importance of the judge's role in the judiciary process. In the past, the U.S. system of justice believed that judges were in the best position to make decisions about fairness and sentencing. However, over time, the discretionary role of the judge has declined as scandals and the electoral process have caused us to lose faith in the idea that a judge can be trusted to make good decisions. In today's judicial system, there are three major problem areas: (a) excessive use of plea bargaining, (b) determinate sentences, and (c) the need to expand jury nullification.

The criminal justice system benefits greatly from the plea-bargaining process. However, it is a potentially coercive process. Hank, a former student, was getting a ride to school in a friend's car. His buddy was driving and sped through a school zone. They were pulled over. Upon giving the driver a ticket, the police officer suspected there might be drugs in the car. After a search, he found crack cocaine. The student had no knowledge of the existence of the drug in the car, but it was under his seat. Therefore, he was charged as an accessory to the crime of transporting a dangerous substance.

After a brief preliminary hearing where bail was set at an amount Hank could not afford, he sat for weeks in jail awaiting trial. The day before his scheduled court appearance, a public defender he had never met came to see him. Hank, who had not been found guilty of anything, had been in jail for about 15 weeks. The lawyer told him, "If you plead guilty, the district attorney will let you off for time served and you can go home. If you insist on proclaiming your innocence and we go to trial, you are looking at 15 years if we lose. What do you want to do?" Hank took the plea and left for home. Of course, he left with a criminal record that previously he did not have. This decision derailed his funding for college, his career choices, and his future. Why was the proposed sentence so long? The answer is determinate sentencing laws.

POLICY IMPLICATION 5

Determinate sentencing refers to legislated sentences given to judges for specific types of crimes. Both federal and state legislatures have created schemas by which individuals are sentenced. For example, a first-offense cocaine distributor would receive a specific number of years, while a second offense would yield more time. On the surface, this seems both efficient and fair. Judges no longer need to adjudicate; they are merely accountants keeping the score of offenses, looking in a book for the punishment, and sentencing someone to the required years of imprisonment or probation.

The problem, of course, is that no two cases are the same, and most have mitigating or aggravating circumstances that might influence the determination of fairness in each specific case. Judicial discretion allows judges to evaluate these circumstances and weigh out the relative fairness. Organizations like Families Against Mandatory Minimums (http://www.famm.org) have records of individuals who had judges apologize for the unjust sentences they were forced to hand down. Our story about Hank is not an isolated case, and millions of other stories like his are, in part, responsible for the boom in incarceration.

Jury nullification refers to the ability of a jury to nullify a law that they see as unjust. In theory, a jury can find the defendant not guilty even though they believe the defendant committed the act for which they are on trial. In the United States, judges almost never inform juries that they can do this. Instead, they order the jury to be determiners of fact, not the law. However, jury nullification can protect people from unjust punishment. The student who takes a ride with a drug dealer is not really a person of which we are afraid. However, based on the way the laws are written, he was guilty. Had he gone to trial and jury nullification was a possibility, he may have been set free without a felony record that would ruin his life.

Jury nullification can allow the jury to accept the evidence of guilt without a corresponding life-ruining conviction. Although some may insist that the determination-of-fact rule is best because it prevents bias from entering legal decisions, the power of the jury to determine the applicability of a law in a specific situation may be preferable. A judge seeking reelection may be more inclined to consider the political consequences of a decision instead of justice. Meanwhile, a jury of peers who have no long-term involvement in the criminal justice system may be more able to ensure that justice is served.

POLICY IMPLICATION 6

Currently in the United States there is a shortage of after-care beds for inmates. No state can claim they have complete placement plans after incarceration (Mellow & Greifinger, 2007). Data suggest that only approximately 10% of released inmates have a placement and plan when they leave prison. The remainder are effectively left to their own devices.

The psychological profile instruments discussed in Chapter 7 should be used in the discharge plan decision-making process. Our experience shows that because of prison overcrowding and under-staffing, discharge planning for inmates frequently doesn't begin until the last 2 to 6 months of their sentence. When visiting Irish prisons a few years ago, John was impressed to discover that discharge planning there started the first day. Newly incarcerated people were asked, "What skills do you need to develop while you're here?" and then plans were created. In the United States, too often inmates are like Avalon and are set up to likely fail upon discharge unless there is a Mary there to try to help them. Thus, we need to increase judicial discretion and eliminate fees charged to inmates for their incarceration.

POLICY IMPLICATION 7

There is a need to address the rising number of juveniles entering the adult criminal system. One question should be considered: Are today's teenagers worse than those a generation ago, or is something else causing this significant rise in youthful offenders? One element that seems to be contributing to this increase is the zero-tolerance policies found in most schools These policies require that students be expelled, and often criminalized, for doing things that years ago might not have been a major offense. Research has shown that enforcement of the zero-tolerance policy tends to be linked to the most vulnerable and disenfranchised students, often the poor and minorities. These students often end up on the wrong end of a rigid rule (Skiba, 2000).

John recalled an incident in which a friend got in a high school brawl over a girl that resulted in a bloody nose and a black eye. Today, in a zero-tolerance school, that same fight would likely result in a report to the police for assault, expulsion from school, and another teen added to a juvenile probation officer's caseload. In John's youth, nothing happened to his friend, the brawler; he now owns a successful business and is a valued member of society.

As we have pointed out, prison rarely corrects adult criminal behavior; it certainly is not going to correct juvenile delinquency. Youthful prisoners have a significantly increased likelihood of being raped and assaulted while in prison (Austin et al., 2000). They also have higher risks of suicide. Unfortunately, most prisons try to avoid these problems by placing juveniles in administrative segregation. This practice borders on cruel and unusual punishment, as teens are locked down 23 hours a day in a single cell just when their psychosocial and moral development is most important for healthy adult functioning. We lock juveniles away; *prisonize* them in a stagnant, wretched environment; and then wonder why they act immature and irresponsible when they are released from prison years later as adults.

Using a progressive discipline model for juveniles is essential. We should use adult incarceration as the absolute last resort. Throwing away 16-year-olds because they did something we don't like is a sure way to continue to grow the Country Called Prison. We must consider the deeds of teenagers in the context of their psychological and social development. The ability to engage in long-range planning is not common in most teens, and so it should not surprise us that they engage in behaviors that we would prefer they not do. Almost everyone recalls episodes from their teenage years that later in life they look back on, shake their head, and ponder, "What was I thinking?" The same is true for teenagers today, many of whom have been labeled as criminals.

Diversion programs for teens are much less expensive to operate than for adults because teens usually live with their parents or guardians, do not have children, and do not need to find employment. The *nothing works* backers would support locking them up. However, we believe that policymakers should divert money from prisons to decarceration and desistance programs that focus on changing behavior. The costs of doing nothing or keeping the status quo are not just in dollars but also in lives. If we could rescue a teen from this detrimental path, we would all be better off for generations to come. We must expand the number of diversion programs for teens and adequately fund them so the programs can be successful. The earlier we divert citizens from the Country Called Prison, the slower the growth rate of that culture and the less expensive it is for America.

We believe that all these issues are interrelated. As is frequently the case, one solution may create a different problem somewhere else. The unintended consequences brought on by mass plea deals, limited judicial discretion, and harsh rules for juveniles have increased the size of the Country Called Prison. We need to make sure that we develop solutions that focus on reducing its population, not just remodeling one component.

POLICY IMPLICATION 8

There is a need to expand mental and addiction health care centers. Every criminologist we know admits that the Country Called Prison has grown in large part due to the War on Drugs and many of our "get tough on crime" policies that began in the 1980s. At the same time, most mental health facilities have been left short of funding and unable to meet the needs of those who are without medical insurance. This often results in the mentally ill and addicted falling through the cracks of America's welfare system to the one place that cannot say no— prison—at a 32% higher cost than treating them in the community (NAMI, 2014).

The tenets of labeling theory apply here. This theory suggests that the labels, or classifications, society puts on things and people create a *self-fulfilling prophecy*. For example, if we define a person with a drug habit as *sick*, then we send that person to a hospital to get *well*. If we define that person as a *criminal*, off to prison they go. Generally, we know that about half of the men and women who go to prison are convicted of drug possession. They are not drug dealers or traffickers; they are merely drug users. Our society has decided to try to punish their addiction, which is a biological problem, not a criminal one. This simply will never work.

Drug abuse and mental illness go hand in hand in prison. The majority of those whom Mary saw frequently while working in prison had a diagnosable mental illness as well as a drug problem. Frequently, they are referred to as *dually diagnosed*. For those involved in the criminal justice system, this will come as no surprise. Many mentally ill people self-medicate with illegal drugs to try to curb the symptoms of their mental illness.

In many states, the prison system is the largest single provider of mental health services. One study showed that about 43% of state and 23% of federal prisoners had a history of mental health problems (Maruschak et al., 2021). About 27% of state and 14% of federal prisoners reported they had a major depressive disorder. An estimated 40% of state prisoners and 26% of federal prisoners who met the threshold for having symptoms in the past 30 days for a serious and persistent mental disorder (SPD) reported they were receiving treatment. Among those not incarcerated for the entire 12 months prior to admission to prison, about 49% of state and 32% of federal prisoners met the criteria for having a substance use disorder (Maruschak et al., 2021). Thirty-one percent of state prisoners and 25% of federal prisoners reported drinking alcohol at the time of offense. Thirty-nine percent of state prisoners and 31% of federal prisoners reported using drugs at the time of offense. Addiction and mental illness are biological disorders that can only be corrected with empirical-based treatment protocols, which are four times less expensive than prison.

Over the past 10 years, more veterans have become drug criminals. When Mary worked in prison with incarcerated veterans, they had usually returned from a war zone within the past 5 years and were suffering from posttraumatic stress disorder. In efforts to self-medicate their terrible psychic pain, many war veterans turn to drugs and alcohol. Instead of locking them up with murderers and rapists, perhaps judges and district attorneys need to "sentence" the offender to take advantage of the services provided by the Veterans Administration. In fact, judges and district attorneys need to use their discretion to sentence all individuals with mental health and addiction problems to treatment facilities, not prisons. These programs are far more effective in controlling addiction and are cheaper as well.

Legislators need to refashion the community mental health system so that people can get continuous and effective help. This will require an increase in both treatment centers and community case-workers who make site visits to individuals who require it. Because of our experiences with those who have serious and perpetual mental health challenges, we support the expansion of civil commitment laws so that individuals who repeatedly avoid self-care and mental health treatments, and who are therefore a threat to themselves, even if not an immediate one, could be committed. We understand that such a stance is controversial and will likely bring up images of insane asylums of the past, with people being "locked away." However, we believe placing individuals in quality mental health centers is far better than simply placing them in prison.

POLICY IMPLICATION 9

We need to make it easier to emigrate from a Country Called Prison. Currently, leaving prison frequently comes with a host of issues, from fines and fees that must be paid to something as simple as just finding work. Let's consider the labels we use for people leaving prison. We call people who have finished their sentence and returned to society "ex-cons." There is no word in the English language that describes the category of people discharged from prison without the use of some form of a word that denotes criminal, convict, or offender. In other words, offenders are labeled and never forgiven.

The concept of "time-out" as a disciplinary strategy for children works best when parents hug their child after time-out is over to demonstrate forgiveness and unconditional love. In the Amish culture, which uses a form of "adult time-out" called *shunning*, the same thing occurs. After the person completes their allotted time of shunning for their misconduct, the community immediately welcomes the person back into full membership and nothing is said again. Many cultures around the world use this same form of social discipline and forgiveness strategy. Major crimes rarely occur in these cultures.

Labeling theory suggests that people behave as we expect them to. Research has consistently shown that students tend to perform better when teachers expect it (Al-Fadhili & Singh, 2006; Kuklinksy & Weinstein, 2001). This is commonly known as the self-fulfilling prophecy. When we continue to refer to people who have completed their punishment as "criminals," "ex-cons," or "ex-felons," then we should not be surprised that they continue to commit crimes. We label them as unchanged, and therefore they don't change. Perhaps the simplest proposal to eliminate the continuation of stigmatizing labels is the automatic expungement of criminal records for nonviolent, first-time offenders.

A few years ago, a college student in John's class admitted that he was a registered sex offender. One night at a party he had relieved himself on the lawn of an apartment complex. A passing police officer saw him and arrested him for indecent exposure. After pleading guilty, he was put on the sex offender registry. As he gave his oral report on criminal justice issues, he told the class that he was lucky because his father was an attorney and that they were already working on getting his record expunged.

Expungement usually applies to first-time offenders and literally means that records from earlier criminal activities are sealed. Therefore, the guilty party no longer needs to worry about background checks discovering their felonious past. It is, in effect, legal forgiveness.

An important point to understand is that expungement is a civil action. The plaintiff must ask the court to declare the records sealed, which usually involves lawyers, money, and time. In the case of this student, he didn't have to find the thousands of dollars it would take to hire a lawyer. But what happens if your father isn't a lawyer? How do you get your record expunged?

Most first-time, nonviolent offenders meet the criteria for expungement after a specific amount of time has elapsed. Unfortunately, most lack the knowledge and financial resources to pull this off. Therefore, we suggest that all nonviolent, first-time offenders be given an automatic expungement after a relatively short period of time, perhaps between 2 and 5 years. While this proposal would take some legislative action, hopefully in a country that prides itself on second chances, this pride will extend to people from the Country Called Prison.

Eastern societies such as Japan practice "reintegrative shaming" (Braithwaite, 1989), which refers to the way the bond can be mended between the offender and society. Until recently, Western cultures tended to use stigmatizing shame; once you've done something wrong, you can never get away from that negative action. Therefore, the individual stigmatized has no way to escape the past. Over the past 10 years or so, the United States has begun to use a restorative justice model that includes such mending activities as restitution and face-to-face meetings between the victim and offender. However, until restorative justice becomes the more traditional way to mend a tear in society, we believe that automatic expungement for nonviolent, first-time offenders can be a way to welcome them back into society. As well as getting on with their lives and feeling less shameful, they will be able to find employment and housing more quickly. Automatic expungement would also reward good behavior and show residents of the Country Called Prison that society wants them back now that they have made positive changes in their lives.

In addition, employment restrictions and practices need to change. You read previously about Avalon's reentry challenges. Employability is a major obstacle to successful reintegration. As one student with a criminal record put it, "If I admit I've been to prison, they don't hire me. If I lie and they check my records, then they don't hire me either. So I decided to try school." Of course, with a drug offense, many of the loans available to most students were not available to this student. So school for this student didn't last long either.

The simple solution to the employment challenge offenders face would be for businesses to simply delete the criminal history question from the employment application and hire based on talent and ability. If businesses are concerned or are hiring for specific positions for which a criminal history might be a cause for concern, then businesses should run background checks. We understand, though, that businesses are often held accountable for employee activities, and so they feel the need to know the criminal histories of potential employees. We propose a kind of "Good Samaritan" law for businesses, so they can hire people from the Country Called Prison without liability should an issue arise.

POLICY IMPLICATION 10

We need to make leaving prison easier. Since nearly 95% of prison residents will leave prison within 10 years of arrival (Hughes & Wilson, 2004), there is a tremendous need to create a support system for these residents when they return to the community. When legal immigrants come to America, support services help them learn English, American customs, and citizenship information so that they can become naturalized American citizens. These same types of acculturation support services are needed for citizens of the Country Called Prison to learn the expectations for becoming prosocial taxpayers.

While many state corrections departments already have some reintegration services, we believe these services should be mandatory. Social workers are aware of the concept of discharge planning. They would never discharge a person in need of oxygen from a hospital unless home medical services were in place prior to discharge. Their ethical standard requires more than that (National Association of Social Workers, 2017). We are proposing the creation of two types of reintegration support services: services that begin in prison and services that are in the community.

We envision prisons having reintegration units where residents live when they are within 1 or 2 years of discharge to begin their preparation for leaving prison. These units will be minimally restrictive and be the equivalent of a halfway house. These units should not be "behind the fence." If prison residents can't be trusted to follow rules and regulations, then they should not be leaving prison in the first place. Too often, prisons keep labeling residents as "bad" because of their original crime, rather than seeing the changes they have made in their lives.

When Gloria first came to prison, at age 19, she was full of meanness. She had been convicted of assault and battery of a shop owner when she was high on drugs and robbing the place. Five years later, she had earned her GED and a certificate in horticulture and was the orderly in charge of maintaining the flowerbeds at the entrance of the facility.

She was going to be discharged in 3 months, and her case manager, who believed in her, had gotten her a job with a friend who had a landscape business. Gloria worked to find a place to live so she wouldn't have to return to her terrible neighborhood and possibly get caught up in drugs again. A reintegration unit could help make this kind of success story happen for every nonviolent person leaving prison.

We envision that residents living in the reintegration units would be given preparation planners and would attend classes on employment, life, interpersonal relationship, parenting, marriage, etiquette, and life planning skills. We hope that the units will function somewhat like a home, with residents sharing in meal preparation, unit cleanliness, and activity planning. Residents would have the opportunity to contact prospective employers. Staff might be able to invite employers to the unit for interviews or they might take residents to interviews at employment agencies or at job sites. Procedures would be in place for finding appropriate housing and obtaining items on the reintegration checklist discussed in the previous chapter. We anticipate that different procedures and programming would be in place for units housing residents under age 50 and those over age 50, since work, family, and aging scenarios would be considerably different.

The creation of reintegration units would not require a great deal of money. Their creation will, however, require a new way of thinking about residents, the purpose of incarceration, and the goal of corrections. Most state correctional departments view their primary goal as protecting the public from dangerous criminals. We agree that the original purpose of prisons was just that, because only the truly dangerous people were locked up. However, times have changed. Private prison corporations would most likely be able to implement reintegration units far more quickly and more effectively than state corrections departments, which tend to be bogged down by bureaucracy and fixed budgets.

As we have pointed out time and again, prisons are full of mostly nonviolent offenders. Yet the goals of prisons have not really changed much. Traditions die hard. We understand most prisons have some type of discharge planning. However, this planning is often focused on the short term. Prison staff just strive to get the person out the door on time. The focus is not on helping residents to stay out. Prison staff have a tremendous opportunity to reduce recidivism by establishing programs that are designed to help residents leave prison with the best possible chance of success.

POLICY IMPLICATION 11

There is a need to expand reintegration support services in the community. In the community, the ideal scenario for reintegration support is to create a type of social work division in state correctional departments. The sole purpose of this department would be to create success stories. To do this, a paradigm shift must occur away from only punishment of criminals toward assimilation.

Many businesses, agencies, and processes are in place in the community that can provide for the needs that former prisoners and their families have. We don't have to reinvent the wheel; we just need to get people connected with existing processes and services. Medical and mental health hospitals and rehabilitation centers have had social work departments for years that help patients with follow-up care in the community after they discharge. This proposed department would focus on providing services that help former prisoners learn appropriate ways to satisfy their innate human needs. Once again, we use Maslow's (1954) hierarchy of needs to discuss the elements that an effective community social work division might contain.

Physiological and safety needs include access to basic survival materials (food, clothing, and shelter), the ability to feel secure, and prospects of obtaining support. People need the proper legal documents to obtain work, rent housing, obtain a car loan, and so on. They need assistance in finding and keeping jobs, which might include coaches who would accompany the person on their first day on the job. They need to be able to obtain medical and mental health services immediately upon release. Allowing someone to wait 3 months to see a psychiatrist is setting that person up to fail. Finally, depending on where the person lives, transportation assistance needs to be made available so they can keep appointments and get to work.

Belongingness and esteem needs include the ability to be accepted and appreciated by others, to have friends, to demonstrate competency, and to gain approval and recognition from others. Former prison residents need to have a support system (not just their family or friends) that is willing and able to assist them for at least 3 years after release. Just as we have learned from the success of Alcoholic Anonymous and Narcotics Anonymous meetings led by recovered addicts, former prison residents should be able to attend meetings with other former residents who have successfully reassimilated, others like themselves who have been successful. We need something like an "offenders anonymous" support group (without the labeling, of course).

At the same time, former residents should be encouraged to become involved in community groups. Community theater, civic organizations, and churches all provide positive social interaction. To break the cycle of prison, those we release should be encouraged to become involved in their communities, and perhaps even be rewarded for it. Almost every town or city has a volunteer organization of some type. If former prison residents were welcomed into such groups, everyone involved would benefit.

Self-fulfillment needs include the ability of people to reach their potential and capabilities as human beings and to help others achieve their potential as well. Satisfying these needs will require long-term strategies through the development of permanency planning and stabilization reform.

One of the most successful reintegration programs around is the Peter Young Housing Industries and Treatment (PYHIT) enterprise (http://www.pyhit.com) in New York, which provides a full range of services. PYHIT began more than 50 years ago when Father Peter Young realized how socially disenfranchised former prison residents were. He realized that addiction was a disease that needed treatment and that a successful reintegration program must include not only treatment but also housing and employment opportunities. Organizations like PYHIT should be implemented in every state if we are going to stop the rising tide of disenfranchised and marginalized people in America.

Avoiding hostile labels, creating automatic expungement of records, reducing the shame of applying for employment, and creating reintegration support services are solutions whose time has come for three reasons. First, and perhaps most important, the nonviolent offender would have a reason, a motivation, to behave properly upon release. Second, odds would be better that former residents would gain meaningful employment, which in the long run would save taxpayers a great deal of money, as well as generate more tax revenue. And finally, these proposals would help remove some of the unintended consequences of mass incarceration by decreasing the population of the Country Called Prison.

SUMMARY

Throughout the implementation of these changes, we support a focus on measurable outcomes to determine program effectiveness. Clearly, no institution can promise a 100% success rate. However, the current paradigm seems content with high failure rates. For example, in California, of the prisoners released in 1995, 66% returned to prison within 3 years (Pew Charitable Trust, 2007); of that group, less than half returned for a new offense. Parole revocation accounted for 36% of the returned residents, which means the individual violated the terms of their parole without committing a new crime. Of that group, half of the parole revocations were for technical violations, such as missing an appointment, not paying a fine, or failing to report a change of address.

Recently Bill's parole was revoked because he missed a meeting with his parole officer. He had a job interview at the same time and thought getting a job would impress his parole officer and allow him to catch up on his unpaid child support (another potential rule violation). Not so. The parole officer never bothered to find out the reason he had missed the meeting; the officer merely issued a warrant for his arrest. Bill was sent back to prison without a court hearing.

Quality should be rewarded, especially since several evidence-based programs with proven success records have been operating for many years, demonstrating that success can be achieved effectively and inexpensively. Prisons (public and private) and programs with high rates of success should get more funding, just as an investor will put more funds into a stock portfolio that is doing well. Prisons and programs with high rates of recidivism should not receive the same level of funding as those that work best.

This chapter has provided some big ideas for your consideration and debate. Stakeholders in the current system are unlikely to immediately embrace these ideas because they make money from today's criminal justice processes. Innovative legislation will need to be passed for any of these changes to go into effect. The Marshall Plan rebuilt the bonds between enemies such as Germany and the United States. It reconnected conquered people such as the French and the Germans, and it set Europe up for rapid, lasting success. Americans can do this again with our prison system since we clearly did this before with the reconstruction of Europe.

Our book has shown that we've built a new nation called prison within America's borders. It is filled with a variety of people: some who are feared, many who are not. Our proposals are for those whom we do not fear. We want to help these people emigrate from the Country Called Prison and assimilate them into their country of birth—the United States. Implementing our proposals will go a long way toward decreasing the prison population and freeing us all from this self-imposed drain on our people and resources. We created the current system; therefore, we can change it.

REFERENCES

Achenbaum, W. A., Howell, J. D., & Parker, M. (1993). Patterns of alcohol use and abuse among aging Civil War veterans, 1865–1920. *Academic Medicine, 69*(1), 69–85.

Ainsworth, M., & Bell, S. (1970). Attachment, exploration, and separation: Illustrated by the behavior of one-year-olds in strange situations. *Child Development, 41*, 49–67.

Alexander, K., Holupka, S., & Pallas, A. (1987). Social background and academic determinants of two-year versus four-year college attendance: Evidence from two cohorts a decade apart. *American Journal of Education, 96*, 56–80.

Alexander, M., & West, C. (2012). *New Jim Crow: Mass incarceration in the age of colour blindness.* New Press.

Al-Fadhili, H., & Singh, M. (2006). Teachers' expectancy and efficacy as correlates of school achievement in Delta, Mississippi. *Journal of Personnel Evaluation in Education, 19*, 51–67.

American Psychiatric Association. (2013). *The diagnostic and statistical manual of mental disorders* (5th ed.).

American Society of Correctional Administrators. (2010). *Staff to inmate ratio survey.* http://www.asca.net/system/assets/attachments/471/Staff_to_Inma te_Ratio_Survey.pdf

Andrews, D. A., & Bonta, J. (2010). *The psychology of criminal conduct.* Anderson.

Antenangeli, L., & Durose, M. R. (2021). *Recidivism of prisoners released in 24 states in 2008: A 10-year follow-up period (2008–2018).* NCJ 256094. U.S. Bureau of Justice Statistics.

Austin, J. (2000a). *Juveniles in adult prison and jails.* Bureau of Justice Assistance.

Austin, J. (2000b). *Multisite evaluation of boot camp programs: Final report.* George Washington University, Institute on Crime, Justice, and Corrections.

Austin, J., & Irwin, J. (2001). *It's about time: America's imprisonment binge.* Wadsworth/Thomson Learning.

Austin, J., Johnson, K., & Gregoriou, M. (2000). *Juveniles in adult prisons and jails: A national assessment.* U.S. Department of Justice, Bureau of Justice Assistance.

Ban the Box. (2018). *Ban the box.* https://employerschoicescreening.com/news/legal-alerts/ban-box-law-employment-application-virginia/#:~:text=Ban%20the%20Box%20Laws%20Finally,laws%20on%20state%20employment%20applications

Bandura, A. (1963). *Social learning and personality development.* Holt, Rinehart, & Winston.

Bauer, S. (2018) *American prison: A reporter's journey into the business of punishment.* Penguin Press.

Baumrind, D. (1967). Child-care practices anteceding three patterns of preschool behavior. *Genetic Psychology Monographs, 75,* 43–88.

Baumrind, D. (1991). The influence of parenting style on adolescent competence and substance use. *Journal of Early Adolescence, 11,* 56–95.

Beccaria, C. ([1764] 1963). *Essays on crimes and punishments* (H. Paolucci, Trans.). Bobbs-Merrill.

Beck, A., Rantala, R., & Rexroat, J. (2013a). *Sexual victimization reported by adult correctional authorities, 2009–2011.* NCJ 243904. Bureau of Justice Statistics.

Beck, A., Rantala, R., & Rexroat, J. (2013b). *Survey of sexual violence in adult correctional facilities, 2009–2011.* NCJ 244227. Bureau of Justice Statistics.

Bentham, J. ([1789] 1970). *An introduction to the principles of morals and legislation* (J. Burns & H. Hart, Eds.). Athlone Publishing.

Berry, K. R., Gilmour, M., Kennedy, S. C., & Tripodi, S. J. (2018). Coming home: Challenges and opportunities to enhance reentry services. In W. T. Church & D. W. Springer (Eds.), *Serving the stigmatized: Working within the incarcerated environment* (pp. 287–306). Oxford University Press.

Blackburn, C., Bonas, S., Spencer, N., et al. (2004). Parental smoking and passive smoking in infants: Fathers matter too. *Health Education Research, 20,* 185–194.

Blomberg, T., & Lucken, K. (2010). *American penology: A history of control* (2nd ed.). Transaction Publishers.

Blonigen, D., Shafer, P., Smith, J., Cucciare, M., Timkol, C., Smelson, D., Blue-Howells, J., Clark, S., & Rosentha, J. (2021, January). Recidivism treatment for justice-involved veterans: Evaluating adoption and sustainment of Moral Reconation Therapy in the US Veterans Health Administration. *Administration and Policy in Mental Health and Mental Health Services Research, 48*(6), 992–1005. https://doi.org/10.1007/s10488-021-01113-x

Blumstein, A., Cohen, J., Roth, J. A., & Visher, C. A. (1986). *Criminal careers and "career criminals."* National Academy Press.

Bocanegra, K. (2017). Community and decarceration-developing localized solutions. In M. W. Epperson & C. Pettus-Davis (Eds.), *Smart decarceration: Achieving criminal justice transformation in the 21st century* (pp. 115–137). Oxford University Press.

Boisvert, D. (2021, November). Biosocial factors and their influence on desistance. In A. Soloman & J. Scherer (Eds.), *Desistance from crime: Implications for research, policy, and practice* (pp. 41–80). NCJ 30149. National Institute of Justice.

Bonczar, T. (2003). *Prevalence of imprisonment in the U.S. population, 1974–2001*. NCJ 197976. Bureau of Justice Statistics.

Bonczar, T., & Beck, A. (1997). *Lifetime likelihood of going to state or federal prison*. NCJ 160092. Bureau of Justice Statistics.

Bovan, R. (2018). *The dedicated ex-prisoner's guide to life and success on the outside: 10 rules for making it in society after doing time* (2nd ed.). Full Surface Publishing.

Bowlby, J. (1960). Separation anxiety. *International Journal of Psychoanalysis, 41*, 89–113.

Braithwaite, J. (1989). *Crime, shame, and reintegration*. Cambridge University Press.

Branden, N. (1994). *The six pillars of self-esteem*. Bantam Books.

Brooks-Gunn, J., Duncan, G., Klebanove, P., & Sealand, N. (1993). Do neighborhoods influence child and adolescent development? *American Journal of Sociology, 99*, 353–395.

Bucklen, K. (2021, November). Desistance-focused criminal justice practice. In A. Soloman & J. Scherer (Eds.), *Desistance from crime: Implications for research, policy, and practice* (pp. 111–134). NCJ 30149. National Institute of Justice.

Bureau of Justice Statistics. (2021). *Drug use and crime*. https://bjs.ojp.gov/drugs-and-crime-facts/drug-use-and-crime#attime

Bureau of Labor Statistics. (2022). *Occupational outlook handbook: Correctional officers and bailiffs*. https://www.bls.gov/ooh/protective-service/correctional officers.htm#:~:text=%2449%2C100-The%20median%20annual%20wage%20for%20correctional%20officers%20and%20jailers%20was,percent%20earned%20more%20than%20%2482%2C600.&text=Most%20correctional%20officers

Burke, K. (1954). *Permanence and change* (2nd ed.). University of California Press.

Burke, P., & Tonry, M. (2006). *Successful transition and reentry for safe communities: A call to action for parole*. Center for Effective Public Policy.

Burnside, A. (2022, April). *No more double punishments: Lifting the ban on SNAP and TANF for people with prior felony drug convictions*. Center for Law and Social Policy. https://www.clasp.org/wp-content/uploads/2022/04/2022Apr_No-More-Double-Punishments.pdf

CA-EDU. (1989). *Characteristics of middle grade students*. California Department of Education. http://pubs.cde.ca.gov/tcsii/documentlibrary/characteristicsmg.aspx

Campbell, D., Levinson, M., & Hess, F. (2012). *Making civics count: Citizenship education for a new generation*. Harvard Education Press.

Campbell, N. M. (2005). *Correctional leadership competencies for the 21st century: Managers and supervisors.* http://nicic.org/Downloads/PDF/Library/020475.pdf.

Carpenter, J. (Director). (1981). *Escape from New York* [Film]. Goldcrest Films.

Carson, E. A. (2020, October). *Prisoners in 2019.* NCJ 255115. Bureau of Justice Statistics.

Carson, E. A. (2021, October). *Suicide in local jails and state and federal prisons, 2000–2019: Statistical tables.* NCJ 300731. Bureau of Justice Statistics.

Carson, E. A. (2022, December). *Prisoners in 2021: Statistical tables.* NCJ 305125. Bureau of Justice Statistics.

Carson, E., & Golinelli, D. (2013). *Prisoners in 2012: Trends in admissions and releases, 1991–2012.* NCJ 243920. Bureau of Justice Statistics.

Carson, E. A., & Kluckow, R. (2023). *Correctional populations in the United States, 2021: Statistical tables.* NCJ 305542. Bureau of Justice Statistics.

Carson, E., & Sabol, W. (2012). *Prisoners in 2011.* NCJ 239808. Bureau of Justice Statistics.

Caudy, M., Tang, L., Ainsworth, S. A., Lerch, J., & Taxman, F. S. (2013). Reducing recidivism through correctional programming: Using meta-analyses to inform the RNR Simulation Tool. In F. S. Taxman & A. Partavina (Eds.), *Simulation strategies to reduce recidivism: Risk need responsivity (RNR) modeling in the criminal justice system* (pp. 167–193). Springer.

Central Intelligence Agency. (2013). *CIA world fact book: Population rankings.* http://cia.gov/library/publications/the-world-fact-book/rankorder/2119rank.html

Chomsky, N. (1975). *Reflections on language.* Pantheon Books.

Choudry, I. (2018, March). *High school dropouts more likely to go to prison.* The Spotlight. https://slspotlight.com/opinion/2018/03/19/high-school-dropouts-more-likely-to-go-to-prison/.

Christian, S. (1998). *With liberty for some: 500 years of imprisonment in America.* Northeastern University Press.

Clear, T. (2007). *Imprisoning communities: How mass incarceration makes disadvantaged neighborhoods worse.* Oxford University Press.

Clemmer, D. (1940). *The prison community.* Rinehart.

Code of Hammurabi. (1770 BCE). http://eawc.evansville.edu/anthology/hammurabi.htm

Collier, J. R., Rosaldo, M., & Yanagisako, S. (1982). Is there a family? In B. Thorne (Ed.), *Rethinking the family: Some feminist questions* (pp. 25–39). Northeastern University Press.

Covey, S. (1989). *The 7 habits of highly effective people: Powerful lessons in personal change.* Simon and Schuster.

Cox, R. (2021). Does the timing of incarceration impact the timing and duration of homelessness? Evidence from "The Transitions to Housing" study. *Justice Quarterly, 38*(6), 1070–1094.

Crime Rate by Country. (2020). https://worldpopulationreview.com/country-rankings/crime-rate-by-country

Cullen, F. T. (2013). Rehabilitation: Beyond nothing works. *Crime and Justice in America, 42*(1), 299–376.

Cullen, F. T., Jonson, C. L., & Stohr, J. K. (Eds.). (2014). *The American prison: Imagining a different future.* Sage Publications.

Darabont, F. (1994). *The Shawshank Redemption.* Columbia Pictures.

Davis, A. T. (2008). *The declining number of youths in custody in the juvenile justice system.* National Council on Crime and Delinquency.

Dawson, P., & Guare, R. (2010). *Executive skills in children and adolescents: A practical guide to assessment and intervention* (2nd ed.). New York, NY: Guilford.

Debus-Sherrill, S., & Yahner, J. (Oct. 2011). Employment after prison: A longitudinal study of former prisoners. *Justice Quarterly, 28*(5), 698–718. https://doi.org/10.1080/07418825.2010.535553

Delaney, C., & Kaspin, D. (2011). *Investigating culture: An experiential introduction to anthropology.* John Wiley & Sons.

Devall, K., Lanier, C., & Baker, L. J. (2022). Painting the Current Picture: A National Report on Treatment Courts in the United States – Highlights & Insights, National Treatment Court Resource Center. https://ntcrc.org/pcp/

Devers, L. (2014). *Plea and charge bargaining, research summary.* Bureau of Justice Assistance, Directory of Representatives. http://www.house.gov/representatives/#state_id

Durose, M., Cooper, A., & Snyder, H. (2014). *Recidivism of prisoners released in 30 states in 2005: Patterns from 2005 to 2010.* Bureau of Justice Statistics.

Dynarski, S. (2003). Does aid matter? Measuring the effect of student aid on college attendance and completion. *American Economic Review, 93,* 279–288.

Edin, K., & Kefalas, M. (2005). *Promises I can keep: Why poor women put motherhood before marriage.* University of California Press.

Edin, K., & Lein, L. (1997). Welfare, work, and economic survival strategies. *American Sociological Review, 62,* 253–266.

Ekirch, A. R. (1985, April). Bound for America: A profile of British convicts transported to the Colonies, 1718–1775. *William and Mary Quarterly, 42*(2), 184–200.

Epperson, M. W., & Pettus-Davis, C. (2017a). *Smart decarceration: Achieving criminal justice transformation in the 21st century.* Oxford University Press.

Epperson, M. W., & Pettus-Davis, C. (2017b). Smart decarceration: Guiding concepts for an era of criminal justice transformation. In M. W. Epperson & C. Pettus-Davis (Eds.), *Smart decarceration: Achieving criminal justice transformation in the 21st century* (pp. 3–29). Oxford University Press.

Equal Justice Initiative. (2013). Children in adult prisons. http://eji.org/childrenprison

Erickson, P., & Erickson, S. (2008). *Crime, punishment, and mental illness.* Rutgers University Press.

Erikson, E. H. (1959). *Identity and the life cycle.* International Universities Press.

Fair, H., & Walmsley, R. (2021). *World prison population list* (13th ed.). Core Publications. https://www.prisonstudies.org/research-publications

Farrall, S. (2021, November). International perspectives and lessons learned on desistance. In A. Soloman & J. Scherer (Eds.), *Desistance from crime: Implications for research, policy, and practice* (pp. 135–162). NCJ 30149. National Institute of Justice.

Farrington, K. (2000). *History of punishment & torture: A journey through the dark side of justice.* Hamlyn.

Fay, D., Borrill, C., Amir, Z., Haward, R., & West, M. (2006). Getting the most out of multidisciplinary teams: A multi-sample study of team innovation in health care. *British Psychological Society, 79*(4), 553–567.

Federal Bureau of Labor Statistics. (2022). https://www.bls.gov/ooh/pro tective-service/correctional-officers.htm#:~:text=%f2449%2C100-,The%20median%20annual%20wage%20for%20correctional%20offic ers%20and%20jailers%20was,percent%20earned%20more%20than%20 %2482%2C600.&text=Most%20correctional%20officers)

Federal Bureau of Prisons. (n.d.). In mate ethnicity. http://www.bop.gov/ about/statistics/statistics_inmate_ethnicity.jsp

Federal Bureau of Prisons. (2023). Inmate Race. http://www.bop.gov/about/ statistics/statistics_inmate_race.jsp

Felson, M. (1998). *Crime and everyday life.* Pine-Forge Press.

Feuerstein, R. E. (1980). *Instrumental enrichment: An intervention program for cognitive modifiability.* Scott, Foresman & Co.

Fisher, W., Silver, E., & Wolff, N. (2006). Beyond criminalization: Toward a criminologically informed framework for mental health policy and service research. *Administrative Policy Mental Health and Mental Health Services Research, 33,* 544–547.

Frank, D., Augustyn, M., Knight, W., et al. (2001). Growth, development, and behavior in early childhood following prenatal cocaine exposure: A system-atic review. *JAMA, 285,* 1613–1625.

Freedmen. (2013). *Civil war home.* http://www.civilwarhome.com/freed men.htm

Garfinkel, H. (1956). Conditions of successful degradation ceremonies. *American Journal of Sociology, 61,* 420–424.

Garnett, M., & Curtin, S. C. (2023, April). *Suicide mortality in the United States, 2001–2021.* National Center for Health Statistics.

Gendreau, P., & Ross, R. (1987, September). Revivification of rehabilitation: Evidence from the 1980s. *Justice Quarterly, 4,* 349–407.

Girard, R. (1986). *The scapegoat.* Johns Hopkins University Press.

Glaze, L. E., & Parks, E. (2012, November). *Correctional populations in the United States, 2011*. NCJ 239972. Bureau of Justice Statistics.

Golding, W. (1954). *Lord of the flies*. Perigee Books.

Gorski, T. (2014). *Post incarceration syndrome*. http://www.tgorski.com/crimi nal_justice/cjs_pics_&_relapse.htm

Gotsch, K., & Basti, V. (2018). *Capitalizing on mass incarceration: U.S. growth in private prisons*. https://www.sentencingproject.org/publications/capitaliz ing-on-mass-incarceration-u-s-growth-in-private-prisons/

Gottfredson, M., & Hirschi, T. (1990). *A general theory of crime*. Stanford University Press.

Grattet, R., Petersilia, J., & Lin, J. (2008). *Parole violations and revocations in California*. U.S. Department of Justice.

Grattet, R., Petersilia, J., Lin, J., & Beckman, M. (2009). Parole violations and revocations in California: Analysis and suggestions for action. *Federal Probation, 73*(1), 2–11.

Green, B. L., Dass-Brailsford, P., Hurtado de Mendoza, A., Mete, M., Lynch, S. M., DeHart, D. D., & Belknap, J. (2016). Trauma experiences and mental health among incarcerated women. *Psychological Trauma: Theory, Research, Practice, and Policy, 8*(4), 455–463. https://doi.org/10.1037/tra0000113

Greenspan, S. (1997). *The growth of the mind*. Addison-Wesley.

Hallett, M. A. (2006). Private prisons in America: A critical race perspective. University of Illinois Press.

Hare, R. D. (2004). *Psychopathology checklist—revised* (2nd ed.). Multi-Health Systems.

Hare, R. D., & Neumann, C. S. (2006). The PCL-R assessment of psychopathy: Development, structural properties, and new directions. In C. Patrick (Ed.), *Handbook of psychopathy* (pp. 58–88). John Wiley & Sons.

Hare, R. D., & Neumann, C. S. (2008). Psychopathy as a clinical and empirical construct. *Annual Review of Clinical Psychology, 4*(1), 217–246. https://doi. org/10.1146/annurev.clinpsy.3.022806.091452

Harlow, C. (2003). *Education and correctional populations*. NCJ 195670. Bureau of Justice Statistics.

Harris, A. (2016). *A pound of flesh: Monetary sanctions as punishment for the poor*. Russell Sage Foundation.

Harrison, L. E. (2006). *The central liberal truth: How politics can change a culture and save it from itself*. Oxford University Press.

Haveman, R., & Smeeding, T. (2007). The role of higher education in social mobility. *Opportunity in America, 16*, 125–150.

Hidayati, N. O., Suryani, S., Rahayuwati, L., & Widianti, E. (2023, February). Women behind bars: A scoping review of mental health needs in prison. *Iranian Journal of Public Health, 52*(2), 243–253. http://doi.org/10.18502/ ijph.v52i2.11878

Hirschi, T. (1969). *Causes of delinquency.* University of California Press.

History of Prisons. https://www.prisonhistory.net/prison-history/history-of-prisons/

Houston Police Department. *Personal safety brochure.* https://www.houstontx.gov/police/pdfs/brochures/english/Personal_Safety.pdf

HUD Exchange. (2022, January). *Are applicants with felonies banned from Public Housing or any other housing funded by HUD? Do the Public Housing Agencies (PHAs), state, or landlords have any discretion in the process that could bar certain felonies?* U.S. Department of Housing and Urban Development.

Hughes, T., & Wilson, J. J. (2004). *Re-entry trends in the U.S.* Bureau of Justice Statistics.

Hurley, M. H., & Hanley, D. (2010). *Correctional administration and change management.* CRC Press.

Institute for Justice Research and Development. (2023). *5-Key model for reentry.* Institute for Justice Research and Development, Florida State University. https://ijrd.csw.fsu.edu/5-key-model-reentry-available-data#

James, L. E., & Glaze, L. E. (2006). *Mental health problems of prison and jail inmates.* Bureau of Justice Statistics.

Janis, I. (1972). *Victims of groupthink.* Houghton Mifflin.

Jannetta, J. (2015). *Transition from jail to community implementation toolkit.* Urban Institute. http://tjctoolkit.urban.org/

Jencks, C. (1994). *The homeless.* Harvard University Press.

Johnston, N. (2000). *Forms of constraint: History of prison architecture.* University of Illinois Press.

Jones, J. S. (2020). Opium slavery: Civil War veterans and opiate addiction. *Journal of the Civil War Era, 10*(2), 185–212.

Jones, N., Marls, R., Ramirez, R., & Rios-Vargas, M. (2021). *2020 Census illuminates racial and ethnic composition of country.* www.census.gov/library/stories/2021

Jonson, C. L., Eck, J. E., & Cullen, F. T. (2014). The small prison. In F. T. Cullen, C. L. Jonson, & M. K. Stohr (Eds.), *The American prison: Imagining a different future* (pp. 215–223). Sage.

Joos, M. (1967). *The five clocks: A linguistic excursion into the five styles of English usage.* Houghton Mifflin Harcourt.

Jung, C., & Campbell, J. (1976). *The portable Jung, a compilation.* Penguin Books.

Kazemian, L. (2021, November). Pathways to desistance from crime among juveniles and adults: Applications to criminal justice policy and practice, NCJ 301503.

Keeshin, B. R., Cronholm, P. F., & Strawn, J. R. (2011). Physiologic changes associated with violence and abuse exposure: An examination of related medical conditions. *Trauma, Violence & Abuse, 13,* 41–56.

Kennedy, R. (2014). *School size matters.* http://privateschool.about.com/od/choosingaschool/qt/sizematters.htm

Kong, A., & Fitch, E. (2002). Using book clubs to engage culturally and linguistically diverse learners in reading, writing, and talking about books. *Reading Teacher, 56*, 352–362.

Koteskey, R. (2014). *What missionaries ought to know about culture stress.* Missionary Care. http://www.missionarycare.com/brochures/br_culturestress.htm

Kozol, J. (1991). *Savage inequalities: Children in America's schools.* Crown Publishers.

Kuklinksy, M. R., & Weinstein, R. S. (2001). Classroom and developmental differences in a path model of teacher expectancy effects. *Child Development, 72*, 1554–1579.

LaBeet, G. (2021). *The end of recidivism: The ultimate guide to transforming the mind of the incarcerated.* Universal Lion Publishing.

Lamb, H., & Weinberger, L. (2005). The shift of psychiatric inpatient care from hospitals to jails and prisons. *Journal of the American Academic Psychiatry Law, 33*, 529–534.

Legner, L. (April 2022). *Kids' screen time: How much is too much?* OSF Healthcare. https://www.osfhealthcare.org/blog/kids-screen-time-how-much-is-too-much/

Lickona, T. (1992). *Educating for character: How our schools can teach respect and responsibility.* Bantam Books.

Lilienfeld, S. O., & Andrews, B. P. (1996, June). Development and preliminary validation of a self-report measure of psychopathic personality traits in noncriminal population. *Journal of Personality Assessment, 66*(3), 488–524. https://doi.org/10.1207/s15327752jpa6603_3

Lipton, D., Martinson, R., & Woks, J. (1975). *The effectiveness of correctional treatment: A survey of treatment valuation studies.* Praeger.

Long, H. (2017). *Private prison stocks up 100% since Trump's win.* https://money.cnn.com/2017/02/24/investing/private-prison-stocks-soar-trump/index.html

Looman, M. (2010). Establishing parental capability as a legal competency in child maltreatment cases. *Annals of the American Psychotherapy Association, 13*, 45–52.

Looman, M. (2012). Grounded strategies that improve self-efficacy. In K. Trotter (Ed.), *Harnessing the power of equine assisted counselling: Adding animal assisted therapy to your practice* (pp. 253–262). Routledge.

Looney, A., & Turner, N. (2018). *Work and opportunity before and after incarceration.* Brookings Institute. https://www.brookings.edu/articles/work-and-opportunity-before-and-after-incarceration/

Loshi, B. (2021). *Life after prison: Getting your life back on track.* GBDR Press.

Lundahl, B. W., Kunz, C., Brownell, C., Harris, N., & Van Vleet, R. (2009). Prison privatization: A meta-analysis of cost and quality of confinement indicators. *Research on Social Work Practice, 19*(4), 383–394. https://doi.org/10.1177/1049731509331946

Lyons, L. (2004). *History of punishment: Judicial penalties from ancient times to the present day*. Diane Publishing.

Marquis, P. (1992). Family dysfunction as a risk factor in the development of antisocial behavior. *Psychological Reports, 71*, 468–470.

Martinson, R. (1974). What works? Questions and answers about prison reform. *Public Interest, 35*, 22–54.

Maruschak, L. M., & Bronson, J. (2021, June). *Indicators of mental health problems reported by prisoners: Prison inmates 2016*. NCIS 252643. Bureau of Justice Statistics.

Maruschak, L., Bronson, J., & Alper, M. (July 2021). *Survey of prison inmates, 2016: Alcohol and drug use and treatment reported by prisoners*. NCI 252641. Bureau of Justice Statistics.

Maslow, A. (1954). *Motivation and personality*. Harper Publishing.

McRaney, D. (2013). *You are now less dumb*. Gotham Books.

Mellow, J., & Greifinger, R. B. (2007, January). Successful reentry: The perspective of private correctional health care providers. *Journal of Urban Health, 84*(1), 85–98. https://doi.org/10.1007/s11524-006-9131-9

Messner, S., & Rosenfield, R. (2008). *Crime and the American dream*. Wadsworth.

Metraux, S., & Culhane, D. P. (2006). Recent incarceration history among a sheltered homeless population. *Crime & Delinquency, 52*(3), 504–517. https://doi.org/10.1177/0011128705283565

Milgram, S. (1965). Some conditions of obedience and disobedience to authority. *Human Relations, 18*, 57–76.

Miller, H. (2006). *Inventory of offender risk, needs, and strengths (IORNS)*. Par Inc.

Millon, T. (1994). *Millon Index of Personality Styles*. Pearson.

Millon, T., Millon, C., Davis, R., & Grossman, S. (2009). *Millon Clinical Multi-Axial Inventory* (3rd ed.). Pearson.

Millon, T., Millon, C., & Grossman, S. (2015). *Millon Clinical Multiaxial Inventory-IV manual* (4th ed.). NCS Pearson.

Moffitt, T. E., & Caspi, A. (2001). Childhood predictors differentiate life-course-persistent and adolescence-limited antisocial pathways among males and females. *Development and Psychopathology, 13*, 355–375.

Montano-Harmon, M. R. (1991, May). Discourse features of written Mexican Spanish: Current research in contrastive rhetoric and its implications. *Hispania, 74*, 417–425.

Morey, L. (2007). *Personality Assessment Inventory*. PAR Inc.

Moschion, J., & Johnson, G. (2019). Homelessness and incarceration: A reciprocal relationship. *Journal Criminology, 35*, 855–887. https://doi.org/10.1007/s10940-019-09407-y

Mruk, C. J. (2006). *Self-esteem research, theory, and practice* (3rd ed.). Springer.

NAMI. (2014). *CIT toolkit: Criminalization of the mentally ill*. http://www.nami.org/Template.cfm?Section+CIT&Template=/ContentManagement/ContntDisplay.cfm&contentID=57465

National Association of Social Workers. (2017). *Code of ethics.* https://www.socialworkers.org/About/Ethics/Code-of-Ethics/Code-of-Ethics-English

National Center for Education Statistics. (2023, May). *Status dropout report.*

National Criminal Justice Association. (2022, April). *Commission to study why so many veterans end up in jail, prison.* National Criminal Justice Association News. https://NCJS.org/crimeandjusticenews/

National Drug Court Resource Center. (2021). *Treatment courts across the United States (2020).* National Drug Court Resource Center, University of North Carolina, Wilmington.

Neumann, C. S., Malterer, M. B., & Newman, J. P. (2008, June). Factor structure of the Psychopathic Personality Inventory (PPI): Findings from a large, incarcerated sample. *Psychological Assessment, 20*(2), 169–174. https://doi.org/10.1037/1040-3590.20.2.169

Noonan, M. (2012). *Mortality in local jails and state prisons, 2000–2010: Statistical tables.* NCJ 23991. Bureau of Justice Statistics.

Nowak, M., & Highfield, R. (2011). *Super cooperators: Altruism, evolution, and why we need each other to succeed.* Free Press.

Nowak, M., & Sigmund, K. (1998). Evolution of indirect reciprocity by image scoring: The dynamics of indirect reciprocity. *Nature, 393,* 573–577.

Office of Disease Prevention and Health Promotion. (2014, August). http://www.health.gov/phfunctions/public.htm

Ogunwole, S. U., Rabe, M. A., Roberts, A. W., & Caplan, Z. (2021, August). *Population under age 18 declined last decade.* U.S. Census Bureau. https://www.census.gov

Patterson, E. J., Talbert, R. D., & Brown, T. N. (2020, July). Familial incarceration, social role combinations, and mental health among African American women. *Journal of Marriage and Family, 83*(1), 86–101. https://doi.org/10.1111/jomf.12699

Payne, R. K. (2005). *A framework for understanding poverty.* aha! Process.

Personal Responsibility and Work Opportunity Reconciliation Act of 1996, Pub. L. No. 104-193. (1996). https://www.govinfo.gov/app/details/PLAW-104publ193

Petersilia, J. (2011). Beyond the prison bubble. *NIJ Journal, 268,* 26–31.

Petersilia, J., Rosenfeld, R., Bonnie, R. J., Crutchfield, R. D., Kleiman, M. A. R., Laub, J. H., & Visher, C. A. (2007). *Parole, desistance from crime, and community integration.* National Research Council.

Peterson, C. M. (1995). *Learned helplessness: A theory for the age of personal control.* Oxford University Press.

Pew Charitable Trusts. (2007). *When offenders break the rules: Smart responses to parole and probation violations.* http://www.pewtrusts.org/uploadedFiles/wwwpewtrustorg/Reports/sentencing_and_corrections/Condition-Violators-Briefing.pdf

Pew Charitable Trusts. (2013). *Sentencing and corrections: Condition violators briefing.* http://www.pewtrusts.org/uploadedFiles/wwwpewtrustsorg/Repo rts/sentencing_and_corrections/Condition-Violators-Briefing.pdf

Piquero, A., Farrington, D., & Blumstein, A. (2003). The criminal career paradigm. *Crime and Justice, 30,* 359–506.

Pisciotta, A. W. (1994). *Benevolent repression: Social control and the American reformatory-prison movement.* New York University Press.

Prins, S. (2011). Does transinstitutionalization explain the overrepresentation of people with serious mental illnesses in the criminal justice system? *Community Mental Health Journal, 47,* 716–722.

Prins, S. J. (2014). Prevalence of mental illnesses in US State prisons: A systematic review. *Psychiatric Services, 65*(7), 862–872.

Pruitt, D. (1999). *Your adolescent: Emotional, behavioural, and cognitive development from early adolescence through the teen years.* Harper Collins.

Rajalakshmi, J., & Thanasekaran, P. (2015). The effects and behaviors of home alone situation by latchkey children. *American Journal of Nursing Science, 4*(4), 207–211. https://doi.org/10.11648/j.ajns.20150404.19

Ramezani, N., Breno, A. J., Mackey, B. J., et al. (2022). The relationship between community public health, behavioral health service accessibility, and mass incarceration. *BMC Health Services Research, 22,* 966. https://doi. org/10.1186/s12913-022-08306-6

Rampey, B., Keiper, S., Mohadier, L., Krenzke, T., Li, J., Thornton, J., & Hogan, J. (2016). *Highlights from the U.S. PIAAC Survey of Incarcerated Adults: Their skills, work experience, education, and training.* NCES 2016040. National Center for Education Statistics. https://nces.ed.gov/pubsearch/pubsinfo. asp?pubid=2016040

Reckless, W. (1970). *Containment theory.* John Wiley.

Reiman, J. (1979). *The rich get richer and the poor get prison.* John Wiley & Sons.

Reiman, J. (1998). *The rich get richer, and the poor get prison: Ideology, class and criminal justice.* Allyn and Bacon.

Renfro, P. (2020). *Stranger danger.* Oxford University Press.

Rocque, M. (2021, November). But what does it mean? Defining, measuring, and analyzing desistance from crime in criminal justice. In A. Soloman & J. Scherer (Eds.), *Desistance from crime: Implications for research, policy, and practice* (pp. 1–40). NCJ 301497. National Institute of Justice.

Rodrigues, L., & Lockwood, D. (2011). Leprosy now: Epidemiology, progress, challenges, and research gaps. *Lancet Infectious Diseases, 11,* 464–470.

Roscigno, V., Tomaskovic-Devey, D., & Crowley, M. (2006). Education and the inequalities of place. *Social Forces, 84,* 2121–2145.

Rose, D., & Clear, T. (2001). *From prison to home: The effect of incarceration and re-entry on children, families, and communities.* U.S. Department of Health and Human Services.

Ross, J., & Richards, S. (2009). *Beyond bars: Rejoining society after prison.* Penguin Group.

Ross, L. (1977). The intuitive psychologist and his shortcomings: Distortions in the attribution process. In L. Berkowitz (Ed.), *Advances in experimental social psychology* (pp. 173–220). Academic Press.

Ryan, W. (1971). *Blaming the victim.* Pantheon Books.

Samenow, S. (2004). *Inside the criminal mind* (rev. and updated ed.). Crown Publishers.

Sawyer, W., & Wagner, P. (2023). *Mass incarceration: The whole pie 2023.* https:// www.prisonpolicy.org/reports/pie2023.html

Schliehe, A., Philo, C., Carlin, B., Fallon, C., & Penna, G. (2022). Lockdown under lockdown? Pandemic, the carceral and COVID-19 in British prisons. *Transactions of the Institute of British Geographers, 47,* 880–897. https://doi. org/10.1111/tran.12557

Schmitt, J. W. (2010). *The high budgetary cost of incarceration.* Center for Economic Policy and Research.

Schrantz, D., DeBor, S., & Mauer, M. (2016). *Decarceration strategies: How 5 states achieved substantial prison population reductions.* Sentencing Project. https://www.sentencingproject.org/app/uploads/2022/08/Decarceration-Strategies.pdf

Schweinhart, L. (2002). *The High/Scope Perry Preschool Study through age 40: Summary, conclusions and frequently asked questions.* High/Scope Educational Research Foundation. http://www.highscope.org/productDetail.asp?intpr oductID=2164

Scott, C. (2010). *Handbook of correctional mental health* (2nd ed.). American Psychiatric Publishing.

Seligman, M. (1975). *Helplessness: On depression, development, and death.* W. H. Freeman.

Sellers, M. P. (1993). *The history and politics of private prisons: A comparative analysis.* Fairleigh Dickinson University Press.

Shichor, D. (1995). *Punishment for profit: Private prisons/public concerns* (Foreword by G. Geis). Sage Publications.

Singer, M. (2013). *Prison rape: An American institution.* Praeger.

Skiba, R. (2000). *Zero tolerance, zero evidence: An analysis of school disciplinary practice.* NCJ 301497. Indiana Education Policy Center.

Smith, A. E. (1934). The transportation of convicts to the American colonies in the seventeenth century. *American Historical Review, 39*(2), 232–249. https://doi.org/10.2307/1838721

Snyder, M. (2013). *The beginning of the end.*

Solomon, A. (2012). *In search of a job: Criminal records as barriers to employment.* National Institute of Justice. http://www.nij.gov/journals/270/crimi nal-records.htm#note1

Soloman, A., & Scherer, J. (Eds.). (2021, November). *Desistance from crime: Implications for research, policy, and practice.* NCJ 301497. National Institute of Justice.

Stefanski, R. (2023, April 1). *Can a felon get a driver's license?* https://www.felonyrecordhub.com/rights/can-felon-get-drivers-license/?expand_article=1

Stephan, J. (2005). *Census of state and federal correctional facilities.* http://www.bjs.gov/content/pub/pdf/csfcf05.pdf

Storti, C., & Bennhold-Samaan, L. (1997). *Culture matters: The Peace Corps cross-cultural workbook.* Peace Corps Information Collection and Exchange.

Substance Abuse and Mental Health Services Administration. (2018). *Key substance uses and mental health indicators in the United States: Results from the 2017 National Survey on Drug Use and Health* (HHS Publication No. SMA 18-5068, NSDUH Series H-53). Center for Behavioral Health Statistics and Quality, Substance Abuse and Mental Health Services Administration. https://www.samhsa.gov/data/

Sutherland, E. (1947). *Principles of criminology.* Lippincott.

Sykes, G. (1958). *The society of captives: A study of a maximum-security prison.* Princeton University Press.

Sykes, G., & Matza, D. (1957). Techniques of neutralization: A theory of delinquency. *American Sociological Review, 22,* 664–670.

Tarullo, A. (2012). Effects of child maltreatment on the developing brain. In T. LaLiberte & T. Crudo (Eds.), *Child welfare 360: Using a developmental approach in child welfare practice* (p. 11). Center for Advanced Studies in Child Welfare, University of Minnesota.

Taxman, F. S., & Murphy, A. (2017). Community interventions for justice-involved individuals: Assessing gaps in programming to promote decarceration (Chapter 12, pp. 193–209). In M. Epperson & C. Pettus-Davis (Eds.), *Smart decarceration: Achieving criminal justice transformation in the 21st century* (pp. 193–209). Oxford University Press.

Testa, M., & West, S. G. (2010). Civil commitment in the United States. *Psychiatry, 7*(10), 30–40.

Travis, J. M. (2005). *Families left behind: The hidden costs of incarceration and re-entry.*

United Nations. (2018). *World drug report 2018.* United Nations Office of Drugs & Crime. https://www.unodc.org/wdr2018/

U.S. Census. (2020). *State population data 2022.* https://www.census.gov/data/tables/time-series/demo/popest/2020s-state-total.html

Vasilenko, S. A., Evans-Polce, R. J., & Lanza, S. T. (2017, November). Age trends in rates of substance use disorders across ages 18–90: Differences by gender and race/ethnicity. *Drug and Alcohol Dependence, 180,* 260–264. https://doi.org/10.1016/j.drugalcdep.2017.08.027

Visher, C. A., Debus-Sherrill, S. A., & Yahner, S. (2011, October). Employment after prison: A longitudinal study of former prisoners. *Journal Justice*

Quarterly, 28(5), 698–718. https://www.ojp.gov/ncjrs/virtual-library/abstra cts/employment-after-prison-longitudinal-study-former-prisoners

Wakefield, S., & Wildeman, C. (2014). *Children of the prison boom: Mass incarceration and the future of American inequality.* Oxford University Press.

Waldram, J. (2009). Challenges of prison ethnography. *Anthropology News, 50,* 4–5.

Weber, M. (1968). Basic sociological terms. In G. Roth & C. Wittich (Eds.), *Economy and society* (pp. 3–62). University of California Press.

Weikart, D. (1985). An early education project that changed students' lives: The Perry school program 20 years later. *Education Digest, 51,* 32–35.

Western, B., & Pettit, B. (2010). Incarceration and social inequality. *Daedalus, 139,* 8–19.

Wildeman, C. (2021, November). The impact of incarceration on the desistance process among individuals who chronically engage in criminal activity. In A. Soloman & J. Scherer (Eds.), *Desistance from crime: Implications for research, policy, and practice* (pp. 81–110). NCJ 30149. National Institute of Justice.

Wilson, J. Q., & Kelling, G. L. (1982). Broken windows. *Atlantic Monthly, 249*(3), 29–38.

Wilson, W. (1987). *The truly disadvantaged: The inner city, the underclass, and public policy.* University of Chicago Press.

World Economic Outlook Database. (2023). International Monetary fund WEO Data. https://www.imf.org/en/Publications/WEO/weo-database/2023/April

World Population Review. (2020). *Crime rate by country.* https://worldpopul ationreview.com/country-rankings/crime-rate-by-country

World Population Review. (2023). *Crime rate by country 2023.* https://worldp opulationreview.com/country-rankings/crime-rate-by-country

World Prison Brief. (2017). *Ten-country prisons project 2017.*

World Prison Brief. (2022). https://www.prisonstudies.org/world-prison-brief-datahttps://www.prisonstudies.org/ten-country-prisons-project

World Prison Brief. (2023). *Highest to lowest: Prison population rate.* https:// www.prisonstudies.org/highest-to-lowest/prison_population_rate?field_ region_taxonomy_tid=All

Zhou, M. (1992). *Chinatown: The socioeconomic potential of an urban enclave* (Conflict in Urban and Regional Development series). Temple University Press.

Zimbardo, P. (2004). The social psychology of good and evil: Understanding how good people are transformed into perpetrators. In A. G. Miller (Ed.), *The social psychology of good and evil* (pp. 21–50). Guilford Press.

Zukerman, B., Frank, D. A., Hingson, R., et al. (1989). Effects of maternal marijuana and cocaine use on fetal growth. *New England Journal of Medicine, 320,* 762–768.

INDEX

For the benefit of digital users, indexed terms that span two pages (e.g., 52–53) may, on occasion, appear on only one of those pages.

Tables, figures, and boxes are indicated by an italic *t*, *f*, and *b* following the page number.

cigarettes as currency, 70–71
citizens of Country Called Prison
   common culture, 43–45
   common history, 56–61
   common language, 68
   common political system, 69–70
   common territory, 65–67
   criminal behavior development
      theories, 77–79
   "good guys/bad guys", 75–77
   material culture/economy, 70–74
   national identity, 61–65
   number of, 52–56, 53t, 54t
   overview, 21
   prisoner crime statistics, 100–2, 101t
   shared values/beliefs/social
      behavior, 68–69
   social learning theory, 79–82, 79t
   See also childhood development;
      demographics of prisoners; mental
      health disorders; proposals for prison
      culture transformation
civic education, 108, 200–2
Civil War era prisons, 29–31
cleanliness, in prison, 138
Clear, Todd, 145–46
Clemmer, Donald, 21, 57, 127
Clinton, Bill, 35
clothing
   in prison culture, 4, 138–39
   providing for discharged prisoners, 182
Code of Hammurabi, 1–2, 3–4
cognitive dissonance, 165
collateral effects of incarceration, 9
collectivist culture, 120–21, 122f
college education, 60–61, 60t
Collier, J. R., 162–63
colonies, prison systems in, 26–27
commitment, 78
common characteristics of Country
    Called Prison
   culture, 43–45
   history, 56–61
   language, 68
   political system, 69–70
   territory, 65–67
communication
   in prison culture, 135–36
   during transformative change, 198
   translation by former prisoners, 171–
      72, 172t

community-based mental health care, 33
community policing, 203
community reintegration support services,
   205, 228–30
community service, 4
compassion, promoting, 149
computer games, 103–4
"con game," 71
consultative register, 172, 172t
containment theory, 78
contraband, 70–71
contract prison labor, 29–30, 31
convict code, 21
cooperation, 147–49
correctional officers, salary of, 19
Corrections Corporation of America, 37
corrections population comparison 2011-
   2021, 12, 12t
corruption, impact of systemic power
   differences on, 117
costs of incarceration
   accountability for, 213–15
   true costs, identifying, 215–16
counties, shifting costs of incarceration
   to, 213–15
countries
   comparison of crime rates, 16–17, 17t
   drug crime rates by, 17–18, 18t
   incarceration rates of richest, 14–16, 15t
   prison populations by, 13–14, 14t
   ranked by rate of incarceration per
      100,000, 14–16, 15t
country characteristics of prisons
   common culture, 43–45
   common history, 56–61
   common language, 68
   common political system, 69–70
   common territory, 65–67
   large collection of people, 46–56
   material culture/economy, 70–74
   national identity, 61–65
   shared values/beliefs/social
      behavior, 68–69
court fees, paying off, 168–69
Covey, S., 176–77, 176t
crime
   crime rates for industrialized nations,
      16–17, 17t
   prisoner crime statistics, 100–2, 101t
   society's view of, 72–73
crime triangle theory, 203f, 203

GED tests, 105, 106-7
gender. *See* men; women
general deterrence, 4-5
general theory of crime, 78-79
geography of Country Called
    Prison, 65-67
Germany
    crime rates in, 17t
    drug crime rates in, 18t
    incarceration rates in, 15t, 16
"get tough" laws, 36-37
Girard, Rene, 119
Gloria (case study), 226-27
Golding, William, 80
"good guys/bad guys", 75-77
Gorski, Terence, 127
Gottfredson, Michael, 78-79
Great Books Foundation, 106
Greek society, punishment in, 2
Green, B. L., 97
Greenspan, Stanley, 83-85, 84t, 157, 157t
Grenada, incarceration rate in, 15t
Grondona, Mariano, 200
group therapy, 184
groupthink, 131-32

habilitation, 61, 200
Hank (case study), 217-18
hard labor, 3t, 6-7, 28-29
Harris, Alexes, 168-69
Harrison, Lawrence, 199-200, 201t
Hawthorne, Nathaniel, 4, 27
health, importance in prison, 138
health care needs, of discharged
    prisoners, 182
Hidayati, N. O., 97
hierarchies in prison, 142-43
Hierarchy of Needs Model (Maslow),
    179-80, 180t, 228-29
Highfield, R., 147-48
Hirschi, Travis, 78, 109-10
Hispanics
    ages of male/female prison inmates,
        47, 47t
    decrease in 10-year prisoner
        populations, 13t
    federal prison admission by crime,
        47-48, 48t
    rate of incarceration, 8-9, 8t
    state prison admission by crime, 48-
        50, 49t

history, in Country Called Prison, 56-61
homelessness, 9, 146-47
homicide
    federal prison admission by race,
        47-48, 48t
    new commitments by gender, 50-51, 50t
    state prison admission by race, 48-50, 49t
    trends in first commitment/parole
        violations, 51-52, 51t
horizontal collectivism, 121
horizontal individualism, 120
houses of correction, 26
housing needs, of discharged prisoners,
    161-62, 182
housing placement, in prisons, 110-13
Huxley, Aldous, 41

identification, of discharged prisoners,
    160-61, 167-68, 181-82
illegal immigrants, 167-68
illegal materials in prison, 70-71
immigration, 31
*Imprisoning Communities: How Mass
    Incarceration Makes Disadvantaged
    Neighborhoods Worse* (Clear), 145-46
incapacitation model, 35
incarceration
    collateral effects of, 9
    costs of, 188
    decrease in prisoner populations 2011-
        2021, 12-13, 12t, 13t
    as epidemic, 22-23, 91-92
    manifest/latent consequences of, 186
    for protection of society, 6-7
    See also prison history
incarceration rates
    as epidemic, 91-92
    increase due to "get tough" laws, 36-37
    by race and ethnicity, 8-9, 8t
    ranking of countries per 100,000,
        14-16, 15t
    of richest countries, 14-16, 15t
income
    of former prisoners, 169, 170t
    prior to incarceration, 58
indentured servitude, 7, 26
India
    crime rates in, 17t
    drug crime rates in, 18t
    incarceration rates in, 15t
    prison population in, 13-14, 14t

indirect reciprocity, 148
individualistic cultures, 120, 122*f*
Inside the Criminal Mind (Samenow), 87–88
institutionalization, reducing, 150–51
institutionalized personality, 127–28, 157–58
internal control, 78, 109–10
internal threats, 63–64
interventions for reducing criminality, 73–74
intimate register, 172, 172*t*
involvement, 78
Iran, prison population in, 13–14, 14*t*
Italy
    crime rates in, 17, 17*t*
    drug crime rates in, 18*t*
    incarceration rates in, 15*t*

jails, early examples of, 25–26
James (case study), 41–42, 74
Jane (case study), 123–24
Janis, Irving, 131–32
Japan
    crime rates in, 17*t*
    drug crime rates in, 18*t*
    incarceration rates in, 15*t*, 16
jargon, 68
Jim Crow era, 9
Jung, Carl, 119
jury nullification, 218–19
juveniles
    beginning of juvenile justice system, 31–32
    decarceration policies, 219–21
    homelessness and, 9
    imprisonment as adults, 10

Kefalas, M., 59
Kennedy, John, F., ix
kindness, 152–53
King, Martin Luther, Jr., 185
kinship, 142, 148

labeling theory, 220–21, 223–26
language
    common, in Country Called Prison, 68
    labeling theory, 220–21, 223–26
    in prison culture, 135–36, 150
    registers, 171–72, 172*t*
    translation by discharged prisoners, 171–72, 172*t*

larceny/theft
    first commitment/parole violations for, 51–52, 51*t*
    new commitments by gender, 50–51, 50*t*
    state prison admission by race, 48–50, 49*t*
latchkey children, 80
latent consequences of incarceration, 186
leadership, transformational, 196–98, 197*f*, 199*t*
learned helplessness, 127, 150–51, 157–58
lease system for prisons, 29
leftover food rule, 137
legal aliens, 53, 72, 160, 167–68
legal codes, historic, 1–3
length of sentence, separating inmates by, 111
lex talionis ("eye for an eye" standard), 1–2, 3–4
licensed professionals, subculture of, 122*f*, 126–27, 129
Lickona, Thomas, 200–2
life roadmaps, 111–12
lifers, placement in housing units, 112
life-span model of psychosocial development, 83–85, 84*t*
literacy, increasing, 105–7
Looman, M., 81–82, 82*b*
Lord of the Flies, The (Golding), 81
Lundahl, B. W., 39

manifest consequences of incarceration, 186
marijuana, decriminalization of, 100
Marshall Plan, 210
Martinson, Robert, 35–36
Maslow, Abraham, 179–80, 180*t*
mass incarceration
    childhood homelessness and, 146–47
    costs of, 188
    decrease in prisoner populations 2011-2021, 12–13, 12*t*, 13*t*
    as epidemic, 22–23, 91–92
    manifest/latent consequences of, 186
    Mass Incarceration Mountain, 10–11, 11*f*
    need to change current system of, 185–86
    See also decarceration; prison history
material culture, 44, 70–74
maturity, levels of, 176–77, 176*t*

paradigm shift, 202
parens patriae principle, 31–32
parenting
  goals of, 82, 82t
  impact on executive functioning skills,
    89–91, 89t
  nurturance, 162–65
  poor attachment, impact of, 159–60, 159t
  styles of, 83, 83t
  tasks of effective, 81–82, 82b
parenting education, 108
parents, incarceration of, 117, 146–47
parole fees, paying off, 168–69
parole violations, 39, 51–52, 51t
Patterson, E. J., 97
Payne, Ruby, 57–58, 172
peer groups, placement by, 110–13
penitentiaries, 27–28
Pennsylvania system, 28
permissive parenting style, 83t
Perry Preschool project, 73–74
personal pride, promoting, 150
Personal Responsibility and Work
    Opportunity Reconciliation Act, 162
Peter Young Housing Industries and
    Treatment (PYHIT) enterprise, 229
Pew Charitable Trusts, 19–20, 36–37
Philippines, prison population in, 13–14, 14t
physiological and safety needs, 228
pillory and stocks, 3t
placement considerations, 110–13
plea bargaining, 217–18
policies for decarceration. *See* proposals for
    decarceration policies
political system, in Country Called
    Prison, 69–70
posttraumatic stress disorder (PTSD), 98–99
Pound of Flesh, A (Harris), 168–69
poverty
  as common history of prisoners, 56–61
  impact on children, 10, 11
  prison communities, 145–47
  secondary interventions for reducing
    criminality, 73–74
power, abuse of, 117–18, 118b
predator/prey separation, 109
pride, promoting, 150
primary interventions for reducing
    criminality, 73
prison communities, 145–47, 152

prison employees
  communication with residents, 138
  cultural stress, 130–31
  groupthink, 131–32
  subcultures in prison, 121–29, 122f
  training social science principles, 151–52
prison history
  Auburn system, 28–29
  Civil War era, 29–31
  in colonies, 26–27
  criminalization of alcohol use, 30–31
  deinstitutionalization era, 32–34
  early examples of prisons, 25–26
  "get tough" laws, 36–37
  incapacitation model, 35
  penitentiaries, 27–28
  Pennsylvania system, 28
  prison labor contracts, 31
  private prisons, 37–39, 38t
  recidivism, 39–40
  rehabilitation movement, 31–32
  "stranger danger," 34
  warehouse model, 34
  workhouses and houses of correction, 26
prisonization, 21, 57, 91
prison labor contracts, 29–30, 31
Prison Policy Initiative, 20
prison populations
  compared to country populations,
    52–56, 53t, 54t
  compared to state populations, 55, 55t
  by country, 13–14, 14t
  decrease in from 2011-2021, 12–13, 12t,
    13t, 100, 101t
  increase during War on Drugs, 34
prison rape, 132, 144–45
prison residents
  cultural stress, 133–35
  institutionalized personality, 127–28
  learned helplessness, 127
  subculture of, 127–29
  See also citizens of Country
    Called Prison
prisons
  funding for, 19–20
  geography of Country Called
    Prison, 65–67
  as places of work, 19
  rehabilitation, 204
  smaller, 109–10, 204–5